Green Beret Instructor's Guide to Everyday Carry

"How Instructors Can Build Safer, Smarter, More Capable Carriers"

Kyle A. Barrington

USArmy Special Forces (Ret)

Kyle "Panda" Barrington
US Army Special Forces (Retired)
Owner: Modern American Combative Arts LLC
Disabled Veteran Owned Small Business

As I penned these final chapters, two grim events weighed heavily on me. A young
Ukrainian woman, fleeing war for the promise of safety in America, was brutally murdered on a train in North Carolina while fellow passengers stood by in silence.
Soon after, the assassination of Charlie Kirk reminded us that political violence has returned to the public square of our nation.

Both events force us to confront a truth: evil does not wait for permission, and it does not respect the unarmed.

I believe fully in the absolute nature of the Second Amendment. Yet with that liberty comes a burden. Carrying a firearm is not simply the exercise of a right; it is the acceptance of responsibility. The gun on your hip is not for vanity or politics; it is for the defense of life, and that weight cannot be taken lightly.

Everyday carriers without training are not guardians but liabilities. Owning a firearm is only the beginning. Mastery requires discipline, humility, and constant learning.

You must hold yourself accountable, because no law, no trainer, and no excuse will shield you from the consequences of a negligent round.

The Founders gave us liberty. It is up to us to wield it with responsibility. Evil prevails when good men stand idle. The protector steps forward.

Carry wisely. Train relentlessly.

Live responsibly.

This is a book that covers aspects of training for pistol shooting, which is by definition inherently a dangerous endeavor. Never try anything presented in the guide without full knowledge and acceptance of the risk associated with that activity.

Always follow the rules of gun safety. These are including but not limited to:

- **Always treat a firearms as if it is loaded, until you are positive that it is not.**
- **Always keep the gun pointed in a safe direction and never point it at anything you are not willing to injure or destroy.**
- **Always keep your finger off the trigger until you have made a conscious decision to shoot.**
- **Always know your target and backstop. Know what is in front of, behind and to the sides of your intended target.**

An accident that takes place is the responsibility of the shooter. This book covers drills and exercises in live-fire and dry-fire settings.

Never have live ammunition near your dry-fire training area and always ensure that your firearm has been inspected and that it is unloaded why performing any dry-fire exercises.

The reader of this book acknowledges and accepts all risks associated with the live-fire and dry-fire activities and herby accepts all risks associated with any and all shooting and related activities.

Acknowledgements:

I do need to thank all the true "Pipe Hitters" that I had the honor of working beside in the United States Army Special Forces. I know that our past does not define us, but mine did lay a very solid foundation.

To all the Instructors that I worked beside in the 3rd Special Forces Group (Airborne) Advanced Urban Combat Course. Thank you MSG Steve Park and MSG Mike Stack for allowing to me teach.

Thank you "Super" Dave Harrington for always sharing your knowledge from the Special Operations Techniques (SOT) and Special Forces Advanced Reconnaissance, Target Analysis and Exploitation Techniques Course (SFARTAETC), and for the friendship.

Thank you to the members of the 3rd Special Forces Group (Airborne) that allowed me to walk beside them into combat and continue to foster the bond that only those that have walked into the fire and returned truly understand. De Oppresso Libre , Nous Defions

Thank you to Northrop Grumman for hiring me after the US Army to teach CQB and Nuclear Warhead recovery operations.

Thank you to Adam Painchaud for trusting me to be a Master Instructor and Adjunct Instructor for the Sig Sauer Academy.

Thank you Sheriff Jeff Brown for deputizing me so that I could see behind that fence.

I want to thank all the staff members of the Firearms Division at the Federal Law Enforcement Training Center. To those who openly shared their knowledge, who were secure enough in their own skills to debate ideas—and when necessary, grab some guns and head to the range to test what truly worked—you pushed me to grow and sharpen my craft. To those who lacked the confidence or ability and chose instead to hide behind students, you too made me stronger, for you reinforced my conviction in my own ideals and skillset. Each of you, in your own way, contributed to making me a better instructor and a more resilient professional.

Thank you to the Federal Agents, Officers and United States Marshals that sought me out and trusted me enough to teach their students and future peers. For having the confidence in me to provide a standard that they would have to strive to meet.

I pray every day that none of my students will ever be forced to use the skills I have taught them. But if that moment does come, I pray they will not fail because of any shortfall in my ability or instruction. I have taught them with my full skillset and with my heart, preparing them to solve complex problems under extreme duress—because I taught them the right way.

Mostly I need to acknowledge and thank my better half, my wife Cindy for loving me and having the patience and fortitude to deal with me and BS for over thirty years, for being my sounding board for this book and my life. As a retired English teacher, she has also been wrapped into my writing adventures and will attest that I am not always as articulate or patient and concise as I should be.

Table of Contents

Romans 13:4
For he is GOD's servant to do you good. But if you do wrong, be afraid, for he does not bare the sword for nothing. He is GOD's servant, an agent of wrath to bring punishment on the wrongdoer.

Finial Thoughts provided by some very good professional firearms instructors and friends of mine-

"High Performance exists in a calm mind and a relaxed body". - Alan Grey

"Do the right thing at the right time every time." - Super Dave Harrington

Preface: A Professional Instructor's Statement

Over the past three decades, I have devoted my career to the study, practice, and instruction of firearms proficiency. My journey has encompassed coaching novice shooters as well as developing and mentoring elite military and federal law enforcement professionals. Each phase has enriched my comprehension not only of shooting fundamentals but also of effective instructional methodologies. Consequently, while this book is crafted for the individual shooter, it is rooted in the principles of advanced instruction, incorporating lesson cues, training philosophies, and insights derived from practical applications.

This volume is not an introductory manual. Instead, it serves as a professional reference for readers who already command a firm foundation in pistol marksmanship and firearms safety. Expanding upon the content of my prior works—*Responsible Citizens Seeking Responsible Training* (ISBN 9780692114452) and *A Green Beret's Guide to Enhanced Pistol Skills* (ISBN 9798218640354)—this book elevates the discourse with broadened instruction, deeper contextual analysis, and refined methodologies suited for dedicated shooters and instructors aiming to amplify their efficacy.

Within these pages, you will encounter drills, techniques, and pedagogical frameworks that I employ in my personal and professional endeavors. These approaches have been tempered in the fires of combat, honed through decades of experience, and articulated with the precision expected of a seasoned instructor. My objective is to furnish resources that bolster both formalized training settings and individual advancement. The stratified instructional structure ensures accessibility for learners while compelling instructors to refine their expertise.

As professionals, we are obligated to perpetually assess our performance, interrogate our presuppositions, and pursue ongoing development. Complacency undermines mastery. I exhort every shooter—particularly instructors—to venture beyond familiar territories in training. Explore diverse disciplines: glean from competitive marksmen, long-range specialists, and combatives authorities. Even when their emphases diverge from yours, their insights often prove unexpectedly pertinent. From competition, I acquired lessons in speed and mechanical precision; from long-range pistolcraft, I derived strategies for accuracy and error mitigation. Every field yields valuable contributions.

Instruction must be anchored in reality. As a lifelong proponent of Everyday Carry (EDC), I maintain that training should mirror potential real-world encounters. Genuine threats transcend static range exercises. Success amid duress hinges not merely on knowledge but on what has been ingrained through realistic, pressurized rehearsals.

One of the most potent instruments for cultivating such skills is dry-fire practice. I have championed dry-fire since my early days in Special Forces. During the Special Operations Techniques (SOT) and Advanced Reconnaissance, Target Analysis, and Exploitation Techniques Course (SFARTAETC), we dedicated two hours nightly to dry-fire, following eight hours of live-fire sessions. Dry-fire was mandatory, not elective. Repetition fosters consistency, and consistency underpins excellence.

My own path recently veered dramatically when I was diagnosed with Stage III throat and tongue cancer. Compelled to reconstruct my physique after shedding over 100 pounds and substantial muscle mass, I scrutinized every motion and technique accumulated over decades. What persisted were the essential fundamentals: principles grounded in biomechanics rather than raw power. These enduring verities form the crux of this book, techniques resilient to stress, exhaustion, and hardship.

My instructional odyssey commenced as a young Green Beret in SOT and SFARTAETC. I subsequently advanced to Special Forces Advanced Urban Combat (SFAUC) Instructor and undertook multiple combat deployments. Post-Army retirement, I trained Air Force nuclear security units via Northrop Grumman. Later, at the Federal Law Enforcement Training Center (FLETC), I held the position of Senior Firearms Instructor for the Survival Shooting Training Program (SSTP) and Reactive Shooting Instructor Training Program (RSITP), contributing to their evolution into the Advanced Pistol Training Program (APTP) and Advanced Pistol Instructor Training Program (APITP).

Furthermore, I established Modern American Combative Arts, served as an adjunct instructor at Sig Sauer Academy, and functioned as a certified NRA Training Counselor, equipping hundreds of NRA instructors. Throughout, my ethos has endured: disseminating lessons steeped in operational veracity, substantiated by rigorous training, and conveyed with pedagogical exactitude.

This is no treatise on abstract theory; it is a compendium of applied proficiency. Whether addressing grip, sight alignment, or trigger manipulation, the principles expounded here are universal and vetted in battle, validated in educational arenas, and polished across a lifetime of pedagogy. Though nomenclature may shift, the fundamentals abide eternally, resonating with historical lineages of combat shooting, such as the Japanese *Ho-Jutsu*, the "Art of the Gun."

This book delineates a layered, principled trajectory toward mastery. Whether you are an armed citizen, a veteran instructor, or a practitioner charged with educating others, I implore you to engage this material with humility, inquisitiveness, and discerning analysis.

We owe our pupils nothing short of excellence, and ourselves the rigor to evolve unceasingly. Let us commence.

We owe our pupils nothing short of excellence!

The Fundamentals abide Eternally

INTRODUCTION

Kyle Barrington is a distinguished Professional Firearms Instructor with an unparalleled depth of experience in Special Operations, tactical training, and firearms education.

As the owner of Modern American Combative Arts LLC—a disabled combat veteran-owned small business dedicated to providing expert education, consulting, and training—Kyle brings a lifetime of elite military service to his civilian endeavors. A retired United States Army Special Forces "Green Beret" Combat Veteran and Senior Non-Commissioned Officer, Kyle served with distinction for sixteen years in one of the world's most demanding roles. He is a graduate of the rigorous US Army Special Forces Qualification Course (SFQC), earning his Special Forces tab, and holds qualifications in

Airborne, Air Assault, and Military Freefall operations. His combat prowess is evidenced by the Combat Infantryman Badge and multiple foreign Parachutists wings, underscoring his operational expertise across global theaters.

Kyle was a founding "plank holder" for the 3rd Special Forces Group (Airborne) Special Forces Advanced Urban Combat (SFAUC) Instructor cadre, where he served as permanent faculty. In this capacity, he instructed in advanced marksmanship, close quarters combat and tactics, and acted as the Primary Breaching Instructor—roles that demanded precision, innovation, and the ability to train elite operators under extreme conditions.

Further enhancing his tactical acumen, Kyle is a graduate of the US Army Special Forces Special Operations Training (SOT) and the Special Forces Advanced Reconnaissance, Target Analysis, and Exploitation Techniques Course (SFARTAETC). He also served as a plank holder for the 3rd Special Forces Group (Airborne) Commander's In-Extremis Force (CIF), a specialized unit tasked with high-risk missions requiring rapid response and flawless execution. Complementing his operational credentials, Kyle holds a Bachelor of Arts in Leadership and a Master of Science in Security Management, providing a scholarly foundation to his practical expertise.

Upon retiring from the Army, Kyle was recruited by Northrop Grumman to deliver advanced marksmanship and close quarters battle (CQB) instruction to United States Air Force Tactical Response Teams responsible for securing and recapturing nuclear missiles within the Continental United States—a testament to his trusted status in safeguarding national security assets.

Kyle's instructional credentials are equally impressive. He is a SIG Sauer Academy Master Instructor and served as an Adjunct Instructor for a decade, honing the skills of law enforcement, military, and civilian shooters in precision firearms handling. Certified as a National Rifle Association (NRA) Instructor since 2001 and an NRA Training Counselor since 2015, Kyle has shaped generations of responsible firearms users.

Currently, Kyle serves with the Department of Homeland Security's Federal Law Enforcement Training Center (FLETC) Firearms Division in Glynco, Georgia. As a Senior Firearms Instructor, he has led as Program Senior Instructor and Coordinator for critical curricula, including the Survival Shooting Training Program (SSTP), Reactive Shooting Instructor Training Program (RSITP), Advanced Pistol Training Program (APTP), and Advanced Pistol Instructor Training Program (APITP). These programs equip Federal agents with the life-saving skills needed to prevail in dynamic, high-stakes encounters.

This book serves as an enhanced instructor training guide, meticulously crafted to empower firearms instructors in refining their ability to instruct, to build safer, smarter and more capable shooters through mentoring and coaching effectively. Drawing from Kyle's extensive background, it distills proven methodologies from Special Forces training halls to federal academies, ensuring instructors can deliver transformative results.

Time is your most valuable commodity. As a professional instructor, it is your solemn duty to optimize every moment of training to elevate your students' proficiency, fostering not just technical skill but adaptive mastery.

Your mind is your most potent weapon. A superior instructor imparts the critical thinking necessary for students to diagnose and resolve shooting-related challenges independently, turning novices into resilient, capable operators.

Your students invest their time, money, resources, and energy in your expertise—honor that trust by exceeding their expectations and delivering uncompromising excellence.

A Superior Instructor imparts critical thinking

Your Students
Invest their
Time, Money and
Resources
Honor that
Trust!

Finally, there is no such thing as "good enough." Preparedness for violence is fleeting; you must be ready to act decisively at the precise moment it is required, within the bounds of your authority. A firearm and good intentions alone are insufficient—seek out responsible trainers, learn relentlessly, and embody citizenship at its highest form. Your students look to you as their guide in this pursuit; do not falter in that responsibility.

Before We Get Started

Let me begin by offering a little context.

I am, both by trade and by passion, a professional firearms instructor. For more than three decades, I've stood on firing lines, on training floors, and in classrooms training **tens of thousands of students** from every walk of life. From first-time gun owners learning to take responsibility for their personal safety, to elite military units and seasoned law enforcement professionals honing their edge, I've had the rare privilege of seeing the **full spectrum** of what it means to carry a gun for a purpose.

That privilege has brought with it a deep responsibility. One that doesn't end with showing someone how to shoot, it starts there. Because as you know, being a firearms instructor means far more than standing behind a bench with a timer or clipboard. It means **building trust**, **shaping mindset**, and **instilling discipline** in others who will one day be accountable for life-and-death decisions. That responsibility never gets lighter but our ability to carry it can grow stronger.

Over the years, my experiences have shaped the way I teach, write, and present information, **always through the lens of a teacher first**. That perspective is reflected throughout this work. It's in the language, the breakdowns, the progressions, and the teaching notes. And it's also in the expectation that the reader isn't just looking to become a better shooter but a better mentor, guide, and protector.

From Shooter to Instructor: A Natural Evolution

If you've read my previous books *Responsible Citizens Seeking Responsible Training: A Guide for Self-Defense with a Pistol* (ISBN: 9780692114452),

OR

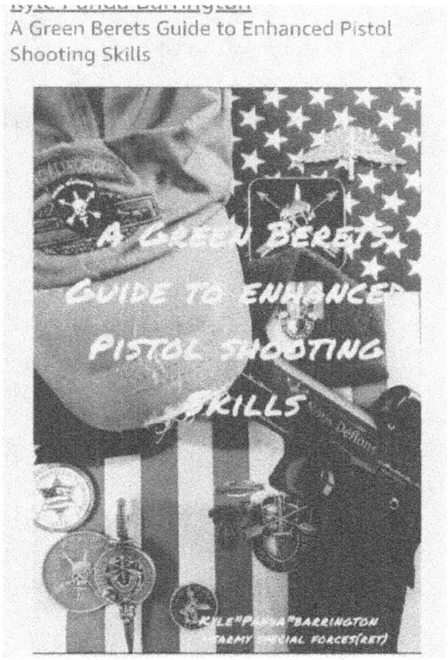

A Green Beret's Guide to Enhanced Pistol Shooting Skills (ISBN: 9798218640354)

You'll recognize some of the foundational material here. Those works were crafted to enhance individual performance and self-reliance with a pistol. They were about helping the shooter become more consistent, more confident, and more capable under pressure.

This book is different.

This volume represents a **deliberate evolution** into instructor-level material. It's for those of you who've gone beyond the basics and who feel the pull to **pass your**

knowledge forward. Whether you're already teaching, mentoring informally, or planning to one day lead others on the range, this book is designed to equip you with **refined skills**, **diagnostic insight**, and **real-world-tested teaching principles**.

A Technical Resource for Firearms Instructors

This book is not a beginner's manual. It's not a plug-and-play certification workbook. It's a **performance-based teaching resource**, a guide for the serious practitioner who either is, or intends to become, a capable, confident, and accountable firearms instructor.

It's written for those who:

- Possess a **firm grasp of pistol marksmanship fundamentals**,
- Maintain a **working or advanced understanding of weapons handling and range safety**,
- And have the **drive to teach others** with clarity, safety, and respect for the responsibility of instruction.

If you are an instructor or aspire to become one this book was built with you in mind. Inside, you'll find:

- Clear explanations of essential and advanced skills
- Instructor notes that highlight **how to teach**, not just what to teach
- **Field-tested methods** that work under pressure
- **Common error diagnostics** that will save time and frustration
- Drills and cueing strategies based on **real students and real results**

Whether you teach civilians, law enforcement, or military personnel—**you'll find information you can apply**.

Not Just Another Manual

Let me be clear—this is not about checking boxes. It's about producing **safe, smarter,** and **more capable shooters** who understand their responsibilities and can perform under pressure.

It's for those of us who want to go beyond simply running the line. This book is for instructors who **refuse to treat teaching like a routine**, and instead approach it as an **honorable craft**—one rooted in discipline, humility, and service.

If that's you, then this book belongs in your hands and in your kit.

My Goal for You, the Instructor

My mission with this volume is simple to provide a **clear, realistic, and practical resource** that helps bridge the gap between **basic instructor credentials** and **true teaching competency**.

I want this book to live in your **range bag**, sit on your **training table**, and follow you through every class you teach. I want you to write in the margins, adapt the drills, share the lessons, and test the concepts. Whether you're refining your own skills, coaching shooters through errors, or building your own curriculum, this book is here to **support your journey as a leader and educator**.

You are in The Right Place
Let's Get Started!

What you'll find here isn't theory for theory's sake, it's **proven, tested, and field-ready material**. It's forged through reps, refined through failures, and delivered with the hope that it will **make your job easier, your classes safer, and your impact greater**.

So if you're ready to train the next generation not just to shoot, but to think, to move, and to survive then let's get started.

You're in the right place.

Instructor Bona Fides

This is the third book I have authored, and my intent is to maintain an instructor-level focus throughout. I will necessarily make certain assumptions, which will be discussed in detail.

First, what constitutes an instructor? Merriam-Webster defines it simply as someone who instructs, a teacher. This broad definition leaves considerable room for interpretation regarding who qualifies as an instructor. In the firearms community, I have found this ambiguity to be particularly concerning.

For those who have read my previous works—***Responsible Citizens Seeking Responsible Training: Guide for Self-Defense with a Pistol*** **(ISBN 978-0691144528)** or ***A Green Beret's Guide to Enhanced Pistol Shooting Skills*** **(ISBN 979-8216403548)**—thank you. You are already familiar with my foundational qualifications and experience, which inform my views on what an instructor should know, embody, and achieve.

My journey as an instructor began in 1989 as a Green Beret, where I served as a force multiplier, and teaching firearms to foreign nationals, fellow U.S. military personnel, and local and federal law enforcement agencies.

Upon becoming a Special Forces Advanced Urban Combat Instructor for the 3rd Special Forces Group (Airborne), I completed my first formal instructor training: the U.S. Army Instructor Training Program at Fort Bragg, North Carolina, a three-week course in instructional methodology that earned me the "H" identifier for my Military Occupational Specialty (MOS).

As a founding member (plank holder) of the 3rd Special Forces Group's Special Forces Advanced Urban Combat (SFAUC) Course, I obtained instructor credentials from the

National Rifle Association (NRA) in Pistol, Rifle, Shotgun, Home Firearms Safety, and Personal Protection in the Home.

Following the events of September 11, 2001, the SFAUC instructors were integrated into the 3rd Special Forces Group's Commanders In-Extremis Force. In addition to combat operations, we trained host-nation hostage rescue and direct-action elements. I also had the privilege of instructing heavy-wall explosive breaching for the Central Intelligence Agency, the Department of Energy, and the National Nuclear Security Administration at a classified training facility.

After retiring from the U.S. Army, I was employed by Northrop Grumman Corporation to teach Close Quarters Battle (CQB) and related skills to U.S. Air Force Tactical Response Force (TRF) units tasked with recapturing nuclear missile silos.

I subsequently joined the Federal Law Enforcement Training Center (FLETC) in Glynco, Georgia, initially teaching Infrastructure Protection in the Counterterrorism Division. All FLETC instructors must complete the two-week Law Enforcement Instructor Training Program. While in Counterterrorism, I also passed the two-week Law Enforcement Use of Force Instructor Training Program.

I eventually transitioned to the Firearms Division, my true passion. This began with the two-week Firearms Instructor Training Course, followed by the Reactive Shooter Instructor Training Program. Before operating independently, new instructors undergo a year-long apprenticeship: shadowing experienced instructors for three months across two 24-student classes, observing multiple iterations of the curriculum. I supplemented this by observing various instructors teaching the same material. The next phase involves co-teaching under supervision, with feedback, culminating in independent instruction of full classes while observed. During this period, I also completed the Law Enforcement Rifle Training Course, Non-Lethal Training Course, and other Firearms Division offerings.

Concurrently, I delivered 80-hour firearms blocks for the U.S. Air Force Office of Special Investigations' Protective Security Operations Course.

Adam Painchaud, Director of the SIG Sauer Academy, offered me an adjunct position contingent on passing the SIG Sauer Academy Master Instructor Course—a week-long, commercially oriented program ending with a demanding course of fire that tolerated no margin for error.

By then, I was instructing for FLETC, the SIG Sauer Academy, and my own company, Modern American Combative Arts LLC. To advance my business, I attended the NRA Training Counselor Workshop at NRA headquarters, a week-long program becoming a certified Chief Range Safety Officer and Regional Refuse to Be a Victim Counselor as well . This enabled me to conduct instructor-level NRA courses in all my certified disciplines.

My primary employment remains with FLETC, where I advanced to Senior Instructor and Program Coordinator for the Reactive Shooter Training Program and Survival Shooting Training Program, which I upgraded to the Advanced Pistol Training Program and Advanced Pistol Instructor Training Program.

In total, this encompasses over 16 years teaching in U.S. Army Special Forces, 10 years as an Adjunct Master Instructor at the SIG Sauer Academy, 17 years (as of this writing) at FLETC, and ongoing work as lead instructor for Modern American Combative Arts LLC.

A conservative estimate places the number of students I have trained at over 200,000. This underscores my belief that experience is paramount and an ongoing process, there is always room for improvement.

I actively seek continuing education from diverse instructors, aiming to attend at least one or two instructor-level courses annually. I have trained under world-class firearms experts across disciplines, not only to absorb tactical insights or new techniques but also to study their instructional methods. These experiences often reinforce existing beliefs while occasionally prompting reevaluation.

My firearms instructor path began under "Super" Dave Harrington, NCOIC of the Shooting Committee at Range 37, Fort Bragg—the U.S. Army Special Forces' hub for marksmanship training. Dave was my primary instructor in the Special Operations Techniques (SOT) Course and later the Special Forces Advanced Reconnaissance, Target Analysis, and Exploitation Techniques Course (SFARTAETC) at the John F. Kennedy Special Warfare Center and School.

I later refined my skills when Dave trained instructors for the SFAUC marksmanship blocks. Today, Dave operates Combat Speed LLC and produces professional videos online; I highly recommend him for continuing education. Every instructor should experience one of his "skull sessions."

My friend and Special Forces Brother passed while I was editing this book.

Dave will be missed by the Special Forces and Shooting communities.

Competent firearms instructors must pursue ongoing education and observe peers in action. At FLETC, with approximately 150 firearms instructors, there are as many approaches, sparking constant debate on best practices.

I encourage instructors to step outside their comfort zones. Though not a competitor, I have attended classes by Ben Stoeger, reinforcing my gun-handling skills and introducing efficient civilian class structures. I adopted his "dead trigger" dry-fire method, teaching it to thousands. I recommend any Stoeger course.

I attended the Special Forces Qualification Course alongside Mike Pannone of CTT Solutions (he in Bravo Company, I in Charlie). Mutual friends and social media led me to his East Coast class, where I focused on his methodologies—outstanding and articulate. I gained valuable insights into appendix carry as a bonus, illustrating how classes yield unexpected benefits.

Brandon Wright, Smith & Wesson's pro shooter, is a 15-year acquaintance from my USAF Protective Security Operations teaching days. I attended his course to evaluate him for FLETC; his live-fire demos reinforced my three-part demonstration philosophy: 50% speed for observation, 85% for proper execution, then slowed again for nuances. Time permitting, push to full speed to model self-challenge.

Serendipity struck when I co-taught with legendary Ken Hackathorn for the SIG Academy for a Japanese Special Operations Forces element in Florida, an affirming experience.

Continuing education is essential in most professions for relevance, yet many firearms instructors neglect it. At FLETC, monthly proficiency ammunition is available, but only about a quarter draw it, the same ones who demonstrate for students.

Instructors build confidence through practice: dry-fire is valuable, but live-fire is indispensable. Professional organizations often mandate annual external training, seek competent sources.

Occasionally, FLETC hosts external instructors, but attendance is predictably low among the insecure, fearing peer scrutiny. As the proverb states, "iron sharpens iron", clashing blades is necessary. Avoiding this hinders growth and disserves students.

Instructors should adopt a proficiency standard. What suffices? As an NRA Training Counselor, I certify many FLETC instructors for external work. The NRA pre-certification requires 20 untimed shots at a 9-inch blank target from 15 yards (two-handed, standing), scoring within a 6-inch spread, a bare minimum.

FLETC demands 255/300 on the Practical Pistol Course (detailed in A Green Berets Guide to Pistol Shooting Skills Courses of Fire section)—generous times, still basic.

From Special Forces, I favor the 300-Aggregate Bullseye at 25 yards: 10 rounds in 10 minutes, 10 in 1 minute, 10 in 10 seconds. Instructor proficiency is 90% (270/300), with balanced scores emphasizing accuracy and speed.

Standards may evolve, but having one is crucial. My enduring benchmark is the "speed bull": 10 rounds in 10 seconds at 25 yards. Upgrading to the full aggregate ensured varied trigger manipulation.

Most schools feature entry/graduation tests that are challenging yet achievable, targeting ~85% pass rates. Civilian instructors often bias toward strengths. A Green Berets Guide to Pistol Shooting Skills Courses of Fire section includes my Modern American Combative Arts evaluation, designed for practicality without bias.

Notable standards herein: Ken Hackathorn's Wizard Drill (five rounds, eye-opening simplicity) and Larry Vickers' 10-10-10 (10 rounds from holster in 10 seconds at 10 yards).

Aspiring professional instructors should join a firearms association, seek mentors, and commit to skill-building through classes.

Firearms training is a martial art with hierarchies, one must strive for excellence.

Never compromise students due to personal deficiencies.

I pray my students never face lethal encounters, but if they do, ensure your instruction equips them for success.

Competent instructors must convey: good intentions and a gun mean nothing in self-defense, preach accountability for every round is absolute.

Teach only within your expertise, demonstrate live-fire for novelties, and walk the walk you talk.

Instructor Truths: Addressing Deficiencies in Instructor Knowledge

In the firearms industry, a myriad of beliefs and methodologies abound. I readily concede that any instructor proclaiming "this is the only way" is likely mistaken.

Many instructors derive their doctrines and qualification standards from their personal capabilities—or, more accurately, their limitations.

If an instructor asserts that "all gunfights occur within 21 feet, rendering training beyond 7 yards unnecessary," one might reasonably infer that they themselves struggle to meet standards at greater distances.

Distance reveals shortcomings, and most instructors hesitate to expose their vulnerabilities to students. At the 7-yard line, anyone can appear competent. Yet, it is essential to recognize that errors persist, even if the target appears acceptable, a dangerously flawed assumption for any competent instructor.

Studies indicate that elite Special Operations personnel experience a 30% to 50% performance degradation in actual kinetic encounters compared to their peak range performance. This effectively halves engagement distances, even for operators firing 2,000 rounds weekly. Average law enforcement officers suffer a 70% to 85% decline, reducing viable hits to roughly 3 feet. Factoring in scoring zones, impacts often fall outside effective areas.

Dismissing training beyond 21 feet fosters a perilous, potentially lethal mindset.

Another common instructor limitation involves advocating a slow, deliberate trigger press: taking up slack, reaching the wall, and gradually building pressure until the shot breaks.

This approach persists among instructors with rudimentary skills. If it dominates your methodology, your students and you will remain at a journeyman level.

Under stress, the human body instinctively squares to the threat, keeps both eyes open, focuses on the target, and rapidly actuates the trigger until the slide locks back, this is a a fundamental physiological response.

Students must eventually confront real-world conditions and learn to operate effectively therein.

I maintain that only instructors proficient at speed from the 25-yard line, and capable of imparting those skills, fulfill their responsibilities.

What constitutes effectiveness at distance with speed? I delve into speed bulls and the 300-point aggregate later in this book, but these form the foundation of my philosophy.

I was taught and firmly believe, that a proficient shooter should draw and hit an A/C-zone target (approximately 11 by 24 inches, akin to the "bottle" on standard qualification silhouettes) in 2.5 seconds at any distance with any handgun.

FBI statistics suggest most gunfights last three seconds and involve three rounds; thus, a 2.5-second single-shot draw enables three rounds in three seconds.

For instance, online videos demonstrate my drawing a SIG P365 subcompact with iron sights and hitting an A/C-zone target at 50 yards in under 2.5 seconds a basic

Never allow instructor
Limitations to
Compromise student
Learning
Instructors must
Self assess, avoiding
Complacency

competency, not an extraordinary feat. With any full-size pistol I own, I achieve the same at 100 yards. This should be the instructional standard.

Distance exposes limitations; speed reveals inefficiencies. Combining both unveils all shooter and instructor deficiencies.

I employ the speed bull as my baseline: 10 rounds in 10 seconds from the 25-yard line on a B-8 bullseye target. Instructor proficiency requires 90 or better; basic competency, 70 or above.

This standard demonstrates mastery of visual cues, sight picture and alignment, trigger control and reset, and recoil management. It also illustrates that the trigger is not manipulated slowly and deliberately.

A student scoring 70 or better possesses foundational understanding and application of shooting fundamentals.

Instructors who deem this unnecessary likely lack the requisite knowledge and skills. I challenge them to refute that it exemplifies high proficiency.

Even the straightforward Vickers 10-10-10 drill—10 rounds from the holster in 10 seconds at the 10-yard line, all within a 10-inch circle, eludes most shooters.

Having trained tens of thousands in military and law enforcement shooters, I use the Vickers drill as an eye-opener. In follow-on sessions for FLETC graduates who passed qualifications, most full-time officers and agents fail initially.

The same holds in advanced pistol instructor classes: many fail to fire all rounds or keep them centered.

This underpins my methodologies. No excuse exists for armed professionals or instructors unable to perform it, a clear indicator of deficient foundational principles.

I often hear dismissals of "competition stuff." Though not a competitor, I collaborate with exceptional ones and engage in informed discussions. Not all competition techniques transfer to everyday carry (EDC) or law enforcement, but gun handling does.

Drawing from personal experience grants insight into diverse disciplines. Instructors must explore other shooting branches for self-improvement.

Bullseye shooters impart sights and trigger mastery; at 50 yards, nuances emerge. You must then integrate speed.

A USPSA Grand Master teaches velocity and efficiency; faster handling, reloads. Movements may be abrupt and prolonged beyond tactical "up-seen-down" timing, but adaptation yields EDC applicability.

Instructors must self-assess, avoiding complacency in "good enough" or student superiority. Qualifying at 300 with ample time does not mirror real-world demands. Seek evaluators and trainers for growth.

As an EDC specialist, I train across disciplines due to broad understanding, but I refer students to experts when needed. For example, teaching a "Girls & Guns" class in

Florida, a participant queried shotgun competition: shooting, reloading while moving to positions, timed. She over-verified shots, inefficiently positioned the shotgun, and halted for dropped shells. I advised rolling the shotgun onto her shoulder (loading port up) while moving immediately post-shot, unfixable errors demand progression. Hold two rounds per load; avoid stops. Efficient handling and movement boosted her scores dramatically.

Readers should grasp the "why" behind my book's tenets. Rooted in Special Forces, they encompass diverse disciplines. As my prior books note, I am a martial artist viewing pistol shooting similarly: proficiency levels vary, styles differ, but skilled practitioners perpetually improve.

I pray daily that students avoid lethal kinetic encounters, but if compelled, ensure my knowledge and demonstrable skills prevent their failure.

Never permit your instructor limitations to compromise your students.

Instructor Observations

I have been a professional firearms instructor for decades. Just when I think I have seen it all, my students prove me wrong. Over time, I have learned that an instructor must also remain a student.

My first overseas Foreign Internal Defense mission as a Green Beret took me to the Dominican Republic for counter-narcotics training. Our task was to teach pistol shooting to the ***Comando de Fuerzas Especiales en República Dominicana***, a group of men who knew they were the top of their food chain and resented "Gringos" telling them how to shoot. The range, built from photographs, sat near a hospital. A two-foot concrete retaining wall ran in front of the berm.

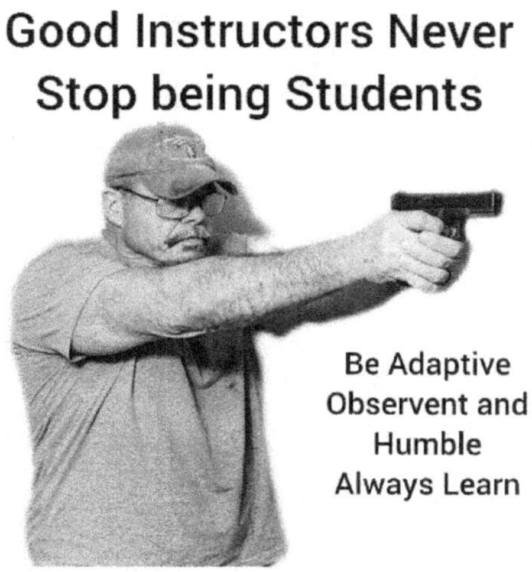

Good Instructors Never Stop being Students
Be Adaptive
Observent and
Humble
Always Learn

It was hot, and we taught through interpreters, learning quickly that Dominican Spanish differed from Mexican or Puerto Rican Spanish. Our challenge was getting the message across. After days of demos and instruction with no real improvement, one Paracaidista sent a .45 round into the concrete wall, and the ricochet hit me square in the shin. It was slow, but big and it hurt.

While my teammate and I stayed behind to watch the range during lunch, a group of Dominican Army hospital nurses passed by. They had never fired pistols, so we offered a quick lesson. They enjoyed it, and we saw an opportunity to teach the Paracaidistas a lesson in humility.

Over several days, we drilled the nurses on the basics—vision, structure, and bullseye shooting without movement. Then, one morning before lunch, we arranged for the nurses to "drop by" in their scrubs. In front of the Paracaidistas, we gave the nurses a five-minute class on stance, grip, and visual focus. A bet was made. The nurses shot exceptionally well, methodically applying what they had learned. The men were stunned. The women had listened, followed directions, and applied a systematic approach, medical training at work. The Paracaidistas took notice.

Understanding Your Student

I once taught a two-day class at NRA Headquarters in Virginia through a SIG Sauer program for NFL players. Most were from Washington or Baltimore, with a few from Miami and Denver. Incredible athletes. One long snapper, in the league for ten years, had never shot a pistol. We outfitted them with SIG 226 X5s for their large hands. I asked how he picked it up so quickly. He said, "I'm a professional athlete. I'm used to being coached and following the process." I learned that if I explained in detail, demonstrated to standard, let them imitate, and then practice, the results could be extraordinary.

At FLETC, I have seen thousands of students. With experience, I can diagnose most shooting issues in seconds. But even after decades, students still surprise me. I have unloaded a Remington 870 with every shell loaded backwards including one chambered through sheer effort. I have seen a pistol loaded with 9mm ammunition on qualification day when the issued caliber was .40, and been told, "I knew it was different, but it still fit."

An instructor must read people. Each student requires a unique approach. Recently, a young woman broke down in tears during on the firing line. She was a Division One college rugby player with a 4.0 GPA, training for a Federal agent position. She was tense in the shoulders, causing unnecessary gun movement. Her tears came from frustration, this was the first skill she couldn't master instantly. One hundred rounds later, with calm coaching and a detailed breakdown of cause and effect, she was calling her shots. Days later, she qualified in the high 90 percentile.

Adapting Your Style

Teaching 18-year-old warriors is easy. The challenge lies in modifying your style for children, seniors, or women. Differences in age, sex, and background create barriers that require adaptation. I have learned the most from teaching people unlike me.

Teaching Green Berets in the Special Forces Advanced Urban Combat course was straightforward, we shared a common reference. Teaching women has been my greatest challenge and my greatest learning experience. Women often require a better answer than men, they want the "why" and the "how," and they are not afraid to ask questions. Many men would rather figure it out alone.

I once taught a "Girls with Guns" class in Florida. I was confident the students were learning, judging by their targets. Later, the range owner told me that one student, Crystal, nearly quit because my delivery was too intense. That was early in my relationship with A Girl & A Gun. My wife began attending these classes, sitting quietly in the back to provide feedback during the drive home. That female perspective changed how I taught younger women at FLETC.

Physical Challenges

Age and physical condition also influence instruction. I taught a woman in her mid-80s with severe arthritis who lived alone and insisted on self-sufficiency. She couldn't rack her pistol, so we developed a method using an empty magazine to lock the slide to the rear, then inserting a loaded magazine. I would never have taught this technique under normal circumstances, but necessity drove innovation.

An 87-year-old man in New Hampshire impressed me by moving slowly to the line with a cane, then sheathing it to draw a 1911 and shoot dime-sized groups. His cane was an ASP-style defensive tool, another lesson in adaptive equipment.

In South Carolina, I met an older man who carried cross-draw. When I asked why, he said his first carjacking taught him that a seat belt made strong-side carry inaccessible. His second carjacking proved that practice still mattered. By the third, with cross-draw, he successfully defended himself. Lesson learned.

Diagnosing Before Adjusting

Many instructors want to "call for fire" and adjust after each shot in an initial assessment. The problem is that one shot tells you little. At FLETC, our ten-round assessment is a grouping exercise. I encourage letting all ten rounds go, then analyzing the group. Ben Stoeger reinforced this in his Doubles Diagnostic, groups tell the real story, fliers included.

Learning From Others

I had the privilege of co-teaching with Ken Hackathorn. Rather than ask questions, I would state my diagnosis of a student's issue and wait to see if he agreed. I didn't want to influence his analysis, a reaffirming approach.

I have also trained under "Super" Dave Harrington, later assisting in his classes. During a class in Savannah, Dave invited me to shoot the Speed Bull Drill beside him. That day, I scored a 96 with my SIG 226; he scored a 94 with his Glock 19. He simply said, "That was a nice piece of work." A very fond memory and shooting reaffirmation!

Final Lesson

Instructing firearms for 35 years has taught me that the best instructors never stop being students. Take classes, teach everyone from children to the elderly and embrace every opportunity to adapt. The next lesson that changes your teaching might come from the most unexpected place.

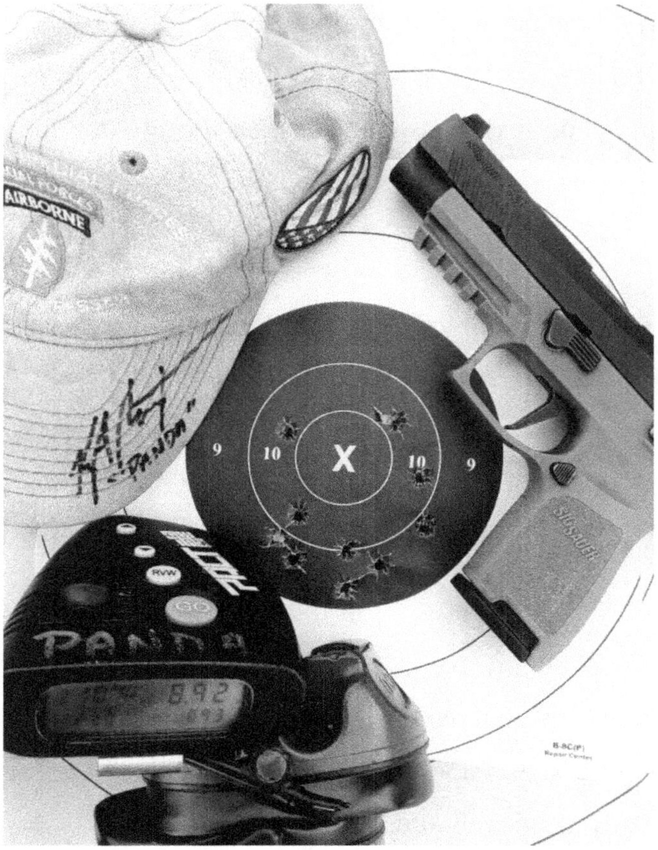

Instructor Lessons Learned

From 35 Years of Firearms Instruction

1. **Always Remain a Student** – No matter how experienced you are, your students will find ways to teach you something new.
2. **Understand the Student Before the Lesson** – Cultural background, personality, and prior experience shape how they learn.
3. **Adapt Your Teaching Style** – Modify tone, pace, and delivery for different age groups, genders, and physical abilities.
4. **Explain the "Why" and the "How"** – Especially for students who thrive on process and reasoning, not just repetition.
5. **Let Performance Speak** – Group drills and assessments reveal patterns better than single-shot corrections.
6. **Innovate When Needed** – Create or adapt techniques when standard methods don't work for a student's needs.
7. **Learn From Other Experts** – Observe, listen, and compare your analysis with other seasoned instructors.
8. **Use Demonstrations Strategically** – Show what "right" looks like, then coach to that standard.

9. **Recognize the Role of Emotion** – Frustration, fear, or pride can all affect performance. Coach through them.
10. **Train Everyone** – Children, seniors, professionals, athletes—each brings unique challenges that will sharpen your skills.

Bottom Line:
The best instructors are adaptive, observant, and humble enough to keep learning. Every student is both a challenge and an opportunity to grow.

Philosophy of Training: Modern American Combative Arts

At Modern American Combative Arts, I hold an unwavering belief that fundamentals form the cornerstone of survival. Everything we undertake from the initial repetition on the range to split-second decisions under threat rests upon a solid foundation of basics executed with excellence. There are no "advanced techniques," only shooters who perform the fundamentals with precision, under pressure, and on demand.

The so-called "advanced" shooter is not defined by greater knowledge but by superior execution. They have internalized core principles so profoundly that their actions transcend conscious deliberation, becoming automatic responses honed through rigorous practice. The truly proficient shooter does not practice until they get it right; they practice until they cannot get it wrong.

Every shooter seeking improvement will inevitably return to the fundamentals, time and again but each time with a deeper layer of understanding. Growth in marksmanship is not a linear progression of techniques; it is a spiral that perpetually circles back to grip, stance, sight alignment, and trigger control, infused with greater insight and purpose.

These elements are not mere motor skills; they are neurological imprints, cultivated through deliberate and consistent repetition, tested under stress, and refined in adversity.

Our training philosophy centers on what we call the Combat Triad:

1. **Marksmanship** – The ability to hit intended targets with precision and repeatability.
2. **Gun-Handling** – The skill of operating the weapon system smoothly, safely, and efficiently.

3. Mindset – The capacity to make timely decisions under pressure, navigating uncertainty and fear with resolve.

This triad must be ingrained in your neuromuscular and cognitive systems, forging a seamless connection between mind and body. Only then can you perform at combat speeds, where visual processing, movement, manipulation, and engagement unfold simultaneously. Such proficiency cannot be simulated or expedited; it must be earned, repetition by repetition.

Paradoxically, it is often the most "advanced" students—the seasoned fighters, warriors, and practitioners—who grasp the imperative of continually recentering on the basics. They possess the humility to revisit fundamentals, recognizing that skills erode, speed can mask errors, and ego impedes progress.

In this book, my aim is to distill and document the hard-earned lessons accumulated over three decades of shooting, teaching, fighting, and evolving. My perspectives on firearms, martial arts, and combative philosophy have transformed through training, real-world application, failures, and insights gleaned from others. I have trained with exceptional shooters, studied under legendary instructors, and stood alongside teammates and warriors in harm's way. Some of the most profound lessons emerged not from textbooks but from lived experience in moments of violence, problem-solving, and post-action reflection.

Though my views have evolved, the principles I share are rooted in enduring truths. You will encounter techniques that embody these principles, not as inflexible dogma, but as tools to foster deeper understanding. I encourage you to approach them not as "the way," but as "a way" one that has proven effective for me and, if adopted and adapted with integrity, will serve you well.

Understand this: the use of firearms in defense of life is, at its essence, a martial art. Like any martial art, true innovations are rare; instead, there are fresh perspectives on timeless elements. Equipment may advance optics, materials, calibers but the core principles persist: vision, structure, trigger manipulation, consistency, predictability, durability, mindset, and composure.

The pistol is more than a mechanical tool; in skilled hands, it becomes an extension of intent capable of projecting force, conveying posture (defensive or offensive), and achieving precision that defies common expectations.

The Truth is a Simple Concept
Hold the Gun
Fire the Gun
Timing
Aim the Gun
Aim Small -Miss Small

There are no secrets. There are no shortcuts. There is only the work. What follows is my contribution to your journey: a presentation of the lessons I have learned, the methods I trust, and the principles upon which I stake my life

On Repetition, Variation, and the Value of Explanation

As a seasoned firearms instructor and the author of this book, I firmly believe in the efficacy of inductive learning, a pedagogical method wherein students construct their own understanding through repeated exposure to concepts, diverse examples, and contextual variations. This approach acknowledges the inherent diversity in learning styles, recognizing that no singular explanation will resonate uniformly with every reader, student, or practitioner.

A foundational principle shaping the architecture of this book is the deliberate integration of repetition and variation. Across its chapters, readers will encounter recurring concepts articulated in multifaceted contexts. At times, these ideas are elaborated in exhaustive detail to illuminate their nuances; in other instances, they are succinctly referenced or distilled to their core essence. Certain chapters expand upon a concept to reveal its profound depths, while others condense it for conciseness, positioning it as a foundational element within a larger discussion.

This repetition is far from gratuitous redundancy; it is purposeful iteration designed to facilitate mastery. In the realm of martial arts and firearms training, a concept akin to the "sky is blue" theory prevails. This notion posits that a fundamental truth may not be fully internalized or even acknowledged until it is conveyed in a manner that personally resonates with the learner. One instructor might articulate it straightforwardly: "The sky is blue." Another may employ poetic imagery, technical jargon, or experiential analogies. Ultimately, the student encounters the explanation in precisely the right formulation at the opportune moment, leading to genuine comprehension. The sky, in essence, "becomes" blue not due to any change in reality, but because the insight has finally taken root.

This philosophy profoundly informs my methodology in both instruction and authorship. If a concept merits inclusion in teaching, it warrants comprehensive exploration. It is incumbent upon me, as an educator, not merely to delineate critical principles but to explicate them through an array of lenses including practical examples, relatable analogies, detailed breakdowns, and visual aids ensuring that readers grasp not only the "how" but also the "why" underpinning each skill and principle.

Anticipate encountering themes reiterated throughout the text and ideas resurfacing in varied scenarios. This design is intentional, mirroring the iterative process of skill acquisition on the firing range or in tactical training environments. Learning in firearms instruction often unfolds through sustained exposure, scaffolded guidance, and multimodal explanations. For instance, when teaching sight alignment, an instructor might first demonstrate it in a static, dry-fire drill, then repeat the concept during live fire under timed conditions, and later vary it in low-light simulations or while incorporating movement. Such layering allows students to internalize the principle across escalating complexities, fostering retention and adaptability. My objective extends beyond mere information dissemination; it is to engrain knowledge so deeply that readers can articulate it confidently, apply it fluidly, and adapt it innovatively in dynamic, real-world contexts whether defending against threats, competing in matches, or instructing others.

By the conclusion of this book, should you encounter a familiar concept, regard it not as repetition but as a pedagogical opportunity. Viewed through the prism of accumulated experience, it may reveal fresh insights, signifying authentic growth in your learning journey.

Sidebar: The Power of Repetition and Variation in Firearms Instruction

Understanding the "Sky is Blue" Theory and Inductive Learning

Inductive Learning Defined
An learner-centered methodology wherein individuals cultivate comprehension by discerning patterns, analyzing examples, and exploring variations, rather than receiving didactic, prescriptive directives.

Firearms Application Example:
Rather than simply declaring, "Maintain a consistent grip," an instructor demonstrates multiple grip techniques (e.g., thumbs-forward for semi-automatics versus revolver-specific holds), allows the shooter to experience outcomes under recoil, and facilitates self-discovery of what "consistent" entails during rapid transitions, one-handed shooting, or in adverse conditions like wet hands or glove use. This inductive process empowers students to adapt grips intuitively, enhancing performance in unpredictable scenarios such as close-quarters engagements or defensive situations.

Why Repetition with Variation Works

Teaching Strategy	Description	Benefit to the Student
Restating Concepts	Reintroducing the same principle across multiple chapters or training modules	Reinforces long-term memory retention and cultivates deeper conceptual understanding
Contextual Reframing	Presenting the idea in diverse drills, tactical applications, or environmental simulations	Develops adaptability and resilience under pressure, such as in dynamic shooting courses or force-on-force training
Progressive Layering	Expanding or condensing explanations based on the instructional focus and learner progression	Aligns with the student's evolving expertise, preventing overwhelm while building mastery over time
Analogies & Metaphors	Employing comparisons (e.g., equating trigger press to "squeezing a lemon" for smoothness) to enhance relatability	Accommodates varied cognitive styles, including visual, kinesthetic, or auditory learners, thereby increasing engagement and recall

The "Sky is Blue" Theory Explained

Individuals internalize truths when they are communicated in a personally resonant manner, often after multiple exposures fail to connect.

Instructor Insight Example:

An instructor may reiterate "Press the trigger straight to the rear" a dozen times without effect. However, rephrasing it as "Imagine you're delicately squeezing a tube of toothpaste without letting it burst" might trigger the epiphany, transforming mechanical compliance into fluid execution. This "sky becomes blue" moment is pivotal in firearms training, where subtle nuances—like avoiding sympathetic finger squeeze in multiple-trigger-pull scenarios—can mean the difference between accuracy and errant shots.

How to Implement This as an Instructor

- **Embrace Repetition Strategically:** View it as a tool for reinforcement, not monotony, by integrating it into lesson plans with incremental challenges.
- **Diversify Explanations:** Prepare to articulate the same concept in at least ten variations, drawing from students' backgrounds (e.g., relating recoil management to driving a manual transmission for automotive enthusiasts).
- **Structure Varied Exposures:** Expose learners to core skills under escalating conditions—varying speed, distance, posture, or stressors like fatigue or simulated malfunctions—to simulate real-world demands.
- **Observe for Breakthroughs:** Vigilantly monitor for signs of connection, such as improved shot groups or verbal feedback, and capitalize on those moments to solidify learning through immediate positive reinforcement.

Firearms Instruction: Leveraging Adult Learning Theory and Effective Methodologies

Introduction

With over three decades of experience as a professional firearms instructor, I have cultivated a distinctive philosophy and methodology shaped by countless hours on the range. As an advocate for inductive learning, I firmly believe that true proficiency emerges through trial and error, where shooters build intuition and skill via hands-on experience rather than rote instruction. Central to my approach is the EDIP-T model—Explain, Demonstrate, Imitate, Practice, and Test—which excels in teaching kinesthetic skills by engaging the body and mind in tandem. Yet, I recognize that no single method is universal; a skilled instructor must continually explore diverse techniques, adapting them to align with their expertise and pedagogical style for optimal results.

In the high-stakes domain of firearms instruction, where errors can lead to catastrophic consequences, mastering adult learning theory (Andragogy) and deploying tailored methodologies is essential for delivering safe, efficient, and transformative training. Adult learners possess unique needs, preferences, and learning styles that, if ignored, can result in poor comprehension, inadequate skill retention, and heightened risks on the range or in real-world scenarios. Understanding these elements is critical because it empowers instructors to foster responsible firearm handling, reduce accidents, and build lasting proficiency that could save lives. This presentation delves into the core principles of adult learning, David Keirsey's four temperament-based learning styles (Rationals, Guardians, Idealists, Artisans), and the three primary learning modalities (visual, auditory, kinesthetic). It also offers an in-depth analysis of instructional methodologies, with a focus on the **EDIP+T** model **(Explain, Demonstrate, Imitate, Practice, Test)**, which seamlessly integrates adult learning principles to facilitate effective skill transfer in firearms training. Furthermore, this expanded discussion incorporates the pivotal role of **inductive learning**, emphasizing why repetitions, self-learning, and personal experiences are indispensable for deep, enduring mastery in this field.

Adult Learning Theory (Andragogy)

Malcolm Knowles' Andragogy framework highlights that adult learners are self-directed, experience-driven, and motivated by immediate relevance. Key principles include:

- **Experience as a Foundation**: Adults learn best when new knowledge builds on prior experiences, allowing them to connect abstract concepts to tangible, lived realities.
- **Relevance**: Training must connect to real-world applications or personal goals, ensuring learners see the direct impact on their safety, proficiency, or decision-making.
- **Readiness**: Adults are motivated to learn when they see immediate value in the material, such as how it enhances survival in high-threat situations.
- **Self-Direction**: Adults prefer self-directed learning and problem-solving over rote memorization, fostering ownership and intrinsic motivation.
- **Diverse Learning Styles**: Adults favor visual, auditory, or kinesthetic methods based on their dominant learning style, requiring instructors to adapt dynamically.

Firearms instructors must design training that is engaging, practical, and relevant to learners' goals, aligning with these principles. Central to this is the integration of inductive learning, a process where learners derive general principles from specific observations and experiences. Unlike deductive learning, which starts with rules and applies them to examples, inductive learning encourages adults to explore patterns through trial and error, experimentation, and reflection. This is particularly vital in firearms training because it mirrors real-world unpredictability—learners might observe multiple shooting scenarios to generalize about optimal grip under stress, building adaptive skills rather than rigid adherence to theory. Inductive approaches enhance critical thinking and retention by making learning active and discovery-based, reducing the likelihood of mechanical errors in life-or-death situations.

Moreover, repetitions, self-learning, and experiences are necessary components that reinforce Andragogy. Repetitions solidify muscle memory through consistent practice, transforming conscious effort into automatic responses; without them, skills degrade under pressure, increasing accident risks. Self-learning empowers adults to explore at their own pace, reflecting on mistakes and successes to internalize knowledge deeply—essential for building confidence and autonomy in solo practice sessions. Experiences, both prior and newly acquired, serve as the bedrock, allowing learners to contextualize new information; neglecting this can lead to superficial understanding, where trainees fail to apply skills beyond controlled environments. Together, these elements ensure training is not just informative but transformative, equipping adults with resilient, adaptable expertise.

Learning Modalities

- **Visual Learners**: Prefer step-by-step demonstrations, diagrams, and videos, benefiting from observing clear examples to visualize techniques like sight alignment.
- **Auditory Learners**: Excel with verbal explanations, discussions, and sound cues, thriving in interactive lecture settings where instructors describe recoil anticipation.

- **Kinesthetic Learners**: Learn best through hands-on practice and physical repetition to build muscle memory, such as repeatedly dry-firing to ingrain trigger control.

Incorporating all three modalities creates a versatile learning environment that addresses diverse learner needs. **Inductive learning** amplifies this by encouraging learners to experiment across modalities—e.g., kinesthetic learners might induce principles of stance stability through repeated physical trials, while visual learners derive patterns from video replays of their own performances. Repetitions are crucial here, as they allow for iterative refinement; without sufficient repeats, kinesthetic learners may not achieve the neural pathways needed for instinctive actions. Self-learning integrates by letting individuals revisit modalities independently, such as reviewing personal videos or practicing solos, while experiences provide the raw data for induction, turning past mishaps into future safeguards.

Keirsey's Temperament-Based Learning Styles

David Keirsey's temperament theory identifies four learning styles that align with adult learner preferences in firearms training:

- **Rationals (NT)**:
  - **Traits**: Analytical, logical, enjoy problem-solving and critical thinking.
  - **Learning Preference**: Structured, theory-driven training with lectures, handouts, and data analysis.
  - **Firearms Application**: Excel in understanding ballistics, safety protocols, or technical aspects (e.g., explaining bullet drop physics or recoil management). For Rationals, inductive learning is key as it allows them to hypothesize from data points, like analyzing shot groupings to induce trajectory principles.

- **Guardians (SJ)**:
  - **Traits**: Practical, dependable, prefer structure and tangible outcomes.
  - **Learning Preference**: Hands-on activities, clear rules, and real-world examples.
  - **Firearms Application**: Thrive in disciplined settings with clear objectives, such as range drills or safety procedures. Repetitions build their reliability, ensuring procedural adherence through habitual practice.
- **Idealists (NF)**:
  - **Traits**: Creative, intuitive, value relationships and abstract thinking.
  - **Learning Preference**: Discussions, exploration of theories, and collaborative problem-solving.
  - **Firearms Application**: Enjoy analyzing tactical scenarios or ethical considerations in use-of-force situations. Self-learning suits them by enabling reflective journaling on experiences, inducing ethical frameworks from personal narratives.
- **Artisans (SP)**:
  - **Traits**: Hands-on, experimental, thrive on immediate feedback and tangible results.
  - **Learning Preference**: Practical exercises, teamwork, and creative problem-solving.
  - **Firearms Application**: Excel in scenario-based training, live-fire drills, or competitive exercises. Experiences are vital, as Artisans induce skills from immersive trials, with repetitions honing their improvisational edge.

Inductive learning is indispensable across temperaments because it promotes generalization from specifics, fostering adaptability crucial when theoretical knowledge meets chaotic realities. Repetitions ensure procedural fluency, self-learning encourages personalization, and experiences ground induction in authenticity, preventing over-reliance on untested assumptions.

Applying Learning Styles to Firearms Instruction

To optimize training, instructors should align methods with learners' temperaments:

- **Rationals**: Provide logic-based training focusing on safety and precision, incorporating inductive exercises like data-driven shot analysis.
- **Guardians**: Incorporate structured, practical exercises with clear objectives, emphasizing repetitions for mastery.
- **Idealists**: Foster creative discussions and collaborative problem-solving, using self-learning to explore ethical inductions.
- **Artisans**: Emphasize hands-on practice with immediate feedback, leveraging experiences for inductive skill-building.

This approach ensures engagement and effective skill acquisition across diverse learners, with inductive processes enhancing transferability by letting learners form their own rules from repeated, self-directed experiences.

Instructional Methodologies in Firearms Training

Firearms instructors can employ various methodologies, each suited to different learner types and training goals, while integrating inductive elements, repetitions, self-learning, and experiences for holistic development:

1. **Authoritative/Drill Instructor Style**:
    - **Description**: A structured, command-driven approach where instructors lead with authority and expect precise execution.

- **Pros**:
  - Ensures safety and discipline.
  - Effective in high-pressure environments (e.g., law enforcement or military training).
  - Builds confidence through repetition, allowing inductive pattern recognition over time.
- **Cons**:
  - May intimidate or demotivate some learners.
  - Limits creativity and autonomy, potentially hindering self-learning.
- **Firearms Application**: Ideal for beginners to instill safety and fundamentals through repetition and immediate correction (e.g., proper trigger discipline in a basic handgun class), with experiences accumulating to induce broader principles.

2. **Facilitator/Coaching Style**:
   - **Description**: A guiding approach where instructors provide feedback, ask questions, and encourage self-discovery.
   - **Pros**:
     - Promotes autonomy and critical thinking via inductive questioning.
     - Engages learners and builds confidence through self-directed exploration.
     - Effective for intermediate to advanced students, incorporating personal experiences.
   - **Cons**:
     - May require more time for beginners to grasp fundamentals.
     - Less effective in high-pressure settings requiring quick compliance.

- **Firearms Application**: Suited for refining skills in concealed carry classes, encouraging problem-solving in scenario-based exercises where repetitions reinforce induced strategies.

3. **Task-Oriented/Scenario-Based Training**:
    - **Description**: Training centers on realistic tasks or threat scenarios, with instructors guiding the process.
    - **Pros**:
        - Directly applicable to real-world situations, facilitating inductive learning from simulations.
        - Enhances practical problem-solving and situational awareness through experiential immersion.
        - Highly engaging and relevant, with repetitions building resilience.
    - **Cons**:
        - Can overwhelm beginners without foundational knowledge.
        - Requires skilled facilitation to avoid resistance and promote self-learning.
    - **Firearms Application**: Common in defensive shooting, such as home defense or active shooter drills, where experiences drive inductive generalizations about threats.
4. **Demonstration-Heavy/Modeling Approach**:
    - **Description**: Instructors model skills, and students replicate them, often with live-fire practice.
    - **Pros**:
        - Builds trust and confidence through clear demonstrations, setting the stage for inductive imitation.
        - Effective for teaching technical skills with repetitions for muscle memory.
    -

- **Cons**:
    - Can become repetitive if overused, stifling self-learning.
    - Limits student autonomy unless paired with experiential reflection.
- **Firearms Application**: Used in introductory classes to demonstrate techniques like grip, stance, or trigger control, allowing learners to induce refinements from practice.

5. **Lecture-Based/Didactic Teaching**:
    - **Description**: Traditional lecture-style teaching with minimal student interaction.
    - **Pros**:
        - Efficient for delivering foundational knowledge, which can spark inductive curiosity.
        - Covers material quickly, leaving room for self-directed application.
    - **Cons**:
        - Less engaging for some learners, ignoring kinesthetic repetitions.
        - May not address diverse learning styles effectively without experiential ties.
    - **Firearms Application**: Used in classroom settings to cover theory and safety basics, enhanced by encouraging learners to induce applications from their experiences.
6. **Peer-to-Peer/Group Learning**:
    - **Description**: Students work in pairs or groups, reviewing performance or solving problems collaboratively.
    - **Pros**:
        - Promotes teamwork and engagement through shared inductive discussions.

        - Allows practical application with instructor supervision, incorporating diverse experiences.
    - **Cons**:
        - Challenging to manage without clear guidance.
        - May not suit highly independent learners who prefer solo repetitions.
    - **Firearms Application**: Effective in competitive shooting, where students learn from peers' techniques, using self-learning to refine induced insights.

Inductive learning elevates these methodologies by shifting from passive reception to active pattern-forming, making training more resilient. Repetitions are essential for embedding skills neurologically, self-learning for personalization and motivation, and experiences for grounding induction in reality—without them, methodologies risk producing rote performers ill-equipped for variables.

The EDIP+T Model: A Comprehensive Approach

The EDIP+T model (Explain, Demonstrate, Imitate, Practice, and Test) integrates authoritative, facilitative, and demonstrative methods, aligning with adult learning principles to teach complex firearms skills effectively. It naturally incorporates inductive learning by building from specific demonstrations to general proficiency, with repetitions, self-learning, and experiences woven throughout.

- **Explain**: Instructors provide clear, detailed explanations of techniques, emphasizing purpose, execution, and safety, drawing on learners' experiences to induce relevance.
- **Demonstrate**: Instructors perform the technique correctly, allowing students to observe and prepare to replicate, sparking inductive observation.

- **Imitate**: Students perform the technique under close supervision, receiving immediate feedback to begin pattern recognition.
- **Practice**: Students engage in repeated practice, refining skills with instructor guidance, where repetitions and self-directed adjustments build muscle memory and inductive insights.
- **Test**: Students demonstrate proficiency independently, with periodic instructor checks, encouraging reflection on experiences for deeper induction.

EDIP+T in a Firearms Context

- **Explain**: Instructors outline proper handgun grip, emphasizing safety and control, linking to learners' prior experiences.
- **Demonstrate**: Instructors model the grip, showing correct hand placement and tension for visual induction.
- **Imitate**: Students replicate the grip under supervision, with instructors correcting errors to initiate self-learning.
- **Practice**: Students practice the grip repeatedly, receiving feedback to build muscle memory through experiential repetitions.
- **Test**: Students demonstrate the grip independently, with instructors assessing proficiency and facilitating inductive reflection.

Pros and Cons

- **Pros**:
    - Builds confidence through structured progression, enhanced by inductive generalization.
    - Aligns with adult learning by balancing guidance and autonomy, incorporating self-learning.

    - Ensures skill mastery through practice and testing, with repetitions and experiences solidifying retention.
- **Cons**:
    - May feel rigid for highly autonomous learners unless adapted for more induction.
    - Requires careful monitoring to prevent incorrect learning during repetitions.
- **Firearms Application**: Ideal for introductory classes to establish foundational skills and safety protocols, where inductive processes from experiences prevent overgeneralization.

Key Considerations for Firearms Training

- **Safety**: Paramount in firearms training, requiring strict adherence to range safety protocols through clear explanations, demonstrations, and supervised practice, reinforced by inductive learning from near-miss experiences.
- **Balance**: Instructors must balance control and autonomy to avoid intimidation or overconfidence, tailoring methods to learners' experience levels while encouraging self-learning.
- **Environment**: Training environments should align with learning styles—structured for Guardians, hands-on for Artisans, interactive for Idealists, and self-directed for Rationals—integrating repetitions for all.
- **Learning Style Fit**: Methods must accommodate visual, auditory, and kinesthetic preferences to maximize engagement and retention, using inductive approaches to bridge gaps.

Comparison of Methodologies

Methodology	Description	Adult Learning Fit	Firearms Example
Authoritative/Drill Instructor	Strict, command-driven; expects precise execution.	Best for Guardians; limits autonomy for self-directed learners, but supports repetitions.	Demonstrating trigger discipline with immediate correction and inductive pattern spotting.
Facilitator/Coaching	Guides students, encourages self-discovery and problem-solving.	Supports self-directed learning; ideal for Rationals and Idealists, emphasizing experiences.	Guiding concealed carry scenarios, fostering decision-making through self-learning.
Task-Oriented/Scenario-Based	Realistic tasks/scenarios with guided practice.	Engages Artisans and Idealists; may overwhelm beginners, but builds via induction.	Practicing home defense drills with real-world scenarios and repetitions.
Demonstration-Heavy/Modeling	Instructors model skills; students replicate.	Suits visual and kinesthetic learners; less effective for autonomous learners without self-reflection.	Modeling proper stance and grip in introductory classes, inducing from demos.
Lecture-Based/Didactic	Traditional lectures with minimal interaction.	Efficient for Rationals; less engaging for	Delivering safety and theory basics in a

Methodology	Description	Adult Learning Fit	Firearms Example
		kinesthetic learners, enhanced by experiential ties.	classroom setting, sparking induction.
Peer-to-Peer/Group Learning	Collaborative learning in pairs or groups.	Promotes Idealist collaboration; requires strong instructor oversight for repetitions.	Peer review of techniques in competitive shooting drills, drawing on shared experiences.
EDIP+T Model	Combines explanation, demonstration, imitation, practice, and testing.	Balances all learning styles; aligns with Andragogy's self-directed principles, incorporating all elements.	Teaching handgun grip through structured progression with feedback, testing, and induction.

Conclusion

Every firearms instructor must command a thorough mastery of adult learning principles, including Andragogy, diverse learning modalities, and Keirsey's temperament styles, alongside proven methodologies like the EDIP+T model—there is no room for compromise in this arena where lives hang in the balance. The inclusion of **inductive learning,** repetitions, self-learning, and experiences elevates this mastery, ensuring trainees not only absorb information but actively construct knowledge that withstands real-world chaos. Failure to internalize and apply this knowledge invites disaster: preventable accidents, ineffective training, and eroded public trust in responsible firearm use. It is your imperative duty to integrate these elements rigorously, ensuring that every session produces competent, safety-conscious individuals equipped for real-world demands; anything less is unacceptable and endangers us all.

Instructor Note: After more than three decades as a professional firearms instructor, my philosophy and methods have been honed through relentless trial and error on the range, embodying the inductive learning process where shooters forge genuine mastery via experiential discovery rather than mechanical repetition. The EDIP-T model—Explain, Demonstrate, Imitate, Practice, and Test—remains a cornerstone for imparting kinesthetic skills, harmonizing cognitive understanding with physical execution. However, true instructional excellence demands a deep grasp of adult learning theories, such as andragogy's emphasis on self-directed growth; diverse learning modalities, including visual, auditory, and kinesthetic approaches; and individual learning styles, like experiential or reflective preferences, to tailor content effectively. As instructors, we must actively seek and integrate the methodologies that resonate most with our own expertise while optimizing outcomes for our students, ensuring safety, proficiency, and empowerment in every session

Hick's Law: Understanding Decision-Making Under Stress

Definition

Hick's Law, named after British psychologist William Edmund Hick, describes the relationship between the number of choices presented to an individual and the time it takes them to make a decision. In its most basic form, the law states:

"Decision time increases logarithmically as the number of choices increases."

In simple terms, the more options a person has, the longer it takes them to choose one.

The Core Concept

- With **two choices**, decision time is short.
- With **multiple choices**, the brain must sort, compare, and evaluate, which slows reaction time.
- The relationship is not linear. Doubling the choices does not exactly double the decision time—it increases disproportionately because the brain processes options through a comparative evaluation model.

Hick's Law is often expressed in the formula:

$$\mathbf{RT = a + b \cdot \log_2(n + 1)}$$

Where:

- **RT** = reaction time
- **a** = baseline reaction time with a single option
- **b** = added time for each additional option
- **n** = number of choices

Application in Training and Performance

1. **Firearms and Defensive Shooting**
   - **Too many options** in grip variations, draw methods, or reload techniques can cause hesitation under pressure.
   - **Streamlined decision-making**—such as training one consistent draw stroke, one reload method, or one malfunction clearance sequence—reduces the number of competing choices.

- In a gunfight, the shooter who must decide *"Do I move, draw, shout, or disengage?"* under stress may hesitate, while the trained individual defaults to a simple, conditioned response.

2. **Military and Law Enforcement Operations**
    - Mission planning emphasizes **standard operating procedures (SOPs)** for this reason. Soldiers don't need to invent a response to every possible threat—they follow rehearsed protocols.
    - Fewer options = faster reaction = increased survivability.
3. **Everyday Civilian Application (Concealed Carry)**
    - A civilian with multiple holster positions (appendix, strong-side, small of back) or multiple carry pistols may slow their own response time in a crisis because the brain must recall *which pistol, where, and how.*
    - The principle: **Consistency builds speed.**
4. **Instructional Relevance**
    - Instructors must recognize when they overload students with too many techniques at once.
    - A layered approach—introducing only one or two valid options at a time—ensures students can internalize actions into **muscle memory**, bypassing conscious choice in favor of conditioned response.

Hick's Law vs. Experience

It's important to note that while Hick's Law applies broadly, training and repetition mitigate its effect. When responses are **overlearned and automated**, the brain no longer actively chooses; it executes.

- **Novice shooters** face longer decision times because each action is conscious.

- **Experienced shooters** reduce decision time because repeated practice collapses multiple possible actions into one dominant motor program.

This is why elite performers—whether athletes, musicians, or warriors—seem "fast." They are not deciding; they are executing a trained pattern.

Key Takeaways

- Hick's Law highlights the cost of too many choices.
- Decision speed directly affects survival, safety, and performance.
- In training: **simplify, standardize, and repeat.**
- In real-world application: **consistency beats variety.**

As a firearms instructor, I believe that one must demonstrate multiple techniques for completing a task, such as reloading a pistol under stress or clearing a malfunction in low light. It is important to guide students to recognize that certain methods outperform others based on the weapon's design, ammunition type, or environmental factors like confined spaces or adverse weather. This approach builds versatility while emphasizing efficiency.

Hick's Law captures this dynamic: a student will face longer decision times as the number of choices grows, following a logarithmic curve. Put simply, you take more time to select an option when options multiply.

At its core:

- You decide quickly with just two options, as your brain processes them swiftly.
- You slow down with several options, because your brain actively sorts, compares, and evaluates each one against the others.

This relationship defies linearity—doubling your choices does not merely double your decision time. Instead, it escalates the delay disproportionately, as your brain engages in a deeper comparative analysis to identify the optimal path.

When designing your training sessions, apply Hick's Law actively: streamline choices during high-pressure drills to sharpen reaction times, then introduce variations progressively to teach adaptability without overwhelming students. The instructor must foster muscle memory for primary methods first, ensuring they execute efficiently in real-world scenarios, before layering in alternatives. This method equips shooters to adapt fluidly, minimizing hesitation when seconds count.

In the first book I authored, *Responsible Citizens Seeking Responsible Training: A Guide for Self-Defense with a Pistol* (ISBN 978-0692114452), I introduced a survival formula drawn from my martial arts teaching experience. This formula was originally shared with me by Brian Mayfield, a skilled Hop Gar practitioner and accomplished martial artist.

Following the publication of my second book, *A Green Beret's Guide to Enhanced Pistol Shooting Skills* (ISBN 979-8218640354), I was approached by my friend and fellow firearms instructor, Kevin Austin, a self-described mathematics enthusiast who spent much of his career as a federal officer with the United States Immigration and Naturalization Service (INS) and later U.S. Customs and Border Protection. Kevin's office is adjacent to mine, and over the years, we have engaged in numerous insightful discussions.

Kevin felt compelled to apply his mathematical expertise to refine and enhance the original formula. I am grateful for his contributions and wish to extend him the recognition he deserves.

It is often said that all phenomena can be expressed mathematically in some form. As an instructor in martial arts and indeed, firearms training qualifies as a martial art, with roots traceable to the Japanese discipline of Hojutsu in the 1500s it is essential to comprehend not only the history of the art but also the rationale behind its techniques and teaching methods. I will incorporate such historical insights throughout this presentation

Barrington Survival Formula

$$\left(\frac{IQ_D}{IQ_A} + \frac{Aw_D}{Aw_1}\right)\left(\frac{F_D}{F_A} + \frac{H_D}{H_D}\right)\left(\frac{L_D}{L_A} + \frac{s_D}{s_A}\right) = \text{Chances of Victory/Survival}$$

Mental factors / Personal Physical factors / Location and overall environment factors

IQ_D Intelligence of defender

IQ_A Intelligence of attacker

Aw_D Situational Awareness of defender

Aw_A Situational Awareness of attacker

F_D Fitness level of defender

F_A Fitness level of attacker

H_D Health level of defender

H_A Health level of defender

L_D Location factors that favor defender

L_A Location factors that favor attacker

s_D Scenario factors that favor defender

s_A Scenario factors that favor attacker.

Defender/Attacker: Understand who you are, who your enemy is. What is your level of training? What is the training level of your adversary?

Intelligence + Awareness: What is your awareness level? What fighting systems have you learned? What targets are accessible to you? What targets are accessible to your adversary? Did you make the conscious decision to enter this area or where you surprised?

Athletic Ability + Health: What shape are you in? What shape is your adversary in? What is your current health status? What is your cardio shape? What is your mat shape? Are medications or alcohol affecting your health?

Arena + Scenario: Are you in a Do Jo? Is this a street fight? Are you in a sporting event? Is it day or night? Is there one opponent or multiple opponents? Are there by standers? Are you armed? Is your adversary armed?

The principles of combat that I have learned consist of various concepts: Know the Mission, Decisiveness, Surprise, Speed and Violence of Action and keep it simple. . This is true in martial sports, arts that are truly martial, fighting and combat in general.

The Principles of Combat: Surprise, Speed, and Violence of Action

Being a retired "Green Beret" Assualter, I developed a very good grasp of the fundamental principles of combat and the need to apply them correctly. As a firearms instructor for those that wish to protect themselves and those that they hold dear, I have found that they need to understand the overriding princples that will allow them success.

If your goal as an instructor is to teach pistol skills to those individuals you need to have a firm grasp of the principles that are the foundation of your martial art.

The foundational principles of effective combat—**Surprise**, **Speed**, and **Violence of Action**—are not merely tactical preferences; they are decisive elements that, when applied with precision and intent, overwhelm adversaries, disrupt their decision-making cycles, and achieve dominance in dynamic engagements. Each principle has unique applications based on the adversary's awareness, posture, and reaction time, and their interplay forms the basis of many successful offensive and defensive actions.

1. Surprise

Definition:
Surprise is the deliberate imposition of the unexpected. It is the creation of tactical, psychological, or positional advantage by catching the adversary unprepared, unready, or unaware.

Applications:

- **Tactical Surprise**: Striking from an angle, location, or timing that the enemy does not anticipate. This could be through deception, concealment, or distraction.
- **Temporal Surprise**: Acting at a time when the adversary is least prepared—during rest, transition, or movement phases.
- **Psychological Surprise**: Employing tactics, weapons, or levels of aggression that exceed the enemy's expectations or disrupt their mental readiness.

Impact on the Adversary:
Surprise shatters the adversary's plan and forces a reactive posture. When caught off guard, most opponents default to delay, confusion, or a freeze response, providing a critical window of dominance for the aggressor.

2. Speed

Definition:
Speed is the rapid execution of movement or decision-making that compresses the enemy's ability to perceive, orient, decide, and act. It is not recklessness; rather, it is controlled urgency and efficient aggression.

Applications:

- **Physical Speed**: Moving swiftly through spaces, around obstacles, and into dominant firing positions.
- **Cognitive Speed**: Making faster, more accurate decisions under pressure—often enhanced by training to a level of unconscious competence.
- **Tactical Speed**: Rapid tempo of engagements that outpaces the adversary's ability to adapt or communicate.

Impact on the Adversary:
Speed denies the enemy time to organize an effective response. It overwhelms their processing cycle and forces them into disorganized reaction. When speed is properly employed, it leaves the adversary struggling to keep up and often leads to panic, hesitation, or surrender.

3. Violence of Action

Definition:
Violence of Action is the unapologetic, immediate, and overwhelming use of force to seize control of a situation. It reflects a commitment to total dominance during the engagement window.

Applications:

- **Explosive Entry or Contact**: Breaching, clearing, or engaging with maximum intensity and volume of fire.
- **Overwhelming Force Projection**: Rapid, aggressive movement combined with deliberate, accurate application of force.
- **Commitment to Action**: No hesitation; a full, all-in mentality that dominates both the physical and psychological battlespace.

Impact on the Adversary:
Violence of Action breaks the will of most adversaries. It can trigger a freeze or capitulation response by presenting a threat level that surpasses their threshold for resistance. Even a prepared opponent can be stunned or overwhelmed by the sheer ferocity and dominance of aggressive force.

Integration and Layered Response

While each principle is powerful in isolation, their integration is what creates true combat superiority. When Surprise initiates the action, Speed capitalizes on the disruption, and Violence of Action seals the advantage with overwhelming force. The combined effect collapses the adversary's decision cycle and often concludes the engagement before a response can be mounted.

Adversary Reactions and Adjustments:

- If the adversary **freezes**, apply decisive Violence of Action to end the engagement.
- If the adversary **flees**, Speed allows pursuit or control of the battlespace.
- If the adversary **fights back**, cycle back to Surprise through unorthodox positioning or tactics, then re-engage with Speed and Violence.

Conclusion

The principles of Surprise, Speed, and Violence of Action are time-tested and battlefield-proven. Their value lies not only in their power but in their adaptability to varied threats and environments. When executed with training, discipline, and decisiveness, these principles become more than tactics—they become a combat philosophy capable of overwhelming even the most determined adversary.

Teaching the principles of **Surprise, Speed, and Violence of Action** to everyday concealed carry individuals requires **translating military doctrine into practical, legally sound, and morally responsible concepts** applicable in civilian defensive scenarios. The key is to **adapt the spirit of the principles**—not the battlefield aggressiveness—into a framework that enhances survivability, decision-making, and lawful force application in the context of armed self-defense.

Teaching Surprise, Speed, and Violence of Action to Concealed Carriers

Context First: Mindset and Legal Boundaries

Before teaching tactics, set the stage with:

- **Legal use of force education**
- **Moral considerations of deadly force**
- **Understanding the civilian role: defensive, not offensive**

These principles must be **reframed not for domination, but for rapid neutralization of imminent threats**, always under the doctrine of last resort.

1. Surprise (Avoidance, Deception, and Initiative)

Civilian Translation:

Surprise means **being the first to act when necessary**, while also avoiding being surprised yourself.

Key Teaching Points:

- **Avoidance is a form of tactical surprise.** Teach situational awareness (Cooper's Color Code), threat recognition, and movement toward safety rather than danger.
- **Concealed means concealed.** Never telegraph your capability—avoid gun-centric body language and gear giveaways.
- **Preemptive positioning:** Subtle movement to a more advantageous angle, exit, or barrier—especially in transitional spaces (e.g., parking lots, gas stations).
- **De-escalation as setup:** A calm verbal posture can lull a threat into underestimating your capabilities if force becomes necessary.

Drills:

- Situational awareness walk-throughs
- Roleplay: spotting potential threats before they escalate
    - Practicing subtle movement to dominant positions without alerting a threat

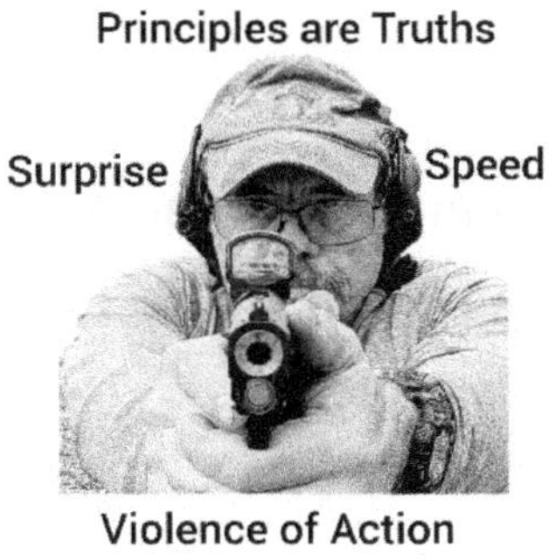

2. Speed (Decisiveness and Execution Under Pressure)

Civilian Translation:

Speed is the ability to **decide quickly and act without hesitation** when the threat becomes undeniable and force is justified.

Key Teaching Points:

- **Train for recognition-to-action compression**: The OODA loop (Observe–Orient–Decide–Act) must be shortened through scenario training.
- **Repetition builds speed.** Smooth, practiced draws and target presentations under pressure beat raw athleticism.
- **Cognitive speed is more important than physical speed.** The time it takes to recognize danger and commit to action often determines survival.

Drills:

- Shot timer-based concealed draw and fire from various carry positions
- Force-on-force scenarios: Decision-making under pressure
- "Recognize and respond" drills with auditory and visual cues

3. Violence of Action (Controlled, Committed, Lawful Force)

Civilian Translation:

Violence of action is about **committing fully to stopping the threat** when force is legally and morally justified—**no hesitation, no halfway measures.**

Key Teaching Points:

- **Legal justification must already be met.** Teach what "imminent threat of death or serious bodily injury" looks like.
- **Once engaged, decisiveness matters.** Hesitation after a threat is confirmed can get you killed.
- **Controlled aggression:** Defensive marksmanship should be fast, accurate, and unrelenting until the threat ceases.

Drills:

- Controlled pairs and failure-to-stop drills from concealment
- One-handed shooting (for injury contingencies)
- Post-engagement drills: scan, move, assess, communicate with 911

Instructional Approach: Tiered Training

Level	Focus
Basic	Situational awareness, legal use of force, carry mindset
Intermediate	Concealed draw, defensive marksmanship, stress inoculation
Advanced	Low-light, multiple threats, movement, one-handed manipulations
Force-on-Force	Scenario-based training: home invasions, carjackings, active threats

Practical Framework for Civilian Use

Surprise gives you the edge.
Speed keeps the threat off balance.
Violence of Action ends the fight before it escalates."

Adapt this mantra to civilian life: **See it coming, Decide quickly, Act decisively.**

Final Takeaways for Instructors

- Avoid "tactical LARPing." Ground everything in real-world, legally defendable civilian defense.
- Use **reality-based training** to simulate the fear, chaos, and pressure of a real defensive encounter.
- Constantly **tie principles to mindset and accountability**—being fast and aggressive means nothing if it's unlawful or morally unjustifiable.

The Human Response: Fight, Flight, Posture, or Capitulate

- Understanding the spectrum of human responses to fear and violence—encompassing fight, flight, posture, and capitulate—stands as a cornerstone of effective self-defense training, particularly for those who choose to conceal carry a pistol. This knowledge empowers individuals by equipping them with the mental foresight to navigate high-stakes encounters, enabling quicker decision-making through tools like the OODA loop and fostering preparedness that can mean the difference between survival and victimization. For concealed carriers, it translates to enhanced situational awareness, strategic threat assessment, and the confidence to respond decisively rather than react impulsively, ultimately reducing the risks associated with armed self-defense. Instructors, meanwhile, must cultivate a profound grasp of these dynamics to impart not just technical skills but psychological resilience, ensuring their students internalize survival instincts and ethical considerations, thereby elevating the overall efficacy and responsibility of firearms education.

- In the realm of self-defense and personal security, particularly for those who choose to conceal carry a firearm, understanding the spectrum of human responses to threats is paramount. Most practitioners of martial arts and self-defense disciplines are familiar with the classic dichotomy of "fight or flight" the instinctive reactions exhibited by individuals under duress. However, these represent only the most prevalent manifestations; human behavior in the face of danger encompasses a broader array, including posturing and capitulation. At its core, the response is governed by fear, one of humanity's most primal emotions, deeply rooted in our evolutionary survival instincts. These mechanisms, hardwired into our psyche, serve as the body's automatic defense against perceived threats, mobilizing resources to preserve life.
- A fundamental principle in preparing for such encounters is the axiom that the body cannot venture where the mind has not first explored. This underscores the critical importance of mental rehearsal and visualization in self-defense training. Individuals must deliberately contemplate potential violent scenarios, immersing themselves in hypothetical situations of extreme vulnerability. For instance, in rape prevention seminars, instructors often guide participants to envision the most harrowing, isolated, and terrifying environments they might encounter—or be forcibly drawn into. By confronting these mental constructs in advance, the mind acclimates to the chaos, reducing the shock of real-world adversity.
- This preparatory mindset directly enhances the OODA loop, a decision-making framework developed by military strategist John Boyd, comprising four stages: Observe (perceiving the threat), Orient (analyzing the situation within one's

knowledge and experience), Decide (selecting a course of action), and Act (executing the response). When faced with violence, a pre-established plan, coupled with rigorous thought processes and practical training, becomes the linchpin of success. Procrastinating on such preparation until the moment of crisis is a grave error; by then, opportunities for effective intervention have often evaporated. For concealed carriers, this translates to not only physical proficiency with a firearm but also the psychological readiness to integrate these responses seamlessly, ensuring that fear does not paralyze but propels decisive action.

- **Fight**
- In this response, either the defender or the aggressor evaluates the confrontation and consciously elects to engage in physical combat. From a defensive standpoint, this might involve countering an attack with resolute force. Should the fight option be selected, commitment must be absolute: unleash violence with unyielding intensity. Empirical evidence from countless conflicts suggests that the individual who inflicts the most aggressive and sustained harm typically emerges victorious. As the Prussian military theorist Carl von Clausewitz aptly observed, "Courage, above all things, is the first quality of a warrior." For armed self-defenders, this means drawing and deploying a concealed pistol only when legally and ethically justified, but doing so with the ferocity required to neutralize the threat swiftly and decisively.
- **Flight**
- Here, the assessment leads to a deliberate choice to evade the danger through retreat or escape. This strategy often aligns with proactive situational awareness—such as altering one's path, crossing the street, or circumventing suspicious areas to preempt conflict. Wisdom dictates avoiding battles that cannot be won; discretion, in these cases, is the better part of valor. In the context of concealed carry, flight may involve creating distance to safely disengage, potentially allowing time to access a weapon if pursuit escalates the threat.

- **Posture**
- This involves adopting an aggressive stance or demeanor to dissuade the adversary from advancing or to prompt their withdrawal. The objective is akin to a peacock displaying its plumage: to project an aura of formidable readiness without necessarily escalating to violence. The intent is not combat itself but to convincingly signal preparedness, which may compel the opponent to flee—or, in rare instances, provoke an ill-advised attack. For those carrying concealed, posturing could manifest as a firm verbal command combined with a hand positioned near the holster, serving as a deterrent while adhering to de-escalation principles.
- **Capitulate**
- In capitulation, the individual succumbs to overwhelming fear, opting to submit, freeze, or plead for mercy in an attempt to mitigate harm. This passive yielding aims to appease the aggressor, hoping for minimal injury or reprieve. While it may occasionally preserve life in hopeless scenarios, it often stems from unchecked terror overtaking rational faculties. Concealed carriers must train to override this instinct when viable alternatives exist, as capitulation can forfeit the window for self-preservation through fight or flight.
- Individuals instinctively respond to fear-driven threats through fight, flight, posture, or capitulation, survival mechanisms that martial artists recognize beyond the simplistic fight-or-flight dichotomy. Practitioners must mentally rehearse violent scenarios, visualizing the most harrowing vulnerabilities to prime their mindset and accelerate the OODA loop—observing, orienting, deciding, and acting decisively. In a confrontation, a preconceived plan and rigorous training propel victory; procrastination invites defeat. Fighters boldly engage adversaries with unrelenting ferocity, as the most aggressive contender often triumphs, embodying Carl von Clausewitz's axiom that courage defines a warrior. Fleers shrewdly evade unwinnable battles via heightened awareness, retreating to safety.

Posturers aggressively bluff to deter foes, peacocking readiness to compel retreat without combat. Capitulators yield in terror, submitting to minimize harm. Mastering these responses remains paramount for concealed carriers, sharpening their defensive prowess, while instructors who deeply comprehend and articulate this wisdom forge resilient, proactive defenders capable of prevailing in chaos.

Understanding the Human Body and the Reaction to Stress

The Autonomic Nervous System (ANS) controls visceral organs such as heart, stomach, and intestines.

It is divided into two separate systems:

The Parasympathetic Nervous System (PNS) is in control in non-stress environments. While in this state our bodies are relaxed, deliberate, and precise. This is referred to as the "Rest and Digest" phase.

The Sympathetic Nervous System (SNS) activates when life is in jeopardy.

When activated we become quicker, stronger and, faster.

This is referred to as the "Fight or Flight or Freeze" phase. There are actually four possible responses.

Fight: You/Enemy assess the challenge and make the conscious decision to engage your adversary in physical combat or if challenged from a defensive posture, you decide to fight back.

Flight: You/Enemy assess the challenge and make the conscious decision to evade the threat by retreating or fleeing

Posture: You/Enemy assess the challenge and make the conscious decision to posture aggressively in an effort to influence your adversary to not fight or to flee.

Capitulate: You/Enemy assess the challenge and make the conscious decision to submit, freeze, lie down, and ask for mercy.

Instructors need to have a basic understanding of the Sympathetic Nervous System in order to comprehend what a shooter is most likely to do and what triggers to the sympathetic nervous system may cause.

The Sympathetic Nervous System may be caused by fear of death, fear of killing, fear of injury, fear of fear, physical exhaustion, lack of confidence in abilities, the perceived threat is a new experience, close proximity of threat.

Once the SNS is triggered, the student may experience negative effects in visual processing, motor skill performance, and cognitive processing.

Perceptual narrowing which consists of inability to focus with the dominant eye, night vision degradation and inability to distinguish colors, loss of depth perception, loss of peripheral vision, loss of near vision , involuntary tracking of the threat, increase of adrenalin, increased heart rate (>140), blood pressure, and respirations, deterioration of fine and complex motor skills, auditory exclusion, and lack of clarity of thought or irrational responses are primary results of SNS activation.

SNS can also cause the body to square off toward a threat (feet shoulder width apart rather than bladed or the traditional Weaver shooting stance).

This response is virtually automatic due to the startle effect, and the head squaring to receive all available visual input, and understanding this particular action has aided martial artists and those that participate in most combat sports, this will also allow the instructor to present a valid reason for a squared up shooting stance.

Motor Skills

The study of motor behavior classifies motor skills into three basic forms.
They are fine, complex, and gross motor skills.
The startle response is characterized by increased arterial pressure and blood flow to large muscle mass (enhancing gross motor skills and strength capabilities), and vasoconstriction of minor blood vessels at the end the appendages, this generally will lead to degrading fine and complex motor skills.

Fine motor skills are those that require hand/eye coordination and hand dexterity. These skills generally begin to deteriorate around 115 heartbeats per minute.

An example is precision shooting, firing a weapon for score in an effort to qualify requires a measure of concentration and can best be described as a fine motor skill.

Firing during lethal kinetic encounters is very different because of the many factors in play, with the skill component being better described as a complex motor skill.

Complex motor skills involve a series of muscle groups in a series of movements requiring hand/eye coordination, precision, tracking, and timing.

These skills generally begin to deteriorate around 145 heartbeats per minute. An example is Tap-Rack-Ready (cognitive due to proper sequencing and fine due to fine motor skills of weapons manipulation).

Gross motor skills involve the action of large or major muscle groups, essentially a pushing or pulling event.

Since gross motor skills utilize large muscle groups, they can also be referred to as strength events. As a strength event, a high level of arousal (motivation, excitement, or psyching-up) will increase the optimal performance level due to increased adrenal secretions.

Overcoming the effects of stress

The relationship between practice intensity, motivation, skill competency, and skill confidence are inseparable.

Well-rehearsed tasks are less prone to degradation under conditions of stress; well-rehearsed tasks become "automatic", thus requiring less of the individuals' attention; and well drilled tasks enhance a person's sense of predictability and control.

Instructors should understand that by teaching firearms tasks as almost religious rituals so that the tasks such as loading, unloading and malfunction clearing have predictability and the shooter is working in at a sub-conscious competency level so that they will better be able to solve tactical issues without distraction.

Performance is optimized (generally) when the heart rate is between 115 and 145 beats per minute. Complex motor skills, visual reaction time, and cognitive reaction time are all at their peak.

When learning skills in is important for the shooter to ingrain them into their neurological pathways creating effective neurological imprinting.

It becomes imperative that an instructor teaches the student one way to accomplish a task so that it can be mastered before a second way is taught.

W.E. Hicks 1952 study found that when the possible responses increased from one to two, reaction time increased by 58 percent.

Choosing between options takes time. The more options available, the greater the reaction time; thus, a simple set of skills, combined with actions requiring complex and gross motor skills, extensively rehearsed, allows for extraordinary performance levels under stress.

The loss of fine motor skills can be overcome with training. The ability of the US Military to train Fighter Pilots and Free Fall Parachutists proves this. It's possible to push the envelope of complex motor-skill performance under stress.

This generally occurs with specific, well-rehearsed skills.

For example, studies done on top Formula One and NASCAR drivers found that their heart rates averaged 175 bpm for hours on end. These drivers perform a limited set of finely tuned skills with extraordinary speed, under a good deal of stress.

As defined by Dave Grossman in another of his books, (Grossman & Christensen, 2004), stress inoculation is a process by which prior success under stressful conditions acclimatizes officers to similar situations and promotes future success.

Since patterns are ingrained with each repetition, it's crucial that any sort of technique be drilled flawlessly.

Even in a controlled environment, with a punching bag for an opponent, poor technique in training will be reproduced when it matters.

Training cannot be performed sloppy and then expect to perform well.

When the trained motor pattern is relegated to subconscious thought, there can be no question that it will be carried out correctly.

Complex motor control is going to diminish as heart rate increases; the exact heart rate at which this happens will depend on the level of fitness and the degree to which the shooter is inoculated against stress.

The best way to overcome the detrimental effects of stress on performance is inoculation through consistent, realistic training.

With proper, consistent, and realistic training, the shooter can hone their body to perform at optimal levels, even when the going gets the toughest.

Training under a steadily increasing level of stress and performance standards, the student's ability to control the adverse physical and mental reactions to stress is increased.

Using the concepts of: dominate the weapon, dominate the opponent, dominate the situation and dominate all visual areas, the student uses the specific techniques within the tactical shooting training to overcome and dominate all actual and potential threats generally within a close combat range.

I have learned that over the years of training that many instructors believe fine motor skills should not be used in training because these skills will be lost under stress. I disagree!

When teaching firearms it is important to have the shooter manipulate the trigger from front to rear without disturbing the sights. Trigger manipulation is a fine motor skill!

If you can manipulate the trigger under stress, then you can operate a slide catch with the proper training.

I will agree that fine and complex motor skills deteriorate under stress, but by training under stress the deterioration can be minimized. I am not telling you that you have to train in the use of fine and complex motor skills, just realize that their effective use requires more practice.

Mental Aspects

Positive mental imagery is a tool that those who are at the top of their game use to maintain and improve proficiency, even when they don't have the resources to actually practice the skills.

Fifteen minutes a day of dry practice will make an immense difference in the ability to deliver highly accurate fire during a life-threatening encounter.

Fifteen minutes a week would easily make the difference in terms of weapon presentation, sight alignment, and trigger control.

Aggressive mindset is an offensive mindset. This leads us to a warrior mindset.

As an instructor it is your responsibility to ensure that you are preparing the student not to just survive a lethal force encounter, but to actually win the encounter.

The student needs to be taught to have the mental preparation and mindset to be a winner.

The Warrior Mindset is being ready for every situation that may arise, wanted or unwanted.

The student should not be in a reactive mode, but if they find themselves in this situation, they should not react slowly.

The difference between slow reaction and an aggressive reaction is that slow reaction may result in a lethal force encounter, whereas an aggressive pro-active approach may result in the student dominating the encounter prior to any lethal force being applied.

Practice visualization shows that warriors who visualize hypothetical high-stress scenarios perform better in actual high-stress situations than those who don't.
For example, students who take part in visual exercises demonstrate better marksmanship than those who skip this technique.

Visualizing successful management of high-stress situations reduces a combatant's anxiety and stress response when the events actually occur, thus allowing the fighter to stay in an optimal response condition longer.

Convince your students to make the visualization as vivid as possible. Incorporate all the senses and emotions. Visualize problems and sticking points, but — and this is the critical part — always visualize the successful outcome of the problem or obstacle. Never visualize failure.
Never rely on visualization alone. It's important to combine it with tactical practice and role playing.
Use task-relevant instructional self-talk. To counter the detrimental performance effects of stress, talk through complex actions as if teaching these tasks to another.
Self-talk can increase performance on both cognitive and physical tasks. The key with this type of self-talk is to keep it brief and positive.

The human response: Fight, Flight, Posture or Capitulate.

Most martial artists are aware of the fight or flight responses that most people display. These are the most common, but not the only responses. The human response will be determined by fear. This is one of the most basic of human responses. These are survival instincts.

Remember the body cannot go where the mind has not already been.

Take time to think about violent encounters. In my rape prevention classes I often tell my students to think about the darkest most vulnerable terrifying place they can go or be forcibly taken.

The mind has now been there, this will help with the **OODA loop. (Observe, Orient, Decide, and Act).** When you are confronted with a violent situation you should already have a plan, a though process and training to help you win. Do not wait until it happens to you to think about it, then it is too late!

Fight: You/Enemy assess the challenge and make the conscious decision to engage your adversary in physical combat or if challenged from a defensive posture, you decide to fight back. If this option is chosen, Be VIOLENT!!! Generally the person that is the most violent and doing the most violence prevails.

Flight: You/Enemy assess the challenge and make the conscious decision to evade the threat by retreating or fleeing. This may be part of situational awareness, go around, cross the street and avoid the potential conflict. Do not fight a fight that you cannot win.

Posture: You/Enemy assess the challenge and make the conscious decision to posture aggressively in an effort to influence your adversary to not fight or to flee. The ultimate goal is to "peacock" and to posture your way out of a fight. The goal is not to fight, but convince your adversary that you are prepared too. This may force your adversary to flee or possibly attack.

Capitulate: You/Enemy assess the challenge and make the conscious decision to submit, freeze, lie down, and ask for mercy. Capitulation is an effort to appease the adversary in hopes of little or no damage being done. Fear has taken over.

Remember and teach your students the old saying passed down amongst warriors: ***"We do not rise to the level of our expectations. We fall to the level of our training".*** **Archilochus'**

Instructors must understand that in a lethal kinetic encounter that, you sink to the level of training and practice and reality the shooter will sink below their best level of training on the range!

Shooting is a very perishable skill.

The best way to overcome the detrimental effects of stress on performance is to inoculate yourself from it altogether through consistent, realistic training.

From a self-defense standpoint, this means you need to do more than just go to the gun range to practice your marksmanship or punch the heavy bag in your garage.

You'll actually need to train your techniques under the same sort of pressure you'd experience in a real-life situation.

The Mind: Cultivating the Warrior's Edge

At the foundation of every elite performer — whether in combat, sport, or crisis lies a **sharpened mind**. The ability to remain calm under pressure, to act decisively in the face of chaos, and to maintain composure in life-threatening encounters is not an accident. It is the result of **intentional mental conditioning**. Skill with a firearm is important. But the ability to access and apply that skill when it counts — under stress, in low light, with lives on the line — is ultimately determined by **mental resilience, clarity, and control**.

Visualization and Mental Rehearsal

One of the most powerful and underutilized tools in the combative practitioner's arsenal is **positive mental imagery**, or **visualization**. This technique is widely employed by top-tier athletes, military professionals, and elite performers to **enhance proficiency**, especially when resources, time, or environmental constraints limit live training.

Even **fifteen minutes of focused dry practice per day**, performed in a safe and controlled environment, can drastically improve performance — particularly in weapon presentation, sight alignment, and trigger control. In fact, **fifteen minutes per week** of deliberate mental and dry-fire practice is often enough to maintain sharpness and build neural pathways that translate to increased real-world survivability.

The critical factor here is **self-motivation**. The responsible armed citizen must take ownership of their training. There is no external accountability in life-and-death moments — only the preparation you've done beforehand will matter.

Aggressive Mindset: From Reaction to Action

A **proactive mindset** — rooted in aggression and purpose — is essential to survival and success in armed conflict. An **aggressive mindset** is not about emotional aggression or recklessness. Rather, it is the mental readiness to seize initiative, dictate tempo, and **fight forward** when danger arises. This is the essence of the **Warrior Mindset**: being mentally, emotionally, and physically prepared to deal with any threat, at any time, even when it's forced upon you.

Once the need for force arises — once your life is on the line — **it is too late to begin learning**. If a citizen has never trained to respond with assertiveness, violence of action, and purpose, how will they suddenly summon those traits when crisis strikes? They won't. You **must train your mind** to respond the way your body will need to perform.

Ask yourself this:
Are you preparing to survive a gunfight, or to win one?

The difference between a slow, reactive mindset and a proactive, aggressive one is stark. The slow-reacting individual finds themselves **in a gunfight** — playing catch-up, under pressure, often behind the curve. The assertive, trained individual finds themselves **in a shooting** — dictating action, executing decisively, and ending the threat. The difference is mindset. And the time to develop it is **before the fight**.

Practical Mental Training Tools

Visualization:
Modern research confirms what warriors have known intuitively: **mental rehearsal improves real-world performance**. Fighters who visualize high-stress scenarios perform better under pressure. They show improved marksmanship, reduced anxiety, and

greater confidence when violence erupts. Why? Because the mind has already "seen" it before — the fight is not new.

- **Make it vivid.** Use all your senses — sight, sound, touch, even smell and emotion. Picture the environment, feel the weapon in your hand, hear the commands, and see yourself performing with precision.
- **Include adversity.** Visualize equipment malfunctions, multiple threats, environmental constraints — and most importantly, visualize yourself **successfully overcoming them**.
- **Never visualize failure.** Always conclude the mental scenario with a successful resolution.

Self-Talk and Instructional Cues:

In moments of stress, our inner dialogue shapes our actions. Use **task-relevant instructional self-talk** — short, positive, clear commands that reinforce action. Examples include:

- "Grip high. Front sight. Press."
- "Tap. Rack. Reassess."
- "Eyes up. Breathe. Move."

This kind of verbal reinforcement, especially when practiced consistently, can significantly improve both **cognitive focus** and **motor function** during high-stress engagements. Science backs this up: athletes and operators who engage in self-talk perform better across a wide range of cognitive and physical tasks.

Role Play and Dry Fire Integration:

Visualization and mental rehearsal must be **paired with physical practice**. Dry fire, scenario-based role playing, and force-on-force drills allow the mind and body to connect

— turning visualization into **habituated action**. These repetitions build a performance base that is not just conceptual but **neurologically imprinted**.

Closing Thoughts on the Mind

"I think anything is possible if you have the mindset and the will and desire to do it and put the time in."
— **Roger Clemens**

Mental preparation is **not optional**. It is a force multiplier that separates those who survive from those who dominate. As a practitioner of the combative arts — whether law enforcement, military, or responsibly armed citizen — your mind is the **first weapon** and the **last line of defense**.

Train it with the same discipline and seriousness you train your body.

Over the years teaching Law Enforcement Officer and Agents at Federal Law Enforcement Training Center in Glynco Georgia I have only had one student out of thousands that has failed. I was teaching a Criminal Investigator Class and the young lady was a Park Ranger that had been picked up to move from uniform Ranger to Criminal Investigator. In the uniform division at the time, the Land Management students had the option to choose any Sig Classic line gun. In her case, her management issued her a Sig 229 in .40 cal. FYI, most law enforcement agencies are issued a weapon selected by their agency for their Academy. Once they graduate they are often allowed to select another pistol off an approved list. This young lady could shoot given time, but with the introduction of timed stages she could not manipulate the pistol controls and adjust her trigger finger to accomplish the tasks required. I had everything done to her pistol that I legally could, short trigger, short reset, minimal grip panels but her hands were just too small. She failed to qualify and I had a long talk with her administration and she was allowed to recycle with a Sig 225 single stack in 9mm. This time she shot in the high ninety percentile at qualification time.

Lesson learned, as a civilian it is very important to choose a gun that meets the needs of the shooter. Too many instructors have favorites or are being payed to push certain pistols for the gun store or range. While working for the Sig Academy I would often be tasked to go to gun stores for promotion days and some of the reasoning of folks was picking a certain gun was quite comical. Husbands would want to pick certain guns out for their wife's because their Cop friend recommended it or they saw So-So shoot it on TV.

Instructors need to understand how to size a pistol to the user, how to work with a recoils spring that will allow a smaller framed individual to rack the slide. Get a gun that fits!

Firearms Industry Guidelines for Pistol Fit

Selecting a pistol that fits the shooter's hand is fundamental to safe, accurate, and effective firearm handling. An ill-fitting pistol can compromise trigger control, sight alignment, and recoil management, leading to reduced performance and potential safety issues. This chapter outlines industry-standard guidelines for assessing pistol fit, drawing from established sources such as the National Rifle Association (NRA), manufacturers like SIG Sauer and Glock, and tactical training experts. These recommendations emphasize ergonomic harmony between the shooter and the firearm, ensuring natural operation across diverse hand sizes and builds. As of 2025, modular designs from leading brands continue to dominate, allowing customization to accommodate individual variations

1. Proper Trigger Finger Placement

The index finger's interaction with the trigger is a cornerstone of pistol fit, directly influencing shot accuracy and preventing unintended sympathetic movements in the grip.

- The distal pad of the index finger—not the joint or fingertip—should rest squarely on the trigger's center when the pistol is gripped naturally
- If stretching or reaching is required, the grip frame is oversized, potentially causing lateral pulls or fatigue. Conversely, excessive finger overlap (e.g., the finger curling beyond the trigger) indicates an undersized grip, risking erratic presses

This placement facilitates a straight-back pull, minimizing muzzle deviation during the press.

2. Grip Size and Circumference

A well-fitted grip ensures comprehensive hand contact, promoting stability and control without strain.

- The shooter should envelop the grip fully, with no voids between the palm and backstrap. The strong-hand thumb and middle finger should nearly touch on the frame's opposite side, ideally meeting at the mid-knuckle line for optimal leverage
- Contemporary pistols, such as the Glock series or SIG Sauer P320, feature interchangeable backstraps or modules to tailor circumference for small, medium, or large hands

This configuration supports a high, firm hold, essential for consistent shooting

3. Natural Point of Aim

The pistol should align intuitively with the shooter's line of sight, reducing the need for compensatory adjustments.

- Upon extending the pistol in a neutral stance, the front and rear sights (or red dot) should align seamlessly with the dominant eye, pointing at the intended target without wrist or arm torque
- Persistent high or low pointing signals a mismatch in grip angle or size, often resolvable with modular adjustments or model selection

This alignment fosters efficiency, particularly in rapid presentations.

4. Control and Recoil Management

A proper fit empowers the shooter to manage the pistol's dynamics during firing cycles.

- The grip should enable unyielding control, preventing shifts under recoil. A high tang engagement—where the web of the hand seats firmly against the beavertail—accelerates sight recovery and follow-up shots

Inadequate fit amplifies muzzle rise, complicating multi-shot accuracy.

5. Thumb and Control Access

Accessibility to controls without disrupting the primary grip is crucial for operational fluidity.

- The strong-hand thumb should reach the magazine release, slide stop, and safety (if equipped) with minimal adjustment. For compact hands, this may favor subcompact models or support-hand assistance training

This ensures seamless manipulations, vital in defensive or competitive contexts

Tools and Techniques for Customization

Industry practices offer versatile solutions for achieving optimal fit:

Grip Inserts and Backstraps: Modular systems in pistols like the Glock Gen5 or SIG Sauer P320 allow rapid size adjustments

Grip Reductions: Custom gunsmithing for extreme small-hand accommodations, though less common with modern modularity

Dry-Fire Fitting: Simulate grips and presses to evaluate alignment and comfort

Laser Bore Sighting or Red Dot Fitting: Verify natural alignment via optics or lasers

These methods, endorsed by the NRA and manufacturers, facilitate personalized setups

Common Misfits and Consequences

- **Oversized Grip:** Induces stretching, weakened hold, and off-axis trigger pulls, degrading accuracy
- **Undersized Grip:** Results in over-wrapping, diminished leverage, and inconsistent groupings
- **Alignment Errors:** Necessitate ongoing corrections, fostering fatigue and imprecision

Summary Checklist for Trainers and Instructors

Utilize this checklist to systematically evaluate pistol fit during training sessions or fittings.

Fit Element	Goal
Trigger Finger Placement	Distal pad centered on trigger for straight-back pull
Full Hand Contact	No palm gaps; fingers wrap naturally, thumb and middle nearly meeting
Sight Alignment (Natural Point)	Sights align intuitively from low ready to target
Control Access	Thumb accesses controls with negligible grip shift
Recoil Control	Pistol remains secure, no shifting during firing

By adhering to these guidelines, shooters can achieve a symbiotic fit, enhancing safety, proficiency, and confidence in their chosen firearm

Concealed Carry: A Comprehensive Guide to Setup, Advantages, Drawbacks, and Training

In today's unpredictable world, where threats to personal safety can emerge without warning, mastering concealed carry stands as a critical pillar of self-defense and empowerment. This subject equips individuals with the tools to safeguard themselves and their loved ones, fostering a proactive mindset that blends vigilance, skill, and ethical judgment to navigate potential dangers effectively. For those who conceal carry a pistol, the benefits extend far beyond mere possession—they gain rapid response capabilities in life-threatening situations, heightened situational awareness that deters risks, and the confidence to maintain normalcy in daily life without compromising security. Instructors bear a profound responsibility to delve deeply into this knowledge, grasping nuances like legal frameworks, biomechanical efficiencies, and psychological preparedness, so they can teach with precision, inspiring students to prioritize safety, proficiency, and restraint over recklessness.

Individuals who embrace concealed carry actively commit to personal protection and accountability, empowering themselves to shield loved ones amid uncertainty while upholding stringent legal, ethical, and practical norms. This guide delves into crafting an optimal setup—choosing dependable firearms like 9mm micro-compacts for superior concealability and capacity, pairing them with robust holsters and supportive belts, and fine-tuning positions for comfort and quick access. Practitioners reap advantages such as stealthy defense that preserves surprise, bolstered security for immediate threat response, and seamless mobility without public alarm, yet they confront challenges including delayed draws, physical strain, heightened legal scrutiny, and the imperative for relentless training. Carriers hone essential skills through dynamic drills in concealment draws, pressure-driven trigger control, tactical movement, and decision-making under duress, transforming armament into a disciplined asset. Ultimately, concealed carry demands unyielding dedication to preparedness and moderation, reinforcing its vital role as a bulwark against vulnerability in a volatile environment.

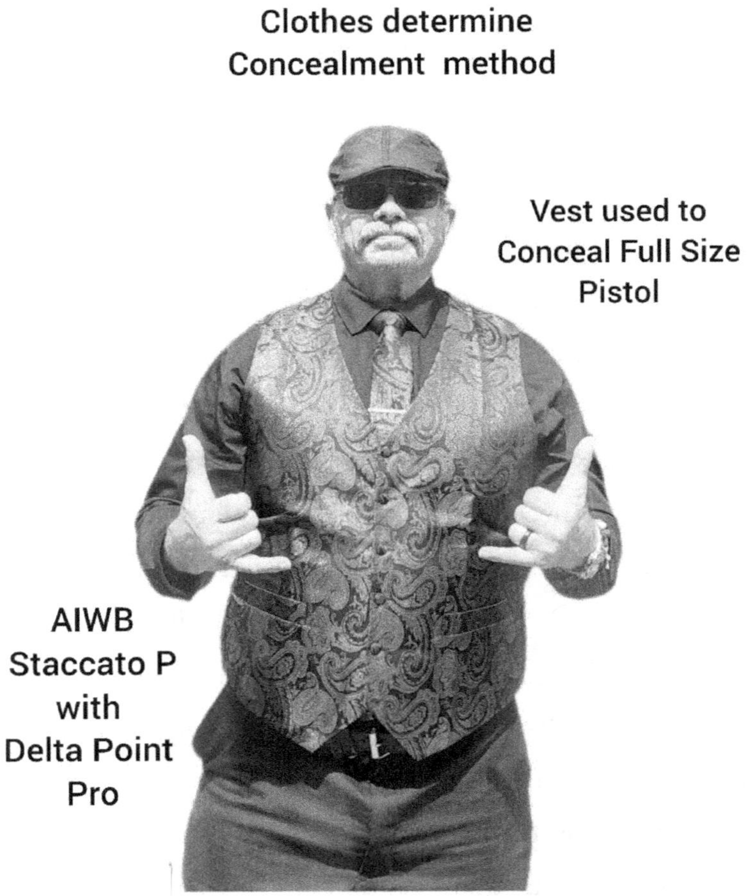

Part I: Setting Up for Concealed Carry

Establishing a reliable concealed carry routine begins with thoughtful selection of equipment and accessories tailored to your lifestyle, body type, and needs. The process emphasizes safety, comfort, and efficiency to ensure seamless integration into daily life.

1. Selecting the Right Firearm for Everyday Carry (EDC)

The foundation of any concealed carry setup is the firearm itself. Reliability is paramount; the pistol must cycle flawlessly with various ammunition types, as malfunctions in a defensive scenario could prove catastrophic. In 2025, 9mm remains the predominant caliber for EDC due to its balanced recoil, effective terminal ballistics, and high magazine capacity, making it suitable for most users.

Consider the form factor based on your concealment requirements and shooting preferences:

- **Micro-Compacts**: Models like the SIG Sauer P365 X-Macro or Springfield Armory Hellcat Pro excel in concealability, often holding 10–17 rounds while remaining lightweight and slim. They are ideal for deep concealment but may sacrifice some shootability due to shorter grips and barrels, potentially increasing felt recoil
- **Compacts**: Options such as the Glock 19 or CZ P-10C strike a versatile balance, offering 15+ rounds, better controllability, and easier handling during extended range sessions. These are favored for their all-around performance but may print more noticeably under tight clothing
- **Subcompacts/Single-Stacks**: Firearms like the Smith & Wesson Shield Plus or Glock 43X prioritize ease of concealment with slimmer profiles and lower capacities (typically 8–13 rounds). They suit slimmer builds or pocket carry but demand more practice to manage recoil effectively

Optics-ready models are increasingly recommended, with footprints like the Shield RMSc or Holosun K-series facilitating red dot sights (RDS) for faster target acquisition. Pair these with suppressor-height or co-witness iron sights as backups in case of optic failure.

Revolvers, such as the Smith & Wesson 642 or Ruger LCR, offer simplicity and reliability for those preferring wheel guns, though they generally hold fewer rounds

2. Choosing a Purpose-Built Holster

A quality holster is non-negotiable for safe and effective concealed carry. It must fully encase the trigger guard to prevent accidental discharges, provide consistent retention (via friction or mechanical means), remain open-mouthed for easy reholstering, and enable one-handed operation. Avoid soft nylon or universal holsters, as they can collapse, snag, or fail to secure the firearm properly

Common holster types include:

Holster Type	Use Case	Pros	Cons
Appendix Inside-the-Waistband (AIWB)	Fastest draw, optimal concealment	Quick access, excellent retention, minimal printing	Potential discomfort when seated; requires precise adjustment
Strong-Side Inside-the-Waistband (3–5 o'clock)	Traditional concealed carry	Familiar draw stroke, aligns with range practice	Slower under stress; more prone to printing during movement
Outside-the-Waistband (OWB) under garment	Winter or layered clothing carry	High comfort, rapid draw	Challenging to conceal without bulky attire
Enclosed Trigger Pocket (e.g., Phlster Enigma)	Deep concealment without belt	Versatile positioning, belt-independent	Steeper learning curve; may shift during activity

Materials like Kydex or hybrid leather-Kydex offer durability and custom fit, while leather provides comfort over time

3. Belt and Clothing Considerations

A sturdy gun belt with internal stiffeners (nylon or leather) is essential to distribute weight and prevent sagging or shifting. Thin belts can cause instability, leading to discomfort or exposure

. Dress strategically around the firearm: opt for darker patterns or prints to obscure outlines, longer untucked shirts or jackets for coverage, and breathable fabrics that resist printing when bending or sitting

4. Carry Position and Comfort Tuning

Positioning impacts access, concealment, and comfort. Appendix carry (AIWB) offers the quickest draw and superior control in close-quarters, with a natural path that minimizes telegraphing. It suits most body types but requires wedge pads or foam inserts to tilt the grip inward and reduce pressure on sensitive areas

. Strong-side carry (around 4 o'clock) is more traditional, accommodating longer torsos, but it can be slower and vulnerable in grapples

Tune for comfort by adjusting ride height (higher for concealment, lower for grip access) and cant angle (forward for AIWB). Experiment with claw attachments to rotate the grip toward the body, minimizing printing

5. Daily Carry Checklist

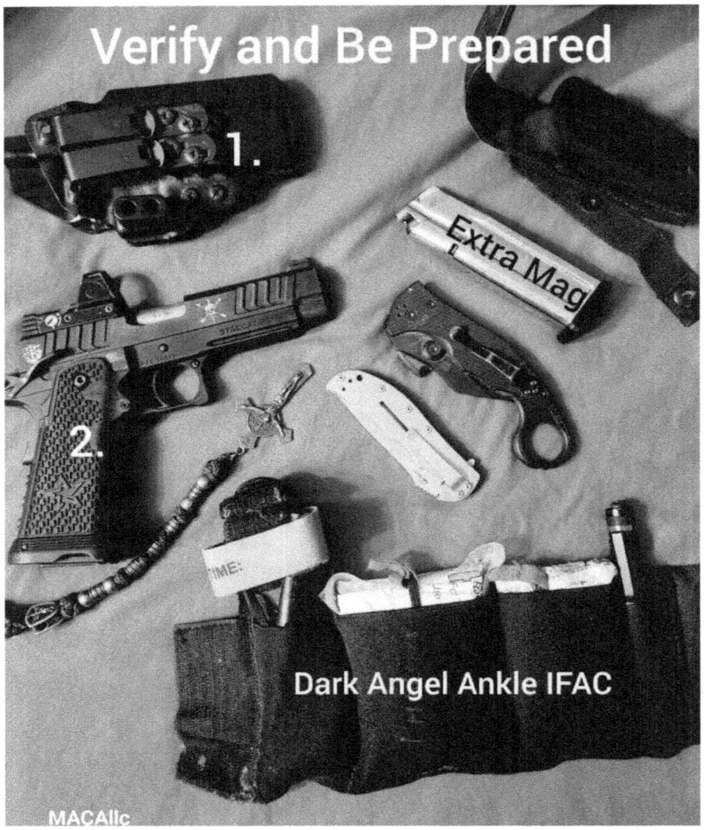

Before heading out, verify:

- Holster security (clips/loops fully engaged).
- Firearm loaded with a chambered round.
- Magazine fully seated.
- No excessive printing under current attire.
- Safe draw capability with your outfit.

Part II: Pros and Cons of Concealed Carry

Concealed carry offers tangible benefits but also introduces challenges that must be carefully weighed. Perspectives vary, with proponents emphasizing empowerment and deterrence, while critics highlight risks to public safety and increased violence potential

Advantages

Advantage	Explanation
Discreet Self-Defense Capability	Preserves the element of surprise, preventing attackers from anticipating or disarming you
Increased Personal Security	Enables immediate response to lethal threats when escape or de-escalation fails
Mobility and Flexibility	Allows unrestricted movement without attracting attention, unlike open carry
Minimal Public Impact	Avoids alarming bystanders, promoting social normalcy
Legal Protections (Where Permitted)	Permits often provide defenses in justified use-of-force cases
Better Retention	Hidden firearms reduce snatch risks during encounters

Drawbacks

Disadvantage	Explanation
Slower Access	Clearing garments and positioning delays draw time without consistent practice
.	
Comfort and Carry Fatigue	Prolonged wear can cause discomfort, especially for certain builds or activities
Increased Legal Responsibility	Requires thorough knowledge of state laws, restricted areas, and justification standards; violations can lead to severe penalties

Printing and Exposure Risks	Accidental reveal may constitute brandishing, inviting legal or social issues
Close-Quarters Challenges	Access and retention complicate in grapples or grounded positions
Higher Judgment Standard	Post-incident scrutiny focuses on decision-making, potentially leading to liability
Training Burden	Demands ongoing skill development beyond basic shooting to ensure safety and efficacy

Critics argue that permissive concealed carry laws correlate with higher violent crime rates, including homicides, by facilitating easier access for prohibited individuals and escalating confrontations

Part III: Training Considerations for Concealed Carriers

Training transforms concealed carry from a mere option into a reliable capability. Focus on practical, scenario-based drills to build muscle memory and decision-making under stress

Essential Skills:

Draw from Concealment: Practice one-handed draws, garment clearance, and consistent grip under timed conditions

Trigger Control under Pressure: Incorporate dry-fire repetitions and live-fire with shot timers to refine smooth presses

Target Identification and Decision-Making: Engage in shoot/no-shoot scenarios, verbal de-escalation, and force-on-force simulations if available

.

Movement and Use of Cover: Train shooting on the move, from cover, and in varied positions (kneeling, supine, seated)

Safe Reholstering: Always visually confirm before reholstering slowly, especially in AIWB, to avoid accidents

One-Handed Operations: Master Dominant- and support-hand shooting, reloads, and malfunction clearances for real-world contingencies

Commit to Personal Protection and Accountability

Final Notes

Concealed carry demands unwavering responsibility: mental preparedness, physical training, and legal awareness. It is not a license for recklessness but a tool for those committed to skill and restraint. As one adage aptly states, "You carry a gun not because you're looking for a fight—but because you're not willing to lose one.

Concealed carry empowers individuals to actively protect themselves and loved ones in an unpredictable world, demanding rigorous commitment to legal, ethical, and practical mastery. This guide equips readers to craft effective setups—selecting reliable 9mm firearms, robust holsters, and strategic carry positions—while balancing stealthy defense, rapid response, and seamless mobility against challenges like delayed draws, legal scrutiny, and ongoing training demands. Practitioners sharpen skills through dynamic drills, mastering concealment draws, precise trigger control, and tactical decision-making under stress. This discipline transforms a firearm into a tool of preparedness and restraint, underscoring its critical role in fostering security, confidence, and responsibility in volatile environments.

Guide for Concealed Carry

A Comprehensive Resource for New and Intermediate Shooters

This guide provides a clear, structured overview of concealed carry fundamentals, including carry positions, equipment selection, draw techniques, and lifestyle adjustments. It emphasizes the pros and cons of each option to help readers make informed decisions. Designed for both self-study and instructional use, the content supports civilian training programs and instructor-led discussions. All recommendations prioritize safety, legal compliance, and practical effectiveness.

Concealed Carry: A Step-by-Step Guide with Pros and Cons

Step 1: Understand Your Purpose

Before selecting gear or carry methods, clarify your motivations and constraints:

- **Why you carry**: Primarily for the protection of yourself and loved ones.
- **Legal boundaries**: Familiarize yourself with local use-of-force laws and concealed carry regulations.
- **Carry frequency**: Determine if it's daily, occasional, or situational (e.g., during travel).

Tip: Your purpose will directly influence your choice of equipment, attire, and training regimen.

Step 2: Select Your Carry Position

Here is a breakdown of common carry positions, including their advantages and drawbacks.

1. **Appendix Inside-the-Waistband (AIWB)**
Position: 11–1 o'clock, forward of the hips.
Access: Offers the quickest draw in most scenarios.
Popular with: Concealed carry permit holders, plainclothes law enforcement, and instructors.

Pros:

- Fastest and most intuitive draw path.
- Superior concealment with minimal printing.
- Convenient access while seated or driving.
- Strong retention for close-quarters encounters.

Cons:

- Elevated risk during reholstering (proximity to femoral artery and genitals).
- Potential discomfort during prolonged sitting.
- Demands rigorous trigger discipline.
- Not suitable for all body types.

2. **Inside-the-Waistband (IWB) – Strong Side (3–5 o'clock)**

   Position: On or behind the hip.

   Access: Traditional and versatile.

   Popular with: Novice concealed carriers transitioning from open carry.

   Pros:

   - Secure holster placement.
   - Effective concealment under longer shirts or jackets.
   - Comfortable for diverse body shapes.
   - Safer reholstering path compared to AIWB.

   Cons:

   - Slower draw than AIWB.
   - Challenging access when seated or in a vehicle.
   - Increased printing under form-fitting clothing.
   - Delayed support-hand assistance during the draw.

3. **Outside-the-Waistband (OWB) with Cover Garment**

   Position: Typically at 3 o'clock.

   Access: Rapid with little obstruction.

   Popular with: Off-duty law enforcement and carriers in cooler climates.

Pros:

- Highly comfortable for extended wear.
- Straightforward access and reholstering.
- Familiar for those trained in duty-style carry.

Cons:

- Difficult to conceal without bulky outerwear.
- Higher risk of printing or exposure.
- May attract attention if the cover garment shifts.

4. **Pocket Carry**

   Position: Front or cargo pocket, using a dedicated pocket holster.

   Access: Discreet but restricted.

   Popular with: Users seeking deep concealment or carrying a backup firearm.

Pros:

- Extremely low-profile and unobtrusive.
- Quick access when standing or walking.
- Ideal for compact pistols.

Cons:

- Very slow from a seated position.
- Holster must remain in pocket during draw.
- Challenging to achieve a full firing grip.
- Limited to small-caliber, low-capacity firearms.

5. **Off-Body Carry (e.g., Purse, Sling Bag, Briefcase)**

   Position: Not affixed to the body.

Access: Variable, depending on setup and practice.

Popular with: Women, travelers, and office professionals.

Pros:

- Optimal concealability.
- Allows for larger firearms without body printing.
- Greater flexibility in clothing choices.

Cons:

- Inconsistent and potentially slow access.
- Risk of separation from the carrier (e.g., theft or misplacement).
- Increased chance of unauthorized access.
- Challenging to train effectively under stress.

Step 3: Choose Appropriate Gear

Holster Essentials

- Must fully enclose the trigger guard.
- Constructed from rigid material (Kydex recommended for AIWB/IWB).
- Secure mounting system (e.g., belt clips or loops that resist failure).
- Incorporate passive or active retention as needed.

The Importance of a Quality Belt

- Opt for a stiff gun belt to distribute weight and maintain holster stability.
- Avoid flexible fashion belts, which can sag, fold, or shift.

Practice Recommendations

Incorporate daily practice with your chosen holster, clothing, and environment:

- Dry-fire draws from concealment.
- Live-fire exercises with timed drills.
- Vehicle-specific draw simulations.

Step 4: Lifestyle Adjustments for Carrying

Category	Key Considerations
Clothing	Opt for longer shirts, darker colors, and looser fits to minimize printing.
Behavior	Refrain from touching or adjusting the firearm in public to avoid drawing attention.
Mindset	Maintain heightened responsibility and awareness as an armed individual.
Fitness	Improve flexibility and core strength to enhance draw, reholstering, and mobility.
Daily Habits	Foster consistency through daily carry, monthly training, and regular gear maintenance.

Step 5: Legal and Ethical Responsibilities

Know Your Laws

- Identify prohibited locations (e.g., schools, government buildings, private property).
- Understand threat response protocols.
- Differentiate between duty-to-retreat and stand-your-ground statutes (state-specific).

Post-Incident Protocol

- Call 911: State, "I was attacked. Please send police and medical assistance."
- Avoid providing a detailed statement at the scene.
- Request legal counsel before further questioning.
- Remain composed, keep hands visible, and comply with arriving law enforcement.

Summary: Concealed Carry as a Lifestyle

Do	Avoid
Carry daily	Carrying only in perceived high-risk situations
Train regularly	Relying solely on initial permit training
Use reliable, tested gear	Improvised or low-quality holsters
Study local laws	Assuming uniformity across states
Stay alert and proactive	Escalating conflicts or displaying the firearm unnecessarily

Layered Breakdown for Concealed Carry (CCW)

For Civilian Defensive Use of Force

Layer 1: Mindset and Legal Foundation

Objectives:

- Grasp the defensive-only ethos of civilian force.
- Cultivate a mindset centered on avoidance, de-escalation, and protection.
- Master laws related to carry, display, and deadly force.

Key Concepts:

- Carry is for life preservation, not law enforcement or confrontation.
- Legal standard: Reasonable belief of imminent death or serious injury.
- Articulate the full context if force is employed.

Instructor Focus:

- Analyze real-world cases for consequences.
- Offer state-specific insights on castle doctrine, stand-your-ground, and retreat obligations.
- Reinforce the hierarchy: Avoid → Escape → Defend.

Layer 2: Concealment, Clothing, and Holster Selection

Objectives:

- Select a secure, comfortable, and accessible configuration.
- Ensure concealment integrates with daily routines, seasons, and activities.
- Train to efficiently overcome concealment barriers.

Key Equipment Variables:

Carry Positions: AIWB, IWB, OWB (concealed), ankle, pocket, off-body.

- **Holster Requirements**:
  - Rigid for safe reholstering.
  - Complete trigger guard coverage.
  - Firm attachment to belt or garment.

- **Garment Selection**:
    - Enables quick one-handed clearance.
    - Tailored to lifestyle (e.g., professional vs. casual attire).

Instructor Focus:

- Conduct dry practice with actual gear and clothing.
- Drill garment-clearing techniques: One-handed sweep, two-handed lift, seated access.
- Stress reholstering safety, particularly for AIWB.

Layer 3: Draw-stroke Mechanics from Concealment

Objectives:

- Develop a consistent, safe, and efficient draw.
- Clear garments, secure a grip, and align with the target.
- Prepare for engagement at any draw stage.

Breakdown:

- Step 1: Clear garment decisively and high.
- Step 2: Establish grip in the holster (avoid fumbling).
- Step 3: Draw upward, rotate muzzle, and press out.
- Step 4: Join hands and extend (or fire from retention if close-range).

Instructor Focus:

- Isolate draw-stroke from garment clearing initially.
- Progress from dry to live fire, increasing speed.

- Incorporate timed drills and retention shooting.

Layer 4: Environmental and Situational Factors

Objectives:

- Adapt to variables like vehicles, crowds, lighting, and proximity.
- Modify draws and engagements based on context.
- Integrate movement and verbal cues.

Situational Considerations:

- **Seated Draws**: Practice in cars, chairs, or with seatbelts.
- **Non-Dominant Threats**: Drill pivots and step-offs.
- **Low Light**: Include flashlight integration and identification protocols.
- **Family Protection**: Emphasize commands, shielding, and cover-seeking.

Instructor Focus:

- Employ force-on-force simulations for decision-making.
- Teach: Move, Communicate, Use Cover, Shoot if Necessary.
- Focus on awareness beyond mechanics.

Layer 5: Post-Engagement Protocols

Objectives:

- Manage legal, tactical, and medical aftermath.
- Handle law enforcement interactions effectively.
- Establish a defensible posture immediately.

Post-Use-of-Force Actions:

- Scan for threats and check for injuries.
- Call 911: Provide essentials; request aid without elaboration.
- Reholster only if safe.
- Upon LE arrival: Identify as victim and cooperate.
- Request counsel before statements.

Instructor Focus:

- Simulate 911 calls and interactions.
- Promote non-confrontational compliance.
- Recommend legal protection plans (e.g., USCCA, ACLDN, CCW Safe).

Layer 6: Psychological, Moral, and Lifestyle Impact

Objectives:

- Anticipate emotional and social repercussions.
- Navigate long-term legal and public challenges.
- Embrace responsible armed living.

Realities to Address:

- Firearm seizure for evidence (possibly prolonged).
- Legal costs, potential prosecution.
- Civil liability risks.
- Impacts on family, career, and relationships.

Instructor Focus:

- Discuss benefits versus consequences candidly.
- Build resilience, accountability, and support networks.
- Advocate for training documentation and insurance.

Optional Add-On Modules for CCW Curriculum

Module	Content
Home Defense Tactics	Defensive positioning, safe rooms, firing angles, family roles.
Vehicle Defense	Seated draws, vehicle as cover, escape strategies.
Low Light & Flashlight	Target identification, one-handed shooting, environmental tactics.
Weapon Retention & Disarm Avoidance	Retention techniques, grappling awareness, entangled firing.
Legal Q&A with an Attorney	Guest sessions for clarifications.

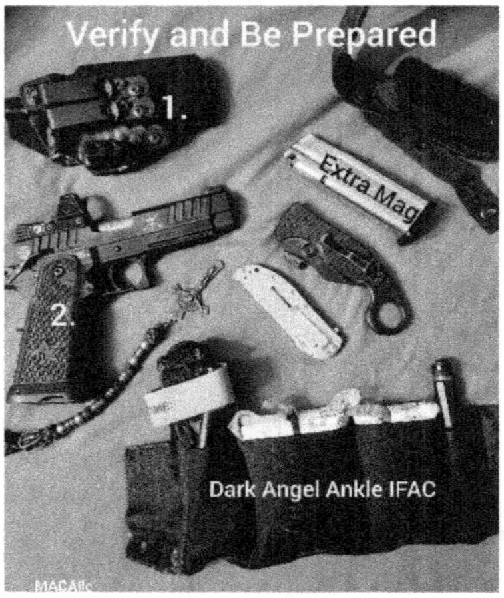

Enhancing Instructor Knowledge: A Paradigm Shift in Pistol Training

As firearms instructors, our role extends beyond imparting basic skills; we must cultivate a deeper understanding of the dynamics that govern effective pistol marksmanship, particularly in high-stakes environments. This chapter challenges conventional approaches, advocating a holistic view where target size, distance, and exposure duration dictate risk levels and engagement strategies. At the core lies the "holy trinity" of pistol shooting: vision (sight package), structure (stance and grip), and trigger manipulation. These elements form an interdependent triangle, essential for success.

The Trinity of Pistol Marksmanship

Visualize this trinity as a balanced triangle, where each vertex represents a foundational component:

1. **Vision – Sight Package**: Determines shooting tempo and feasibility—how quickly can we engage, and when is the shot viable?
2. **Structure**: Encompasses stance, grip, and all elements that establish a stable foundation for the shooter.
3. **Trigger Manipulation**: The precise control required to execute the shot without disrupting alignment.

Analogous to close-quarters battle (CQB) principles, maintaining at least two components ensures viability, though integrating all three yields optimal results. Terminology may evolve, but the underlying concept endures: harmony among these elements is paramount.

- **Attack Targets**: Engaged predictively with Confirmation 1 or 2, based on size, distance, and risk—prioritizing speed for imminent threats.
- **Control Targets**: Addressed reactively with Confirmation 2 or 3, emphasizing precision for managed risks.

The shooter's structure (grip and stance), required visual confirmation, and corresponding trigger technique must synchronize seamlessly. Through inductive or discovery learning—where students explore and internalize concepts via guided experimentation—shooters discern the optimal grip, then align trigger methods with sight confirmations. As training advances, they grasp the interrelated yet variably weighted roles of structure, vision, and trigger in diverse engagements.

Let the journey of discovery commence.

Beyond Traditional Precision: Adapting to Real-World Demands

Conventional firearms instruction often prioritizes precision shooting, advocating a deliberate, smooth trigger press to preserve sight alignment for pinpoint accuracy within the pistol's effective range. While invaluable for foundational marksmanship, such methods falter in dynamic, unannounced deadly force encounters, where time is compressed and predictability absent.

Instructors must recognize the spectrum of pistol disciplines—each tailored to specific contexts—and adapt accordingly. My foundational pistol training, as a Green Beret, originated in the Special Forces Special Operations Techniques (SOT) Course and the Special Forces Advanced Reconnaissance, Target Analysis, and Exploitation Techniques

Course (SFARTAETC) at the John F. Kennedy Special Warfare Center and School, Fort Bragg, North Carolina.

Special Operations units thrive on accuracy delivered at speed: "Accuracy First!" The inaugural event—a B8 bullseye at 25 yards with a 70/100 minimum set the tone. Subsequent day's involved even-numbered shooters standing in front their targets while odds fired, then reversing roles, with targets spaced a mere yard apart center-to-center. This proximity, initially daunting, instilled unwavering confidence in precision, allowing assaulters to change targets downrange amid live fire from flanks.

This experience solidified my ethos: Accuracy is paramount in lethal kinetic engagements, yet it must be swift and efficient, lest it prove counterproductive.

Distinguish among:

- **Precision Shooting**: Untimed, methodical accuracy.
- **Accurate Shooting at Speed**: Essential for kinetic encounters.
- **Speed Shooting**: Often prioritized in competitions.

Recall these definitions:

- **Training**: Acquisition of skills, acts, or methods; **failure is permissible** and instructive.
- **Competition**: On-demand demonstration of marksmanship and handling; **failure incurs penalties.**
- **Combat**: Application of skills in dynamic, adversarial settings; **failure is fatal.**

What, then, are you preparing your students for? As instructors, define the destination first this shapes methodologies, sequencing, and priorities. The techniques must support the Principles and herein primarily target everyday carry (EDC) practitioners, accounting for physiological and psychological responses under survival stress.

Elite military and law enforcement operators' worldwide train to acquire sights rapidly, apply fundamentals at peak velocity, and sustain supreme accuracy an advanced proficiency demanding deliberate practice at speed.

In real-world scenarios, encounters unfold in seconds. Competent instructors differentiate untimed precision from time-compressed accuracy, where temporal constraints expose flaws in grip, presentation, or trigger control.

Data from deadly force incidents and stress studies indicate traditional methods inadequately prepare students. Instructors should integrate threat recognition, movement, and innovative technologies for realistic practice and assessment, fostering confidence in high-pressure responses.

Targets are pivotal: Early Special Forces training used B8 bullseyes for measurable accuracy, evolving to silhouettes and realistic, faced targets to build mindset for lethal encounters. Align targets, methodologies, and technologies with training phases and objectives.

Consider your audience and purpose; overlaps exist across disciplines, but factor pistol type, concealment, and desired outcomes.

National statistics on law enforcement officers killed in the line of duty reveal approximately 80% of lethal encounters occur within 20 feet, with 50% at 5 feet or less and half in low-light conditions. Percentages hold steady annually, though raw numbers fluctuate.

This prompts queries like, "Why train beyond 21 feet?" Yet, distance amplifies weaknesses; adding speed exacerbates inaccuracies. The "good guy" often reacts defensively, while adversaries act proactively.

Years of instruction affirm: Anyone can excel at 7 yards with vague hits. True proficiency demands more. Special Forces assaulters, firing thousands of rounds weekly, perform at 50–70% of peak in real engagements. Grandmaster competitors fare similarly practice accelerates problem-solving, but shooting degrades.

Competitors "dirt dive" stages, adapting plans post-execution. Assaulters leverage intelligence and layouts, yet two-way ranges disrupt finesse. Law enforcement averages an 85% miss rate historically, compounded by movement, low visibility, and congestion.

EDC carriers, often reactive from holster draws, benefit from assault indicator training and OODA loop discussions.

Thus, limiting to 7 yards invites failure. A "good" group low-left in the 10-ring at 5 yards signals breakdown, magnified by distance, time, and speed. Mastery at 25 yards enhances survival inside 10.

Target shooting (static range) contrasts tactical: Known variables permit smooth triggers, centered stances (Isosceles/Weaver), and perfect shots. Tactical demands gunfight velocity, unknown timings, distances, rapid triggers across focal continua, natural stances, movement, and tactical accuracy.

Instructors must comprehend the Sympathetic Nervous System (SNS) activation in jeopardy: Heightened speed, strength, and agility via "Fight or Flight" (with "Posture" or "Capitulate" variants, detailed earlier). Build on natural responses to formulate effective techniques.

The Trinity of Pistol Marksmanship: A Professional Framework for Precision Shooting

Elevating a shooter's performance hinges on redefining their understanding of the interplay between vision, body mechanics, and trigger control. The "Trinity of Pistol Marksmanship" — comprising **Vision**, **Structure**, and **Trigger Manipulation** — forms a dynamic framework that governs a shooter's ability to engage targets effectively. These three elements create a performance envelope, where the shooter's actions are dictated by real-time environmental data, such as target size, distance, and presentation time. This framework empowers shooters to prioritize their actions based on the demands of the situation, ensuring adaptability and precision in both defensive and competitive contexts.

The Trinity Defined

- **Vision**: The foundation of shot execution, vision determines the sight package required — the level of sight alignment and confirmation needed to engage a target. It dictates how quickly a shot can be fired and whether the shot is viable based on visual input.
- **Structure**: Encompassing biomechanical elements like stance, grip, and upper body alignment, structure provides the stability needed to manage recoil and maintain consistent shot placement.
- **Trigger Manipulation**: The deliberate act of pressing the trigger in alignment with visual confirmation and structural stability, ensuring the shot breaks without disrupting the pistol's alignment.

These three components are interdependent, forming a triangle where optimal performance arises from their harmonious integration. Much like close-quarters battle

(CQB) doctrine, where maintaining two of three principles (speed, surprise, violence of action) can still achieve success, shooters can often perform adequately with two of the Trinity's components. However, true mastery is achieved when all three are synchronized.

Contextual Engagement: Attack vs. Control Targets

The Trinity framework adapts to the nature of the target and the associated risk. Targets are broadly categorized as **Attack Targets** or **Control Targets**, each requiring a tailored application of the Trinity:

- **Attack Targets/Predictive Targets**: Large, close, or fully exposed targets that present low risk. These are engaged predictively with minimal to moderate visual confirmation (Confirmation 1 or 2), prioritizing speed and efficiency.
- **Control Targets/Reactive Targets**: Smaller, distant, partially obscured, or high-risk targets requiring greater precision. These demand reactive engagement with enhanced visual confirmation (Confirmation 2 or 3), prioritizing accuracy over speed.

Shooters must learn to assess target characteristics and adjust their application of vision, structure, and trigger manipulation accordingly. This adaptive process is cultivated through inductive, discovery-based learning, where shooters internalize how each component of the Trinity supports the others based on real-time feedback.

The Instructor's Role

The instructor's primary responsibility is to guide shooters toward discovering how to dynamically balance the Trinity's components based on situational demands. Rather than merely teaching mechanics, instructors facilitate an environment where shooters learn to prioritize vision, structure, or trigger manipulation based on the target's characteristics and the shooter's capabilities. This approach fosters adaptability, enabling shooters to make informed decisions under pressure.

Layered Breakdown by Shooter Level

Beginner Level

Objective: Introduce the Trinity and build awareness of the interplay between vision, structure, and trigger manipulation for consistent shot execution.

- **Vision**: Teach the fundamentals of sight picture, emphasizing dot clarity (for red dot optics) or iron sight alignment. Introduce the concept of a "sight package" as the visual input required to confirm a shot.
- **Structure**: Focus on establishing a consistent grip and stance to ensure predictable recoil control. Emphasize proper hand placement and body alignment to minimize movement.
- **Trigger**: Introduce trigger press isolation through dry-fire drills, allowing shooters to focus on smooth, controlled trigger movement without visual distractions.

Instructor Tip: Use a physical or visual representation of the Trinity triangle to illustrate the three components. During debriefs, ask students which component they feel breaks down under stress to encourage self-awareness.

Intermediate Level

Objective: Develop contextual understanding, enabling shooters to adapt their application of the Trinity based on target demands.

- **Vision**: Introduce Confirmation Levels 1, 2, and 3, teaching shooters to match the appropriate sight package to the target's difficulty (e.g., size, distance, or presentation speed). Emphasize the transition from static sight alignment to dynamic tracking.
- **Structure**: Challenge shooters to test grip consistency and recoil management using timed drills and group size tracking. Encourage experimentation with grip pressure to optimize stability.
- **Trigger**: Introduce concepts like trigger prep and staging, linking trigger control to visual confirmation. Help shooters discover the level of trigger precision required for different target types.

Discovery Drill: Set up two contrasting targets — one large and close (Attack Target), one small and distant (Control Target). Instruct shooters to engage both using varied grip pressures, sight packages, and trigger speeds. Debrief to discuss how adjustments to the Trinity affected performance.

Advanced Level

Objective: Enable shooters to dynamically prioritize the Trinity's components under stress, making real-time adjustments based on risk and time constraints.

- **Vision**: Shift focus from static sight acquisition to dynamic tracking of the dot or front sight through recoil. Teach shooters to interpret sight movement as a diagnostic tool for shot execution.
- **Structure**: Develop structural diagnostics to identify and correct breakdowns under recoil, such as wrist collapse or inconsistent shoulder tension. Emphasize adaptability in maintaining stability across varied shooting positions.

- **Trigger**: Link trigger manipulation to cognitive load, emphasizing intentionality for high-risk shots. Develop pre-shot cueing (e.g., "Is this an attack or control shot?") to guide decision-making.

Instructor Tip: Encourage shooters to "triage the Trinity" before each drill. Ask them to identify which two components are most critical for the task and why, then test their hypothesis through live-fire exercises. Debrief to refine their decision-making process.

Conclusion

The Trinity of Pistol Marksmanship provides a comprehensive framework for shooters to navigate the complexities of target engagement. By mastering the interplay of vision, structure, and trigger manipulation, shooters can adapt to diverse scenarios with precision and confidence. Instructors play a pivotal role in guiding this discovery, fostering an environment where shooters learn to assess and prioritize the Trinity's components based on real-time demands. Through progressive training and intentional practice, shooters can unlock their full potential, achieving mastery in the art and science of pistol marksmanship.

All Things VISION!

The First and Guiding Factor in the Holy Trinity of Shooting

Vision Dictates Everything

Firearms instructors teaching everyday carry (EDC) skills must ensure students understand that vision governs all shooting aspects. Vision dictates accuracy and speed in lethal kinetic encounters and, more importantly, grants permission to draw and use a weapon.

Before drawing the pistol, shooters process visual information: What is the target? What lies beyond the target? What surrounds the target? Does the target pose an actual threat?

Instructors emphasize that guns and good intentions mean nothing without positive target identification. Shooters must bet lives on visual confirmation.

Once students process information, navigate their OODA loop, and confirm the decision to act, they initiate actions to engage successfully in a kinetic lethal encounter.

In pistol application, vision represents the visual information from the sighting package that guarantees acceptable accuracy as fast as possible. The sighting package encompasses the sight picture, enabling shooters to achieve required accuracy to eliminate threats.

Instructors remember speed's crucial role: Shooters beat adversaries to the draw, but only with required visual confirmation to eliminate threats.

Shooters use as much of the sighting package as needed—whether iron sights (front and rear, or front only), optics, or lasers. As tactical distances increase, the sighting package must become more precise to ensure accuracy.

The sighting package employs the method that best allows accurate threat engagement at the given distance.

Shooters hold preferences, and no definitive sight picture exists. Trained shooters weigh considerations like distance, lighting, and environment when choosing sighting packages for accurate shots.

Sight Alignment: Fundamentals for Iron Sights and Mini Red-Dot Sights (MRDS)

Sight alignment aligns weapon sights. For iron sights, center the front sight blade in the rear notch, following traditional principles: equal height and equal light. Proper alignment ensures correct pistol presentation toward the target area.

For pistols equipped with mini red-dot sights (MRDS), traditional alignment gives way to an intuitive, streamlined process. Mastering this requires understanding mechanics and consistent technique.

Sight alignment stands as a key fundamental. Manufacturers place sights on pistols for use; proper alignment ensures round placement and accountability.

During training, shooters achieve the best sight alignment in basic presentation drills. Speed drills demonstrate quick acquisition and alignment during presentation.

Sight Picture: Integrating Sights with the Target

The sight picture correlates the front sight blade, rear aperture, and target as seen by the shooter. Center the blade's top edge in the rear aperture.

Instructors ensure students place the blade's top edge on the target's largest visible mass—center on the torso, disregarding the head, as eyes naturally center the mass (though not always true center mass).

The sight picture correlates the front sight blade, rear aperture, and target.

Students using iron sights understand that human eyes focus on one object at different distances. Shooters identify the target, align sights for a proper picture, center sights on a blurry target, then shift vision from front sight to target and back.

The eye's last focus always lands on the front sight: A clear front sight blurs the rear and target.

With MRDS, shooters become target-focused. Shift focus to the target, keep both eyes open, and place the dot on the target while maintaining surroundings awareness.

MRDS on pistols alter sight alignment fundamentals compared to iron sights.

Feature	Iron Sights	MRDS (Mini Red-Dot Sight)
Alignment Focus	Front sight post and rear notch	Single focal plane – red dot only
Sight Alignment Needed	Front and rear level and centered	Only the dot placed on target
Eye Focus	Front sight (sharp)	Target (dot superimposed)

Instructor Note: Target-Focused Shooting Techniques

Target-focused aiming excludes point shooting, kinesthetic shooting, or proprioception-reliant styles. It involves focusing on the target while looking through sights, similar to red-dot use.

Traditional iron-sight instruction teaches focus shifts. Under stress in kinetic encounters, both eyes stay open (or closed). Proper training activates kinesthetic ability: Present the pistol correctly while focusing on the assailant.

Red-dot sights grow ubiquitous, reducing iron-sight use. Target-focused iron-sight skills transfer directly to red dots, where target focus avoids reticle blur.

World-class competitors train twice as long with MRDS-equipped pistols before iron-sight competitions. MRDS teaches efficient presentation, translating to faster iron-sight acquisition and better both-eyes-open, target-focused shooting.

Target-focused iron-sight shooting, a learned skill based on human physiology, allows journeyman shooters effective engagement to seven yards and trained shooters to 25 yards or beyond. Instructors avoid letting personal shortcomings affect students.

Kinesthetic and Visual Skills: Synergistic Performance

Shooting fast and accurately combines kinesthetic and visual skills: "The body points, but the eyes verify." Proper training blends these synergistically for superior performance.

Sights verify skeletal alignment. Shooters sometimes need this verification; often, they do not. Train to present the gun with aligned sights using kinesthetic awareness, ingraining the reflex into neurological imprinting, then stress-condition for reliable duress performance.

Kinesthetic-visual integration is not 50/50. At closer ranges, kinesthetics dominate with vision supporting. Target-focused shooting emphasizes kinesthetic alignment, with eyes bringing the gun to target.

Stressors disrupt kinesthetic alignment, degrading precision. Vision maintains alignment and keeps the gun on target, especially during movement. At mid-ranges, vision monitors closely to ensure sights stay positioned.

Five Distinct Levels of Focus: Speed, Distance, and Confirmation

Focus levels vary by speed and distance.

- **Level One: Peripheral Focus** – Awareness of surroundings without deep engagement, useful for multitasking. In shooting, apply to single threats at extreme close range for fast hits—no sight or target focus. Shots rely on body feel. This forms spatial orientation (Confirmation One): Present the pistol parallel to the ground, with slide and front sights (or red-dot housing) covering the target for quick, large-target acquisition.
- **Level Two: Selective Focus** – Concentrate on specific stimuli, ignoring distractions (e.g., multiple close targets). Generally Confirmation One: Align gun and body on the first target; sights may enter peripheral vision. Once indexed, the gun appears where the shooter looks. If target-focused, look through sights.
- **Level Three: Sustained Focus** – Maintain attention over time for complex tasks. Requires greater control (Confirmation Two): Color confirmation of dot/sights in the target area with minimal movement. Loosely align iron sights over medium-range targets; red dots move acceptably. Enables fast, accurate engagements. Common for standard distances; shift focus target-to-sights. For closely spaced distant targets, focus on front sight lift; for difficult shots, monitor trigger pressure and sight movement.
- **Level Four: Deep Focus** – Intense concentration leading to flow. Focus on front sight lift in recoil (irons) or stable red-dot settlement with no movement (Confirmation Three): Clean, stopped/stable sight package for high-risk or distant targets.

- **Level Five: Hyper Focus** – Extreme concentration, losing time track. For difficult long-range or small targets (Confirmation Three): Stable sight picture for high-risk or distant targets.

At longer or higher-risk ranges, use traditional sight focus for irons (soft to hard) to ensure hits without sacrificing accuracy. For MRDS, stop and settle the dot in Confirmation Three.

To shoot well at speed with Confirmation Three, hold sights aligned by feel (kinesthetic awareness) and process visuals without hard focus.

Acceptable Sight Picture and Engagement Strategy

In tactical shooting, speed proves crucial: Beat adversaries to the draw, but only with required accuracy to eliminate threats. Instructors ensure students understand EDC prioritizes accuracy/speed over speed/accuracy.

Accurate shooting demands two unarguable elements: Point the muzzle at the target and manipulate the trigger without added muzzle movement.

To ensure muzzle pointing, use the preferred sighting package correctly.

Holding a correct sight picture is noble, but everyone shakes. Practice perfectly; seek focus and alignment for best success. Vision dictates accuracy and speed.

Always better the sight picture with each round.

If the muzzle points at the target on shot break, the bullet hits.

In kinetic encounters or competition, locate the target, align the gun, maintain alignment during fire, allow rapid recoil recovery, and place follow-ups if needed. Visual requirements vary by shot difficulty.

Recall the five focus levels for speed and distance.

With proper training, shooters see sights and achieve accurate hits at speed. Practice seeing sights; they appear when needed.

At the range, practice visual confirmations and levels at 100%, transitioning to risk-appropriate cues.

Know a "10" (perfect) sight picture to settle for a "2" under duress. Proper presentation places sights in the visual path.

Studies claim sights vanish under stress or elevated heart rates, but correct training proves shooters see what's needed for fight-stopping hits.

Achieve this by always practicing the best sight picture, regardless of distance—perfect practice!

Instructor Considerations and Debates

Shooting and instructing feature differing opinions on vision for engagement strategies. Instructors understand and form opinions on key concepts.

- **Single Threat at Extreme Close Range**: Fast hit with no sight or target focus—body feel. As a "use the sights" advocate, practice perfect sight pictures in dry-fire; under stress, sights align properly.

- **Multiple Targets at Extreme Close Range**: Align gun and body on first target; sights peripheral. Once indexed, gun appears where looked. If target-focused, look through sights.
- **Standard Shooting Times and Distances**: Shift focus target-to-sights; monitor sight-trigger for difficult shots.

"Float the dot. Shoot the shot" aids older shooters struggling with focus: Accept movement, center the front sight dot, and then trigger without disturbing it. Applies to red dots. Zero red dots (e.g., EMR or Sig Romeo 1) for distance; know offsets. Pistol optics revolutionize pistols like rifles.

Peripheral or "soft focus" sighting sees sights without hard front-sight focus—misnamed "target focus." Needs differ by range: Close centerline hits vary from 5–7 yards. Precise centerline requires feeling and seeing differently from body hits—return to front sight and alignment.

Shoot well at speed with soft focus by holding sights aligned by feel and processing visuals without hard focus.

Soft focus techniques date to firearms' invention and earlier archery. High-speed competition uses them for decades; they succeed in lethal force, combat, and hunting.

For stress success: Bring weapon to target with aligned sights; task-focus on appropriate sight picture for the hit.

Avoid point shooting (unsighted fire); time is better spent on structured sighted training.

Traditional training focuses on front sight, centering in rear notch, blurring rear and target during trigger press without disturbance.

Under deadly close-range, some find front-sight focus difficult and switch to point shooting—kinesthetic alignment with vision steering, old-west style.

Point shooting faces interference from physical processes, differing range from gunfight results.

Most instructors overlook locking support wrist and pointing thumbs with bio-indexing, enhancing sights—aiming in three complementary ways.

Responsible shooters account for every round.

Instructors failing complementary enhancements often favor point shooting.

Responsible handlers cannot teach unsighted fire.

Instructors teach accountability for every round. As citizens, remember training's purpose. See sights on every shot; account for impacts, rounds hit desired targets.

Master seeing moving sights on target through follow-through, awaiting realignment before next trigger, for proficiency.

EDC tactical shooting prioritizes acceptable-zone hits with speed secondary.

Exclude contact engagements from initial sight requirements (shooter touches target); however, follow-ups require movement and improving sighting for placement.

Use proper sighting package as needed for accurate shots. Kinesthetic and peripheral awareness suit close tactical shooting; increase sight focus with distance.

Shooters always use sufficient sighting package to identify targets visually.

Sighting package variations: Traditional hard-focus front blade in rear notch; slide/hammer as focal for index; flash front without rear reference; soft-focus target with front/rear.

For MRDS: Window framing with housing; housing as alternate flash; floating dot in window; true target focus past dot, floating over hard-focused target.

Sight alignment: Center front blade in rear notch with equal light. Dot fronts: "Put the baby in the cradle" in U-shaped rear. Traditional and dot irons differ in point of aim/impact.

Train best alignment in presentations to teach proper pistol alignment for advancing proficiency. Speed drills confirm quick acquisition and referencing.

Sight picture: Correlate blade, aperture, and target. Center top edge in aperture on largest mass (torso center).

Eyes focus on one object at distances; last on front sight, blurring rear/target. Shooters decide consciously what focuses.

Use sights for target alignment. Strive for perfect at range and dry-fire.

Reference pre- and post-shot for proper presentation.

Target-focused irons: Learned by experience and pistol time. Bodies under stress look both-eyes-open at threats.

Visual sight reading from initial shot through recoil eludes most via instruction alone—appreciated through implementing iron sights under time constraints.

Target focus with irons ties to configuration: Rear window width vs. front width. Optimal: Thinner front for wider light bars, more feedback.

For target focus, look at impact spot—not outline; focus specific point.

This mirrors real encounters: Target focus, present pistol, reference sighting as needed for distance.

For micro red dots (MRDS): Aim realistically with target focus. Pick small target spot; drive pistol between eyes and target. Both eyes open, focused on target.

Find spots, not whole targets—not 8-inch rings, but centers. Smaller spots yield better impacts.

Proper presentation floats dot in housing over target. Dot focus causes climbing impacts.

Understand sighting methods via relationships to target size, distance, risk, and presentation time.

Proprioception

Proprioception is one of those underlying, often overlooked, performance factors in shooting that separates "mechanical" shooters from highly skilled ones.

Definition

Proprioception is the body's sense of position, movement, and force without relying on vision. It's sometimes called the "sixth sense" of body awareness. In pistol shooting, it's what allows you to know where your hands, arms, and pistol are in space—even without consciously looking at them.

In Relation to Pistol Shooting

1. **Grip Consistency**
    - Proprioception helps you replicate the same grip pressure and hand alignment on the pistol every time.
    - Skilled shooters can “feel” if their grip is slightly off without needing to visually confirm.
2. **Presentation to Target**
    - When drawing from the holster, proprioception allows you to present the gun so the sights or red dot naturally align with your eyes.
    - With training, your body learns the exact angles and motions required so the gun "arrives" on target consistently.
3. **Trigger Control**
    - Proprioceptive awareness lets you sense the trigger press, reset, and weight without overthinking.
    - It helps you feel micro-errors in finger placement or excessive tension.
4. **Stability & Balance**
    - It controls stance, posture, and recoil management.
    - Your nervous system constantly makes micro-adjustments in balance and muscle tension to keep you stable under recoil or when moving between targets.

Vision gives you permission
Proprioception builds Precision

In Relation to Shooting Drills

Proprioception develops best under **repetition and feedback**, which is why certain drills are so valuable.

- **Dry Fire Reps**: Builds proprioceptive "maps" of the draw, trigger press, and reload.
- **Blind Draw Drill**: Present the pistol to eye level with eyes closed, then open eyes to check alignment—this sharpens proprioceptive alignment of sights to eyes.
- **Target Transitions**: Teach proprioceptive control of speed, stopping the gun precisely on new targets without overswing.
- **Strong-Hand/Support-Hand Only Shooting**: Forces your proprioception to adapt and refine motor control with reduced contact.
- **Low Light / No Light Drills**: Especially valuable because they force reliance on proprioceptive awareness instead of pure vision.

Bottom Line

Proprioception in pistol shooting is your **internal feedback system** that makes movements smooth, consistent, and repeatable. Visual confirmation (seeing the sights) tells you "when" you can shoot, but proprioception is what makes sure the gun, hands, and trigger are where they should be without conscious thought.

Instructors can think of it this way: *vision gives permission, proprioception builds precision.*

Sight Package: What Do We Need to See and When Do We Need to See It?

Overview from *A Green Beret's Guide to Enhanced Pistol Shooting Skills*

In the pursuit of marksmanship excellence, shooters must continually refine their sight picture, adapting fluidly to achieve greater precision with successive shots. This adaptive process integrates visual confirmations—categorized as Levels 1, 2, and 3—with corresponding trigger manipulations, enabling engagements tailored to target distance, size, and risk. These confirmations, along with associated trigger techniques, receive deeper exploration in subsequent sections on targets, shooting dynamics, and engagement protocols.

1. **Spatial Orientation (Confirmation One)**
   This level emphasizes the pistol's overall alignment parallel to the ground, with the slide, front sights, or red dot optic housing obscuring the target area. It facilitates rapid sight acquisition for large, proximate targets. Trigger

manipulation aligns with this speed, often involving a "slap" to expedite discharge without preparatory staging.

2. **Color Confirmation (Confirmation Two)**
   Here, the sight package presents with minimal oscillation: iron sights loosely aligned over mid-range targets or the red dot traversing an acceptable zone. This yields swift engagements with adequate accuracy. Trigger action requires at least preparatory engagement to the initial resistance wall, culminating in a controlled press upon visual acceptance.
3. **Clean Sight Package (Confirmation Three)**
   Demanding utmost stability, this confirmation mandates a halted, unwavering sight picture—ideal for high-risk or distant targets. Trigger preparation deepens, initiating during presentation and progressing continuously rearward until discharge as stability solidifies.

Shooters must recognize that trigger manipulation intensifies with improving sight pictures pre-shot; once initiated, rearward motion persists uninterrupted. The target's relationship to the sights dictates engagement timing and velocity, underscoring the need for instructors to master these subtleties for effective student guidance.

Instructor-Level Insights: Spatial Orientation and Trigger Manipulation in Confirmation One Engagements

At the instructor level, a nuanced grasp of Confirmation One—high-confidence shots at close range with expansive target zones—is essential for imparting controlled velocity and discipline. This tier prioritizes gross visual cues, kinesthetic awareness, and expedited mechanics to deliver combat-effective accuracy without undue deliberation.

Defining Spatial Orientation in Context

Spatial orientation entails instinctive alignment of the pistol's slide, muzzle, and bore axis with the intended impact zone, bypassing refined sight verification. It leverages:

- Kinesthetic and proprioceptive feedback for hand-eye coordination.
- Predictable grip and presentation pathways honed through repetition.
- Peripheral indexing via blurred sights or red dot artifacts.
- Neuromuscular imprinting from extensive dry fire to embed positional consistency.

Neuromechanics of Spatial Orientation

- **Visual System:** Maintain target fixation, relegating pistol position to peripheral detection as a soft blur.
- **Upper Limbs:** Rigid arm and wrist structures ensure repeatable recoil management.
- **Neural Integration:** Muscle memory automates alignment, drawing on subconscious pathways for minimal cognitive latency. For red dot users, a streaking or blurred dot suffices; iron sights rely on front post flashes sans precise notch alignment.

Pistol Alignment Dynamics

- Predictive pointing targets vital zones (e.g., center mass or cranial areas) via gross indexing.
- Recoil tracking depends on grip integrity and visual cues, privileging velocity over meticulous verification within acceptable hit margins.

Trigger Manipulation: Aggressive "Slap" Technique

Confirmation One compresses trigger control for rapidity:

- Execute forceful, jab-like presses, eschewing preparatory stages.

- Omit deliberate resets; allow recoil to facilitate finger return.
- Engage mid-pad on the trigger face, completing full strokes swiftly with complete disengagement between shots.

Neuromechanical Elements:

- Subconscious automation minimizes delays, fostering reactive responses.
- Grip stability is paramount, as high-speed inputs tolerate no recovery pauses.

Often misconstrued as error, "trigger slapping" constitutes a purposeful method for balancing expedition and efficacy in close-quarters scenarios.

Synergistic Integration: Orientation and Trigger

Component	Execution in Confirmation One
Visual Focus	Target-centric
Pistol Orientation	Kinesthetic and gross visual indexing
Trigger Behavior	Rapid, assertive slap per shot
Recoil Control	Grip-driven; seamless follow-ups
Decision Process	Predictive, pre-visual confirmation

Training Drills for Spatial Orientation and Trigger Integration

1. **Single-Shot Draw (3–5 Yards):** Target-fixate while aligning to center mass; break upon orientation.
2. **Bill Drill (6 Shots at 7 Yards):** Sustain awareness through recoil; analyze splits and groupings.
3. **Trigger Isolation (Dry Fire):** Present aggressively, slap while preserving alignment.
4. **Modified Dot Torture:** Employ 3–4-inch circles; prioritize gross references at pace.

Instructor Guidance:

- Vigilantly identify flinch disguises, where "slaps" mask poor follow-through.
- Verify grip robustness, as recoil amplifies foundational flaws.
- Leverage high-speed video or timers for objective speed-accuracy assessments.

Instructor-Level Insights: Color Confirmation and Trigger Preparation in Confirmation Two Engagements

Confirmation Two bridges rapid point-shooting and precision alignment, demanding visual cues of color or shape within target zones alongside staged trigger control. This suits mid-range (5–10 yards) or partially obscured targets, elevating visual discipline over Confirmation One.

Overview of Color Confirmation

This visual threshold verifies sighting system presence in the hit zone sans perfect stability, accommodating moderate constraints.

Red Dot Sights:

- Target-focused, with the dot visible and contained within vital areas despite motion.
- Accept arcs or streaks if bounded; reject external appearances or overcorrections.

Iron Sights:

- Predominantly target-focused, with momentary sight-plane shifts.
- Front post color/shape overlays center; tolerate minor notch misalignments.
- Accept flashes on-target; reject absent or shadowed sights.

Trigger Manipulation Breakdown

- Initiate contact during presentation.
- Prep through slack to the resistance wall concurrently with alignment.
- Finalize break upon confirmation, sans further verification.
- Reset in recoil for subsequent preps.

Neuromechanical Synchronization

Process	Visual Cue	Tactile Response
Target Indexing	Identify threat	Stabilize grip
Presentation	Dot/post enters field	Initiate trigger movement
Confirmation	Element in zone	Reach wall
Discharge	Color affirms	Complete press

Training Applications and Drills

1. **Press Prep (Dry Fire):** Mount to small targets; prep to wall, hold on cue.
2. **Half-Split Transitions:** Shift from Confirmation One to Two pacing.
3. **3-2-1 Sequencing:** Escalate from full zones to tighter circles, integrating levels.

Comparative Summary

Component	Confirmation One	Confirmation Two
Target	Large, proximate	Medium, moderate confidence
Visual Focus	Fully target	Target with overlay
Iron Sights	Glimpse/flash	Front color/shape visible
Red Dot	Blur/streak	Dot in zone
Trigger	Slap	Prep to wall, cue break
Time	Maximal speed	Controlled rapidity
Accuracy	Acceptable broad hits	Refined zonal impacts

Instructor-Level Insights: Clean Sight Package and Deep Trigger Preparation in Confirmation Three Engagements

Confirmation Three mandates supreme precision for distant, diminutive, or high-stakes targets, subordinating speed to unwavering control.

Defining the Clean Sight Package

This entails a static, unyielding alignment: zero motion, clear superimposition over precise zones.

Red Dot Variant:

- Target-focused with immobilized dot in narrow areas (e.g., cranial T-box).
- Ensure perfect eye-dot-target congruence.

Iron Sights Variant:

- Front-sight focused, with equal height/light in notch.
- Stabilize entirely over the zone.

Visual Summary

System	Focus	Alignment	Movement Tolerance
Red Dot	Target with exact dot	Centered in zone	None
Iron Sights	Front sight	Equal height/light	None

Deep Trigger Preparation Explained

- Commence early, eliminating slack progressively.
- Sustain tension through "the wall" during final aiming.

- Break solely on stability, yielding a near-surprise discharge.

Timing and Sensory Alignment

Input	Action
Visual: Sights halt	Finalize press
Tactile: Tension peaks	Smooth continuation
Auditory: N/A	Slight surprise break

Drills for Mastery

1. **B8 Bullseye (25 Yards):** Deliberate preps on repair centers; score consistency.
2. **3-Inch Dot (10–15 Yards):** Break on stasis; emphasize patience.
3. **Wall Drill (Dry Fire):** Present and press sans sight deviation.

Comparative Elements

Element	Description
Target	Small/distant/high-consequence
Visual Focus	Precise dot or front sight
Sight Package	Fully stabilized
Trigger	Deep, continuous prep
Time Pressure	Negligible; precision reigns
Movement	Absolute stasis
Mental Cue	Break on halt

Instructor Guidance:

- Instill patience against premature breaks.
- Enhance sight visibility if needed.
- Enforce trigger isolation to prevent sympathetic inputs.

Instructor Talking Points: Explaining Visual Confirmations to Novice Shooters

Introduction:
"Visual confirmation governs how much sight information you require before firing, with three levels balancing speed and accuracy based on shot difficulty. Closer, easier targets permit haste; distant or risky ones demand deliberation."

Confirmation One: Prioritizing Speed

- **Use Cases:** Close (3–5 yards), large targets, immediate threats.
- **Visuals:** Sight flash or dot blur; target-focused.
- **Trigger:** Quick slap.
- **Rationale:** Velocity trumps precision for broad, proximate hits.

Confirmation Two: Balanced Approach

- **Use Cases:** Mid-range (5–10 yards), moderate targets.
- **Visuals:** Dot in zone or loose irons; target with sight reference.
- **Trigger:** Prep to wall, break on cue.
- **Rationale:** Merges rapidity with assurance.

Confirmation Three: Emphasizing Precision

- **Use Cases:** Extended ranges (10+ yards), small/high-risk targets.
- **Visuals:** Stabilized dot or perfect irons; sight-focused.

- **Trigger:** Deep prep, clean break.
- **Rationale:** Ensures exact impacts where errors are intolerable.

Student Comparison Chart

Confirmation	Target Type	Distance	Sight Picture	Eye Focus	Trigger Work	Priority
1 (Speed)	Large/close	0–5 yds	Flash/blur	Target	Quick slap	Speed
2 (Balanced)	Medium	5–10 yds	Dot in zone/loose irons	Target w/reference	Prep to wall	Speed + Control
3 (Precision)	Small/far	10–25+ yds	Stopped/stable	Sight	Deep prep	Accuracy

Reinforcement Strategies:

1. **Analogies:** "Confirmation One punches a balloon; Three threads a needle."
2. **Experiential:** Vary distances in drills; query perceptual shifts.
3. **Drill Alignment:** Match exercises to levels for progressive mastery.

In my second book *"A Green Berets Guide to Enhanced Pistol Shooting Skills (ISBN 979821640354)"*, I introduced the structural components; that I believe through observation and teaching tens of thousands of students, which a shooter must learn to incorporate to be successful.

Since this book is being written at an instructor level, it is time to provide a more detailed breakdown of this concept.

Here is a **refined and anatomically detailed breakdown** of the pistol shooting structure principles, ideal for instructor-level training and advanced shooter refinement. This version clarifies **why each element matters**, what **anatomical structures are involved**, and how **breakdowns affect shot placement**—especially point of aim (POA) vs. point of impact (POI).

Shooting Structure: Anatomical and Mechanical Breakdown

A shooter must create a **solid, repeatable skeletal and muscular structure** that both supports recoil management and promotes visual efficiency. Breakdowns at any level—from **posture to grip pressure** create disruptions in POA vs. POI.

1. **Head Up, Eyes Up**

Instruction: *Look where you want to shoot. Bring the gun to your line of sight.*

- **Cervical spine** should remain vertical and neutral (not compressed or flexed).
- The **orbital axis** (eyes) must align with target-level focus.
- Eyes should drive the movement: the **hand–eye connection** ensures fast target acquisition.

Why it matters: Lowering the head introduces **neck tension** and creates downward pressure that can cause the front sight to dip, especially under recoil.

2. Nose Over Toes

Instruction: *Weight forward over the balls of the feet.*

- Promotes **anterior weight distribution** and forward engagement of the **center of mass (COM)**.
- Shoulders, hips, and knees aligned to form a **forward-ready fighting stance**.
- Engages the **hip flexors**, **gluteus medius**, and **tibialis anterior** for balance.

Why it matters: A backward or upright posture will shift recoil force into the lumbar spine and heels, resulting in muzzle rise or shooter instability.

3. Shoulders Relaxed, Not Raised

Instruction: *No unnecessary tension. Raise your head to relieve shoulder tightness.*

- Relaxes **upper trapezius**, **levator scapulae**, and **sternocleidomastoid** muscles.
- Promotes clean scapular function, prevents shoulder fatigue.

Why it matters: Tense shoulders disrupt natural arm movement, affect fine motor control, and reduce endurance.

4. Chest–Arm Triangle High and Even

Instruction: *Elbows out, triceps above nipples, form a triangle from arms to chest.*

- Forms an equal triangle between both **humeri (upper arms)** and the **sternum**.
- Shoulders slightly rolled forward for consistent elbow alignment.
- **Triceps brachii** are engaged and stabilize the shooting platform.

Why it matters: Uneven arms shift the gun laterally or vertically, leading to irregular recoil paths and lateral POI shifts.

5. Forearm Tension from Elbows to Wrists

Instruction: *Tension begins at the elbow and carries through to the wrist joint.*

- Engages **brachioradialis**, **flexor carpi radialis**, and **extensor carpi radialis longus**.
- Both arms should feel equally firm and "alive" from elbow to grip.

Why it matters: Inconsistent forearm tension compromises stability during recoil impulse and may affect sight recovery.

6. Engage Both Wrist Tendons ("Locked Forward")

Instruction: *Wrist flexor tendons should be evenly tensed in a forward-locked position.*

- **Flexor carpi ulnaris** and **flexor carpi radialis** keep the wrist angled forward.
- Prevents upward recoil and keeps muzzle level post-shot.
- **Isometric tension** applied equally on both hands.

Why it matters: A "broken" or "limp" wrist causes the muzzle to lift erratically, delaying target reacquisition.

7. Thumbs High—Within Mechanical Limits

Instruction: *Thumbs as high as possible without interfering with the slide.*

- Activates **thenar eminence** (thumb pad group) for leverage.

- Strong-side thumb slightly forward; support-side thumb forward and slightly higher.

Why it matters: High thumbs aid in recoil tracking and muzzle indexing but must not ride the slide or block ejection.

8. Palm Pressure Drives Grip

Instruction: *Both palms push into the frame—support hand applies more pressure.*

- Use **hypothenar eminence** and **thenar pad** to apply inward and forward pressure.
- Support hand provides **60–70% of grip tension**, strong hand ~30–40%.

Why it matters: Dominant-hand overpressure leads to trigger jerk; support-hand dominance gives stability and steering.

9. Do Not Adjust Fingers After Initial Grip

Instruction: *Set the grip during the draw. No fidgeting afterward.*

- Involves **intrinsic hand muscles**: **lumbricals, interossei, flexor digitorum profundus**.
- Changing pressure mid-string destabilizes the recoil control loop.

Why it matters: Re-gripping creates movement of the muzzle and interrupts neural pathways for consistency.

10. Support Index Finger Indexes Trigger Guard

Instruction: *Support index finger should drive into the underside of the trigger guard.*

- Creates **tactile feedback** and establishes indexing reference.
- Activates **flexor digitorum superficialis** for firm engagement.

Why it matters: Builds reference and consistency in grip—helps in low light or under stress to reinforce hand alignment.

11. Support Fingers Fit Knuckle Notches of Strong Hand

Instruction: *Index and middle fingers nest into the strong-hand finger grooves.*

- Achieves **interlocking grip geometry**
- Maximizes skin-to-frame contact and mechanical advantage

Why it matters: Inconsistent finger placement allows the gun to shift in the hand under recoil.

12. Strong-Hand Fingers Pull Rearward

Instruction: *Middle, ring, and pinky fingers apply rearward pressure into the backstrap.*

- Uses **flexor digitorum profundus** and **flexor digitorum superficialis**
- Anchors the gun into the palm for better muzzle control

Why it matters: Lack of rearward pressure lets the gun torque or roll upward under recoil.

13. Strong-Hand Thumb Applies Forward Pressure

Instruction: *Thumb and palm push forward, opposing the pull of the fingers.*

- Creates **isometric tension** along the longitudinal axis
- Engages **opponens pollicis** and **abductor pollicis brevis**

Why it matters: Completes the front-to-back tension loop and stabilizes the gun longitudinally.

14. Trigger Finger Moves Independently

Instruction: *Trigger finger isolates movement—no sympathetic movement with other fingers.*

- Requires neural independence via **motor cortex training**
- Only **flexor digitorum profundus** of the index finger should activate

Why it matters: If other fingers move with the trigger finger, POI shifts laterally—classic trigger jerk or milking.

15. 360° Vise Grip

Instruction: *Hands provide all-direction pressure: side-to-side, front-to-back, diagonal.*

- Form an **isometric tension net** around the gun
- Prevents any shift during recoil impulse
- Arms, hands, and tendons create a cohesive recoil control system

Why it matters: Anything less than full circumferential tension = movement of the muzzle = variable POI.

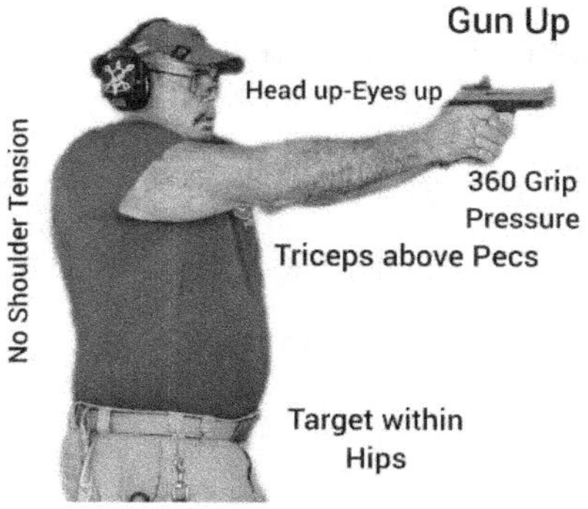

Summary for Instructors

Structure Element	Anatomical Focus	Diagnostic Error When Missing
Head/Eyes Up	Cervical spine, eye axis	Muzzle dips, poor indexing
Weight Forward	Hips, knees, ankles	Recoil pushes shooter off balance
Wrist Locked	Flexor/extensor carpi	Muzzle flip or delay in sight recovery
360° Grip	Intrinsics + forearm flexors	Gun shifts in hand, delayed follow-ups
Isolated Trigger Finger	FDS/hand proprioception	Group shift, lateral POI errors

Instructors need to understand and also be able to relate the same information to various students in various shooting disciplines.

I spend most of my days training Law Enforcement Agents/Officers, so with that in mind, as an instructor I must get a "buy in" from my students. To accomplish this a good instructor needs to understand the why.

Combat-Ready Shooting Structure for LE & CCW

"Structure drives consistency, consistency drives survivability."

A solid structure underpins accuracy, recoil control, and speed. For LE and CCW, structure must remain **stable under pressure**, **agile under movement**, and **repeatable under stress**—whether from a duty rig or concealment.

1. Head Up, Eyes Up – "See to Solve"

- **Context:** You don't draw unless you've identified a threat. Head and eye position dictate awareness and speed of response.
- **Instruction:** Look directly at the target. Bring the gun up to your line of sight, don't lower your head to the gun.
- **Anatomy:** Neutral cervical spine; engage **levator scapulae** and **superior trapezius** gently to hold posture.
- **Failure Result:** Head forward/down causes poor indexing and increased sympathetic shoulder tension, slowing response.

2. Nose Over Toes – Combat Posture

- **Context:** Forward balance enables explosive movement, stable recoil control, and force projection.
- **Instruction:** Slight forward lean from the **ankles**. Nose over your toes. Weight over **balls of the feet**.
- **Anatomy:** Engages **glutes**, **hip flexors**, **quadriceps**, **gastrocnemius**, and **tibialis anterior**.
- **Failure Result:** Leaning back = muzzle rise, disrupted recoil control, and delayed follow-up shots.

3. **Relaxed Shoulders, Head Lifts You**

- **Context:** Muscle tension adds inconsistency and fatigue, especially during prolonged incidents.
- **Instruction:** Shoulders down and relaxed. Lift your head tall—don't pull it forward.
- **Anatomy:** Minimize activation of **upper traps**, **sternocleidomastoid**, and **scalenes**.
- **Failure Result:** Tense shoulders raise elbows, tighten grip unconsciously, and reduce endurance.

4. **Chest–Arm Triangle (Symmetry = Control)**

- **Context:** This structure absorbs and redirects recoil across both arms evenly.
- **Instruction:** Elbows slightly out, triceps above nipple line. Arms form an isosceles triangle.
- **Anatomy:** Engage **deltoids**, **triceps**, **pectoralis major**, and **latissimus dorsi**.
- **Failure Result:** Uneven triangle leads to lateral muzzle jump and slower sight tracking.

5. **Forearm Tension Elbow to Wrist**

- **Context:** Consistent forearm tone stabilizes the gun during movement and recoil.
- **Instruction:** Keep both arms "alive" from the elbow forward. Not stiff, but firm.
- **Anatomy:** Active **brachioradialis, flexor carpi radialis, extensor carpi radialis longus**.
- **Failure Result:** Slack forearms = shock absorbed in the wrists = delayed return to target.

6. **Wrist Tendons Locked Forward**

- **Context:** Forward wrists reduce muzzle rise and keep the gun on target during rapid strings.
- **Instruction:** Flex wrists slightly forward (isometric lock), keep even tension on both sides.
- **Anatomy: Flexor carpi ulnaris**, **flexor carpi radialis**, **extensors** stabilize the wrist.
- **Failure Result:** Weak wrist = muzzle flip + poor shot placement during stress fire.

7. **High Thumbs, Slide-Clear**

- **Context:** Thumbs help track recoil and improve control without interfering with slide or controls.
- **Instruction:** Support-side thumb rides high and forward; strong-side thumb just under it.
- **Anatomy:** Uses **thenar eminence**, **opponens pollicis**, and **adductor pollicis**.
- **Failure Result:** Low or wrapped thumbs delay sight return and decrease lateral control.

8. **Palm Pressure = Gun Control**

- **Context:** Under recoil, grip pressure must be 360° and centered.
- **Instruction:** Strong hand pulls rearward, support palm drives inward and forward.
- **Anatomy:** Pressure from **thenar/hypothenar pads**, and **interossei** stabilize the grip.

- **Failure Result:** Gripping too hard with the gun hand = flinching, trigger jerk, poor POI.

9. No Finger Adjustment After Draw

- **Context:** Fidgeting with grip during a draw can shift POA and slow the shot.
- **Instruction:** Set it and forget it—your draw must end in your shooting grip.
- **Anatomy:** Intrinsic finger control from **lumbricals, flexor digitorum profundus**.
- **Failure Result:** Loss of grip geometry and shot timing under stress.

10. Support Index on Trigger Guard (Index Point)

- **Context:** Tactile contact under the trigger guard builds hand alignment memory under concealment stress.
- **Instruction:** Push index finger up under the trigger guard as a mechanical stop.
- **Failure Result:** Poor grip reference increases rotational error and gun shift.

11. Support Fingers Fit into Strong Hand Knuckles

- **Context:** Interlocking geometry maximizes surface contact and recoil direction.
- **Instruction:** Index and middle fingers nest into strong hand grooves naturally.
- **Failure Result:** Gaps = gun shift = inconsistent point of impact on follow-up shots.

12. Strong Hand Fingers Pull Rearward

- **Context:** Anchoring the gun rearward fights muzzle lift and roll.
- **Instruction:** Middle, ring, and pinky fingers pull straight back into the backstrap.

- **Anatomy:** Uses **flexor digitorum profundus** and palm flexors.
- **Failure Result:** Gun lifts out

13. Strong Side Thumb Pushes Forward

- **Context:** Creates isometric tension from front to back.
- **Instruction:** Apply counter-pressure with the thumb web and pad forward.
- **Failure Result:** Inconsistent recoil path without this balancing force.

14. Trigger Finger Must Move Independently

- **Context:** Trigger control is the #1 accuracy driver in close-range defensive shooting.
- **Instruction:** Isolate trigger finger movement—no sympathy from other fingers.
- **Failure Result:** If grip fingers move with the trigger = lateral group shifts, classic milking.

15. 360° Vise-Like Grip

- **Context:** Defensive and law enforcement shootings demand recoil control under duress.
- **Instruction:** Apply full, circular pressure—front to back, side to side, diagonal.
- **Failure Result:** Incomplete pressure leads to twist, lift, or lateral muzzle movement.

Summary for LE & CCW: Combat Relevance

Structural Element	Why It Matters in the Real World
Head Up, Eyes Up	Improves threat ID, maintains visual control
Nose Over Toes	Helps fight during recoil or physical contact
Shoulders Relaxed	Reduces fatigue, maintains fine motor skill
Triangle Structure	Keeps gun level and recoil consistent
Wrist Lockout	Reduces rise, improves follow-ups
Thumb & Palm Positioning	Affects both slide reliability and recoil tracking
Grip Geometry	Prevents gun shift under stress
Trigger Finger Isolation	Preserves accuracy when it matters most

Instructor Training Guide: Combat-Ready Shooting Structure for LE & CCW

Purpose:

To equip instructors with the anatomical understanding and instructional cues necessary to teach consistent, high-performance shooting structure tailored for Law Enforcement (LE) and Concealed Carry (CCW) contexts.

1. Head Up, Eyes Up – "See to Solve"

Objective: Maintain threat focus and target clarity.

- Instruct: "Look directly at what you need to shoot. Bring the gun to your eyes, not your head to the gun."
- Anatomy: Neutral cervical spine, eyes level.

- Common Errors: Head forward/down, creates downward muzzle angle and shoulder tension.
- Fix: Mirror drills, dry fire with visual focus on a point.

2. Nose Over Toes

Objective: Promote combat stance and recoil control.

- Instruct: "Lean forward from the ankles. Nose over toes."
- Anatomy: Engages hips, glutes, and anterior chain.
- Common Errors: Leaning back, heel loading.
- Fix: Wall lean drills, recoil control while moving.

3. Shoulders Relaxed

Objective: Reduce fatigue and maintain range of motion.

- Instruct: "Lift the head, let the shoulders fall."
- Anatomy: Upper traps, SCM, levator scapulae.
- Common Errors: Raised shoulders under stress.
- Fix: Relaxation drills, emphasize breathing cadence.

4. Chest-Arm Triangle

Objective: Symmetry in support and recoil management.

- Instruct: "Elbows out, triceps above the nipple line."
- Anatomy: Triceps, deltoids, pecs.
- Common Errors: Uneven extension, dropped elbows.
- Fix: Mirror stance drills, triangle with laser training.

5. Forearm Tension

Objective: Stabilize pistol platform.

- Instruct: "Tension from elbows to wrists, not stiff but engaged."
- Anatomy: Brachioradialis, forearm flexors/extensors.
- Common Errors: Limp wrists or stiff arms.
- Fix: Elastic band tension drills, shot recovery timing.

6. Wrist Tendons Locked Forward

Objective: Minimize muzzle rise.

- Instruct: "Lock both wrists slightly forward."
- Anatomy: Flexor carpi ulnaris/radialis.
- Common Errors: Collapsing wrists on recoil.
- Fix: Recoil tracking drills, laser dot control.

7. High Thumbs

Objective: Guide and manage recoil.

- Instruct: "Thumbs high and forward, but clear of the slide."
- Anatomy: Thenar eminence, opponens pollicis.
- Common Errors: Wrapped thumbs, riding the slide.
- Fix: Re-grip drills, dry fire press with high thumbs.

8. Palm Pressure

Objective: Stabilize grip structure.

- Instruct: "Press palms inward, support hand stronger."
- Anatomy: Thenar/hypothenar pads.
- Common Errors: Overgripping strong hand.
- Fix: Pressure pad drills, strong vs. support hand analysis.

9. Grip Consistency

Objective: Avoid shifting under stress.

- Instruct: "Establish grip on the draw. Don't fidget."
- Anatomy: Flexor digitorum profundus/superficialis.
- Common Errors: Readjusting grip after draw.
- Fix: Draw-to-shot timer drills, concealment reps.

10. Support Indexing on Trigger Guard

Objective: Create tactile reference point.

- Instruct: "Drive the support index under the trigger guard."
- Anatomy: Finger flexors and proprioceptive nerves.
- Common Errors: Low or floating support hand.
- Fix: Indexing drills, reference point pressure checks.

11. Interlocked Fingers

Objective: Maximize surface contact.

- Instruct: "Nest support fingers into the strong hand notches."
- Anatomy: Interossei, lumbricals.
- Common Errors: Gaps in grip geometry.
- Fix: Interlock drills, pressure mapping.

12. Rearward Pressure with Strong Hand Fingers

Objective: Anchor gun into the backstrap.

- Instruct: "Pull back with middle, ring, and pinky."
- Anatomy: Finger flexors.
- Common Errors: Floating pinky or uneven pull.
- Fix: Pressure squeeze drills, one-hand isolation checks.

13. Forward Pressure with Thumb

Objective: Counterbalance rearward pull.

- Instruct: "Drive strong side thumb forward."
- Anatomy: Opponens pollicis, adductor pollicis.
- Common Errors: Thumb not engaged.
- Fix: Isometric thumb-push drills.

14. Trigger Finger Isolation

Objective: Maintain shot precision.

- Instruct: "Only the trigger finger moves."

- Anatomy: Index flexors (FDP), motor isolation pathways.
- Common Errors: Milking or sympathetic grip.
- Fix: Finger isolation drills, trigger reset training.

15. 360° Vise Grip

Objective: Create full grip enclosure.

- Instruct: "Grip front to back, side to side, top to bottom."
- Anatomy: Full hand musculature.
- Common Errors: One-directional pressure only.
- Fix: Grip ring drills, live fire follow-up shot analysis.

Final Coaching Tip:

"Structure is subconscious control of recoil under conscious decision-making."

LE context: Train for structure under movement, barricades, low light.

CCW context: Emphasize structure from concealment, in confined space, or crowd environment.

Quick Structure Checklist for LE & CCW

1. Use this during instruction, dry fire evaluation, or live fire assessment.
2. Head up, eyes on threat – bring sights to eye level
3. Nose over toes – aggressive forward stance
4. Shoulders relaxed – eliminate unnecessary tension
5. Chest–arm triangle – elbows out, triceps above nipples
6. Forearms alive – tension from elbow to wrist
7. Wrists locked forward – resist muzzle rise
8. Thumbs high – forward, clear of slide
9. Palm pressure – support hand applies more pressure
10. Grip set on draw – no re-adjusting under stress

Index finger of support hand under trigger guard

11. Support fingers locked into strong hand notches
12. Strong hand fingers (middle, ring, pinky) pull rearward
13. Strong hand thumb drives forward into grip
14. Trigger finger moves independently
15. 360° vise grip – pressure in all directions

Building the Shooting Structure from the Ground Up

Mastering the foundational elements of a solid shooting structure—encompassing stance, posture, and grip—stands as a cornerstone of proficient pistol handling, directly influencing accuracy, recoil control, and overall safety in high-stakes situations. For individuals who conceal carry a pistol, this knowledge empowers them to respond swiftly and effectively to threats, minimizing errors under stress while enhancing their confidence and legal defensibility through precise, controlled actions that prioritize de-escalation and precision over panic. Instructors, meanwhile, must cultivate a profound grasp of these principles to impart not just mechanical skills but also the nuanced rationale behind them, enabling them to tailor instruction to diverse body types, scenarios, and skill levels, ultimately fostering safer, more competent shooters who can adapt and excel in real-world applications.

A solid shooting structure is fundamental to effective pistol handling, providing the foundation for accuracy, recoil management, and safety. This chapter outlines the key elements of stance and posture, starting from the feet and progressing upward. By establishing a stable, aligned, and tension-free structure, shooters can achieve consistent performance across various scenarios. We will then explore popular stances, their advantages and drawbacks, and recommendations for specific applications, before transitioning to grip techniques.

Establishing the Foundation: From Feet to Shoulders

Begin with the lower body to create a balanced platform that supports the entire shooting posture. The goal is to ensure stability, mobility, and natural alignment with the target while minimizing unnecessary tension.

1. **Feet: Flat and Positioned for Balance**
   The feet should remain flat on the ground, with the possible exception of the toes digging slightly into the surface for enhanced grip.
    - The strong-side foot (gun side) is generally positioned about halfway back relative to the instep of the support-side foot.
    - Smaller shooters may prefer a slightly more aggressive stance, aligning the toes of the strong-side foot with the heel of the support-side foot.

- The toes of both feet should point toward the target to promote proper hip alignment.
- Feet should be spaced approximately shoulder-width apart.
- Key contributions of the feet:
  - **Stability**: A solid platform that minimizes unnecessary movement, with balanced weight distribution (typically shifted slightly forward onto the balls of the feet). Feet positioned shoulder-width apart or slightly wider help resist recoil and maintain control.
  - **Mobility**: The ability to move quickly in any direction as needed, facilitated by slightly bent knees that keep the shooter agile.

2. **Knees: Unlocked for Flexibility**
   Keep the knees unlocked and slightly bent to lower the center of gravity, enhancing balance and readiness for movement.
3. **Hips: Squared to the Target**
   Present the hips straight toward the target, avoiding an open or rotated position to maintain natural alignment.
4. **Chest: Aligned and Relaxed**
   The chest should face the target squarely, in harmony with the hips. Avoid using muscle tension to "force" the pistol toward the target; the structure should guide alignment naturally.
5. **Shoulders: Relaxed and Tension-Free**
   Maintain relaxed shoulders without shrugging, rolling, or dropping the chin. Ensure no tension originates from the shoulders, as this can disrupt the overall posture.
6. **Elbows: Unlocked and Elevated**
   Keep the elbows unlocked and positioned above the chest (with triceps aligned above the nipple line). Extend the pistol as far from the face as possible without locking the elbows to optimize sight alignment and recoil absorption.

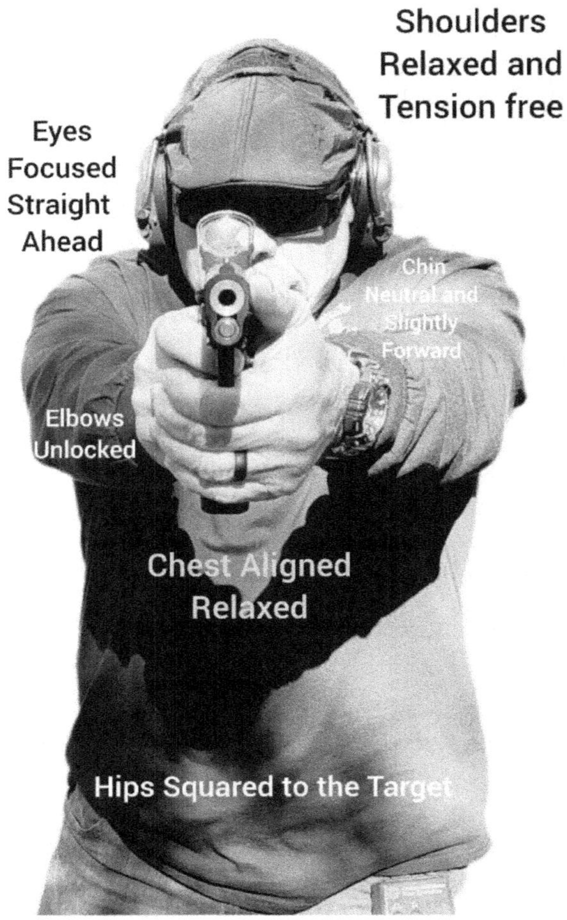

7. **Chin: Neutral and Slightly Forward**

Hold the chin in a neutral, upright position, slightly forward so the nose is even with or just ahead of the toes. This promotes a subtle "nose over toes" posture without aggressive leaning.

8. **Eyes: Focused Straight Ahead**

Direct the eyes straight toward the target, selecting a small, specific spot for precision focus.

A well-constructed stance from the feet to the shoulders, as described, delivers stability and mobility. It also provides additional benefits essential for effective shooting:

1. **Recoil Management**
   - A forward lean in the torso, combined with extended arms, enables the body to absorb and manage recoil more efficiently.
   - This setup facilitates quicker sight recovery and return to target after each shot.
2. **Consistency and Repeatability**
   - A stance that is straightforward to replicate across shots and environments.
   - It fosters muscle memory, enhancing accuracy through uniform positioning.

3. **Comfort and Endurance**
    - The posture must be sustainable for extended periods without inducing fatigue.
    - It minimizes tension, which could otherwise compromise grip and trigger control.
4. **Alignment with the Target**
    - Naturally directs the pistol toward the target.
    - Supports proper sight alignment and sight picture with minimal adjustments.

Popular Shooting Stances

Several established stances meet these criteria, each with strengths and limitations tailored to the shooter's experience, physique, and operational requirements. The Isosceles, Weaver, and Modified Isosceles are among the most common.

1. Isosceles Stance

Description:

- The shooter faces the target squarely.
- Arms are extended straight forward, forming an isosceles triangle with the body.
- Feet are shoulder-width apart, with weight shifted slightly forward.

Pros:

- Simple and intuitive, making it easy for beginners to learn.
- Effective recoil management, as body mass directly absorbs the force.
- Ideal for body armor, presenting the full plate toward the threat.
- Facilitates faster target transitions due to symmetrical posture.

- Well-suited for red dot sights, maintaining natural dot alignment in the window.

Cons:

- May feel stiff or less flexible for some users.
- Results in more perceived recoil in the arms compared to stances with greater muscular involvement.
- Potentially less stable under stress, particularly if balance is compromised.

2. Weaver Stance

Description:

- A bladed posture with the support-side foot forward.
- The strong arm is extended straight, while the support arm is bent.
- Employs push-pull tension between the hands for control.

Pros:

- Superior recoil control through muscular tension, effectively managing muzzle rise.
- Natural for those familiar with rifle shooting due to similar positioning.
- Enhances agility, resembling a fighter's stance for close-quarters maneuvers.
- Reduces the shoulder profile, offering potential advantages in cover or concealment.

Cons:

- More complex to teach, requiring coordination and developed muscle memory.
- Suboptimal for body armor, as the side profile exposes vulnerabilities.

- Less effective with red dot sights, as the head may not align squarely behind the optic.
- Can lead to muscle fatigue during prolonged use, especially in the support arm.

3. Modified Isosceles Stance

Description:

- A hybrid combining elements of Isosceles and Weaver.
- Feet are slightly staggered for improved balance.
- Arms are nearly straight like in Isosceles, but the body is subtly bladed.

Pros:

- Balanced recoil control, leveraging both body mass and muscular tension.
- Enhanced mobility from the staggered foot placement.
- Greater stability under recoil, with forward weight bias supporting rapid follow-up shots.
- Excellent for tactical applications, blending armor compatibility with readiness for movement.

Cons:

- Demands practice and may not feel intuitive for beginners.
- Risk of inconsistency if shooters inadvertently shift toward pure Isosceles or Weaver.
- Lacks standardization, with minor variations potentially impacting repeatability.

Shooters construct a robust shooting structure by prioritizing stability from the feet upward, positioning them flat and shoulder-width apart with toes aimed at the target, unlocking knees for agility, squaring hips and chest forward, relaxing shoulders, elevating unlocked elbows, maintaining a neutral chin slightly advanced, and focusing eyes intently on a precise spot. This deliberate alignment delivers superior recoil absorption through forward lean and extended arms, ensures repeatable consistency via muscle memory, sustains comfort during prolonged sessions by eliminating tension, and naturally orients the pistol toward the target for effortless sight alignment. Among popular stances, the Isosceles offers simplicity and symmetry ideal for beginners and armored users but may amplify perceived recoil; the Weaver excels in muscular control and mobility for dynamic environments yet risks fatigue and suboptimal optic alignment; while the Modified Isosceles balances both, providing tactical versatility though demanding practice for mastery. Instructors who deeply comprehend and dynamically teach these elements empower concealed carriers to wield pistols with precision and poise, underscoring the subject's vital role in elevating personal defense from reactive instinct to disciplined expertise.

Over the years, I have come to believe that the essence of effective recoil management lies in its profound importance yet inherent simplicity, transforming what could be a daunting challenge into a seamless extension of the shooter's form. By adopting a forward lean in the torso paired with extended arms, the body absorbs and dissipates recoil forces with remarkable efficiency, allowing for rapid sight recovery and a swift return to target after each discharge. This foundation not only promotes consistency and repeatability—enabling effortless replication across varied shots and environments while building muscle memory for enhanced accuracy through uniform positioning—but also prioritizes comfort and endurance, ensuring the posture remains sustainable over prolonged sessions without inducing fatigue or excess tension that might impair grip and trigger control. Ultimately, such alignment naturally orients the pistol toward the target, facilitating impeccable sight alignment and picture with minimal adjustments, empowering shooters to achieve precision, control, and confidence in every engagement.

Anticipation in Shooting: Causes, Mechanics, and Diagnostics

One of the most frustrating pet peeves I encounter as a seasoned firearms instructor surfaces when I assess troubled or failing law enforcement shooters. I start by asking them to pinpoint their issues, and they almost always echo their previous instructor's diagnosis: "I'm anticipating." This vague label irritates me because anticipation does not function as a universal scapegoat for poor marksmanship. In reality, shooting errors stem from a web of interconnected breakdown points, each demanding precise identification and targeted correction. Competent instructors bear the responsibility to scrutinize the shooter's entire structure from behind the gun—observing stance, grip, arm extension, and body alignment in real time—and dissect the true culprits, whether flawed fundamentals, physiological responses, or equipment mismatches, to foster genuine improvement rather than superficial fixes. If an instructor understands the finer points of creating the proper structure, then the ability to diagnose shooter problems becomes easier.

To truly expound on this, let's first define anticipation in the context of firearms training. Shooters "anticipate" when they subconsciously brace for recoil before the shot breaks, often causing the muzzle to dip, push, or jerk off target. This manifests as low-left hits for right-handed shooters (or low-right for lefties) on diagnostic targets. Instructors love this term because it sounds insightful and shifts blame to the student's mindset. However, it oversimplifies the problem. True anticipation rarely occurs in isolation; it often signals deeper flaws in technique that trigger the flinch as a symptom, not the root. For instance, a weak or inconsistent grip allows the pistol to rotate excessively during recoil, prompting the shooter to overcompensate on subsequent shots. Similarly, poor stance—such as standing too upright without a forward lean—fails to absorb energy, amplifying perceived recoil and breeding that anticipatory twitch.

Consider the multiple breakdown points that masquerade as mere anticipation. Grip issues top the list: if the shooter fails to achieve a high, firm hold with both hands compressing inward and rearward, the gun shifts unpredictably, eroding confidence and inviting preemptive movements. Stance breakdowns follow closely; a balanced, athletic posture with feet shoulder-width apart and weight forward on the balls of the feet channels recoil straight back into the body, but many students default to a rigid, rear-weighted position that exacerbates muzzle rise. Trigger control represents another frequent offender—jerky pulls or staging the trigger midway disrupt smooth shot breaks, mimicking anticipation's effects. Sight alignment and focus compound these: if the shooter fixates on the target instead of the front sight, or allows parallax errors in red-dot optics, hits scatter wildly, leading instructors to wrongly cry "flinch!" Equipment factors play a role too; ill-fitted holsters, mismatched ammunition, or even vision problems like uncorrected astigmatism can induce compensatory behaviors that resemble anticipation.

As instructors, we must commit to rigorous analysis from behind the gun, a vantage point that reveals truths the shooter themselves often misses. Position yourself directly in line with the muzzle, and watch the entire kinetic chain during live fire. Does the muzzle flip upward excessively? That points to insufficient arm extension or elbow lockout. Observe the slide's cycle: erratic ejection patterns suggest grip inconsistencies. Track the shooter's shoulders and torso—hunching or leaning back indicates fear of recoil, while a forward-aggressive posture promotes control. Use tools like slow-motion video capture or laser training aids to quantify these observations, stripping away subjectivity. This methodical breakdown transforms vague complaints into actionable insights: "Your grip slips because your support hand rotates counterclockwise—let's reinforce it with this drill."

Ultimately, mislabeling errors as anticipation harms students by delaying progress and eroding trust. Law enforcement officers, in particular, cannot afford such shortcuts; their lives depend on split-second accuracy under stress. By embracing a holistic diagnostic approach, instructors empower shooters to address root causes, build resilient fundamentals, and achieve consistent, confident performance. This not only resolves the immediate pet peeve but elevates the craft of instruction itself.

Anticipation is not a single "flinch" but a family of *pre-ignition disturbances*—movements initiated by the shooter *before* the pistol discharges. These movements occur within milliseconds of the shot and are often subconscious, originating from a combination of **neuromuscular reflexes, startle responses, and learned compensation habits**.

Each type of anticipation recruits different muscle groups—from the fine motor control of the distal phalanges (trigger finger) to gross motor bracing of the shoulders, torso, and even the lower body. Understanding which body parts are engaged, and *how*, allows the instructor to rapidly diagnose and correct errors on the range.

Primary Anticipation Types and Involved Body Parts

1. Recoil Management Flinch

Muscles Involved:

- **Forearms & wrists:** Flexor carpi radialis, flexor carpi ulnaris (downward push)
- **Hands:** Thenar eminence (thumb pad) applying forward pressure
- **Upper arms:** Biceps (pull) and triceps (brace)
- **Core:** Rectus abdominis and obliques tighten to stabilize
  Mechanics: Shooter pushes the muzzle forward or down in an attempt to "meet" the recoil before it happens. Often results in low hits.

2. Noise Startle Response

Muscles Involved:

- **Neck:** Sternocleidomastoid contracts, causing slight head recoil
- **Shoulders:** Trapezius tightens, causing a “shrug”
- **Face:** Orbicularis oculi (blinking) and masseter (jaw clench)

  Mechanics: Body reacts to the expected sound with micro-tensing that disrupts the sight picture at the moment of discharge.

3. Visual Blink Anticipation

Muscles Involved:

- **Eyes:** Orbicularis oculi (eyelid closure)
- **Forehead:** Frontalis (raising brows during blink reflex)

  Mechanics: The blink occurs microseconds before the break, eliminating the visual reference needed for precise alignment.

4. Body “Crash” or Collapse

Muscles Involved:

- **Shoulders:** Deltoids and trapezius contract
- **Chest:** Pectoralis major pulls arms inward
- **Spine/Core:** Erector spinae and rectus abdominis flex forward

  Mechanics: The shooter compresses the upper body forward and down to “absorb” recoil before it arrives, shifting the muzzle low or off-target.

5. Trigger Slap or Jerk

Muscles Involved:

- **Trigger Finger:** Flexor digitorum profundus and flexor digitorum superficialis (rapid pull)
- **Forearm:** Flexor carpi radialis stabilizes but can over-engage

- **Hand:** Entire hand may tighten sympathetically
  Mechanics: The shooter "punches" through the trigger instead of pressing straight to the rear, throwing shots laterally or low.

6. Grip Clench Anticipation

Muscles Involved:

- **Hands:** Flexor pollicis longus (thumb) and flexor digitorum (fingers)
- **Forearms:** Pronator teres and wrist flexors
  Mechanics: Both hands suddenly squeeze tighter just before the break, dipping the muzzle or shifting point of impact.

7. Breathing Disruption

Muscles Involved:

- **Diaphragm:** Sudden tightening or release
- **Intercostals:** Rib cage muscles contract
- **Core:** Abdominals tense
  Mechanics: Breath-holding or forceful exhalation shifts upper body stability and moves the sight package.

8. Pre-Ignition Push / Heeling

Muscles Involved:

- **Hands/Wrist:** Thenar muscles push forward
- **Forearm:** Wrist extensors activate
- **Shoulder:** Anterior deltoid engages to drive muzzle upward/forward
  Mechanics: Heel of the hand presses into the backstrap to "control" recoil before it occurs, producing high or diagonal hits.

9. Lower-Body Bracing

Muscles Involved:

- **Legs:** Quadriceps (front knee lock), gastrocnemius (calf tension)
- **Hips:** Gluteus maximus and hip flexors tighten
- **Core:** Lower abdominals brace the pelvis

  Mechanics: Sudden weight shift or knee lock changes upper body alignment, pulling sights off target.

Professional Diagnostic Table: Anticipation Patterns

Anticipation Type	Primary Body Parts Engaged	Observable Target Signature	Likely Cause	Corrective Drill
Recoil Management Flinch	Forearms, wrists, core	Tight low grouping, often centered	Bracing for recoil	Ball-and-dummy drill, surprise break training
Noise Startle Response	Neck, shoulders, facial muscles	Random miss pattern, inconsistent	Reaction to sound	Dry fire with hearing protection layering
Visual Blink Anticipation	Eyelids, forehead	Poor follow-through, shots wander	Flinch to muzzle flash	Flash acclimatization dry fire
Body Crash/Collapse	Shoulders, chest, core	Low-left (RH shooter), body tension visible	Over-bracing	Video slow-mo feedback, wall drill
Trigger Slap/Jerk	Trigger finger, forearm	Lateral spread, often low	Timing the shot	Trigger reset drills, cadence shooting
Grip Clench Anticipation	Hands, forearms	Low-center grouping	Sympathetic hand squeeze	Grip isolation drills, coin-on-sight dry fire

Anticipation Type	Primary Body Parts Engaged	Observable Target Signature	Likely Cause	Corrective Drill
Breathing Disruption	Diaphragm, intercostals	Slight vertical stringing	Breath-hold under stress	Controlled breathing cadence drills
Pre-Ignition Push / Heeling	Hands, wrist, shoulder	High/diagonal impacts	Overcompensation	Support-hand-only fire for recoil isolation
Lower-Body Bracing	Legs, hips, core	Erratic vertical displacement	Whole-body bracing	Dynamic stance drills, balance board shooting

Instructor Note: a firearms instructor's should gain extensive knowledge—honed through years of dedicated study, practical application, and mastery of diagnostic technique that should equip them to dissect anticipation issues beyond mere symptoms, pinpointing root causes like grip flaws or stance imbalances for precise corrections. This expertise imposes a profound responsibility to students: to provide thorough, individualized guidance that builds trust, enhances safety, and fosters lasting proficiency, ensuring no shooter endures superficial fixes that could compromise performance in critical moments.

Grip: At the Instructor Level

In the domain of advanced pistol instruction, a profound examination of the grip's intricacies is indispensable. This entails a nuanced comprehension of the interplay among its constituent elements, which collectively underpin shooting efficacy. As previously articulated, the foundational trinity of pistol marksmanship comprises vision (sight package), structure (encompassing stance and grip), and trigger manipulation. The relative emphasis and integration of these pillars vary according to the scenario at hand.

In high-stakes lethal encounters, where accelerated action is imperative for survival—and temporal constraints are unforgiving—the grip emerges as a pivotal fulcrum for success. Its establishment assumes heightened significance in such kinetic environments, as well as in practical shooting disciplines where velocity is paramount. The shooter must forge a comprehensive 360-degree vise around the pistol grip, thereby asserting dominance over the firearm.

This vise-like hold empowers the shooter to sustain control, facilitate recoil management, and expedite recovery. A more robust grip enhances tolerance for assertive trigger operations, while also orienting the weapon toward the threat with minimal reliance on meticulous sight alignment for tactical precision. Ultimately, an effective grip must embody **consistency, predictability, and durability**.

Certain gripping methodologies prove more efficacious than others; however, the selected approach must prioritize uniformity. This ensures invariant firearm behavior with each discharge. **Consistency** begets **predictability**: The pistol recoils uniformly and resettles reliably, enabling the shooter to track the sight package amid recoil due to its foreseeable trajectory.

Durability is equally critical. The grip must endure unwavering pressure and tension across the requisite volley of shots. Any degradation—such as slippage or loosening—erodes predictability, which in turn undermines consistency.

The optimal grip hinges on two principal facets: the judicious application of pressure and the maximization of friction.

Anatomical and Biomechanical Foundations of the Grip

This exposition delves into the grip's role in fostering consistency, predictability, and durability, illuminated through anatomical and biomechanical lenses. Such insights equip instructors to convey these principles with precision, enhancing shooter performance.

1. Grip Consistency and Predictability

- **Biomechanical Rationale**: Consistency arises from the body's capacity to replicate the grip configuration reliably. Proprioceptors—sensory receptors in the hands and forearms that detect positional cues—require a stable, repeatable hold to minimize recoil variability and bolster shooting reliability.

- This uniformity yields a foreseeable recoil pattern, facilitating swift follow-up shots and sustained accuracy.
- **Anatomical Insights**: Synchronized engagement of forearm and hand musculature is essential, with balanced tension across flexors and extensors. This orchestration stabilizes the grip under duress, preventing deviations.

2. Head and Eye Positioning

- **Head Up, Eyes Up**: The eyes serve as the primary conduit for aiming; thus, maintaining an upright head aligned with the target is vital for precision.
- Anatomically, this posture relaxes the sternocleidomastoid and associated neck muscles, averting tension in the shoulders and upper back that could compromise stability.
- **Aim Small, Miss Small**: Concentrating on a diminutive focal point leverages the fovea's acute central vision. Proper head alignment permits independent eye and neck mobility, mitigating extraneous strain.

3. Shoulder Relaxation and Elbow Positioning

- **No Shoulder Tension**: Shoulder rigidity impairs grip integrity. Elevating the head alleviates this, preserving fluidity in the arms.
- **Muscles Involved**: The deltoids and trapezius govern shoulder posture; their tension induces arm rigidity, hindering recoil absorption and realignment.

4. Forearm Tension from Elbows to Wrists

- **Biomechanics**: Engaging musculature from elbows to wrists—via flexors and extensors—fortifies recoil control. This tension locks the wrists forward, channeling energy efficiently.
- **Anatomical Details**:
    - Brachioradialis: Stabilizes wrist and elbow.
    - Flexor Carpi Radialis and Ulnaris: Facilitate forward wrist flexion.
    - Extensor Carpi Radialis: Counterbalances flexors for a rigid lock.

5. Wrist Tendons and Locking Forward

- **Wrist Locking Mechanism**: Active tendon engagement prevents backward collapse under recoil. Balanced flexor activation (e.g., Flexor Carpi Radialis and Ulnaris) sustains forward stability.

6. Thumb and Palm Positioning

- **Thumbs High**: Position thumbs maximally elevated without impeding slide function, curbing muzzle rise and averting limp-wristing. The thenar eminence presses firmly against the backstrap.
- **Pressure Distribution**: Support-hand dominance in pressure application optimizes recoil mitigation, with strong-hand alignment ensuring aim integrity.

7. The Role of the Fingers

- **Strong Hand**: Middle, ring, and pinky exert rearward force, securing the grip via flexor tendons. Anatomically, palmar interossei aid in finger compression.
- **Support Hand**: Index and middle fingers nest in strong-hand knuckle grooves for uniform pressure.

- **Trigger Finger**: Operates autonomously to preclude sympathetic disruptions, isolating flexor tendon action.

8. 360-Degree Grip Pressure

- **Vise-Like Grip**: Omnidirectional pressure engages flexors (e.g., Flexor Digitorum Superficialis) and extensors (e.g., Extensor Digitorum Longus), governing recoil holistically.
- **Durability**: Unyielding pressure sustains focus on trigger work, obviating mid-sequence adjustments.

9. Misconceptions about Grip Pressure

- **Dispelling Myths**: Antiquated notions (e.g., "hold until it shakes, then ease") have evolved; contemporary emphasis favors support-hand predominance for recoil mastery.
- **Special Forces Legacy**: Wrist-rolling and thumb-pointing techniques lock tendons, enhancing control—a precursor to modern methods.

A meticulously formed grip, when consistent and predictable, applies optimal tension and friction, neutralizing trigger anomalies at engagement ranges.

Grip Establishment from the Draw

The grip originates with the strong hand during the draw, leveraging the holster's stability. This hand must:

- Seat the thumb-pointer web high into the tang/beavertail.
- Assert control from the top and rear.
- Disengage holster mechanisms via thumb.

- Apply front-to-rear pressure as the support hand converges.

The support hand stages across the body for efficient union. Strong-hand fingers (middle, ring, pinky) wrap forward, ideally abutting the trigger guard with equitable pressure. Thumb and palm contribute rearward friction, while the trigger finger indexes rigidly along the frame.

Upon holster clearance and barrel parallelism, the two-handed grip forms. Strong-hand pressure remains constant; alterations induce instability. Support-hand palm overlays the rear, fingers interlock at knuckles, with index high under the trigger guard.

This configuration yields a vise-like enclosure, mitigating trigger perturbations and enabling rapid manipulation with negligible sight disruption.

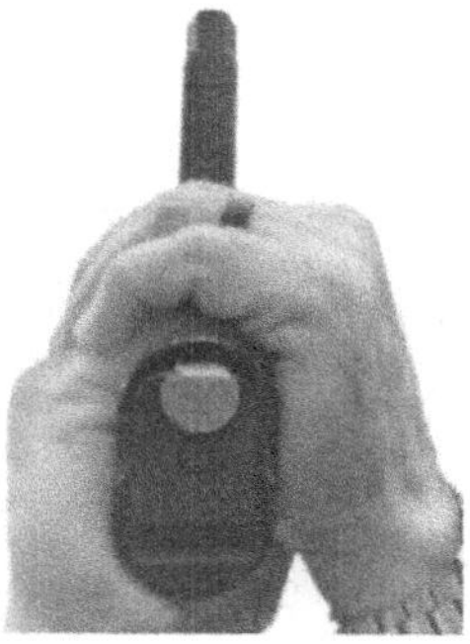

Quick Review: 13 Points of Proper Pistol Grip Structure

1. **Head & Eyes Up**: Upright posture; eyes fixed on a precise target point. "Aim small, miss small."
2. **Relaxed Shoulders**: Tension-free; head elevation dissipates strain.
3. **Forearm Tension**: Uniform from elbows to wrists for foundational control.
4. **Wrist Tendons Engaged**: Locked forward with isometric balance.

5. **Thumbs High**: Maximized elevation sans mechanical interference.
6. **Palm Pressure In**: Inward drive; support hand predominates.
7. **Frozen Finger Pressure**: Immutable once set.
8. **Support Index Finger Placement**: Firmly under trigger guard for lateral stability.
9. **Support Finger Integration**: Even pressure into strong-hand knuckles.
10. **Strong Hand Fingers (Rearward Pressure)**: Middle, ring, pinky secure durability.
11. **Strong Thumb Forward Pressure**: Counters rearward forces.
12. **Trigger Finger Isolation**: Independent motion.
13. **360° Vise-like Tension**: Multi-directional for comprehensive recoil mastery.

Inductive Learning

Employ inquiry-based methods, wherein shooters discern optimal support pressure, friction, and thumb placement through iterative observation and experience, rather than didactic instruction. Repetitions reveal personalized efficiencies.

Grip efficacy manifests in rapid engagements: Minimal sight lift, with symmetric rise and return velocities, signaling structural and grip synergy.

A steadfast, predictable grip, imbued with apt tension and friction, obviates trigger concerns at fighting ranges.

Instructor Checklist: Pistol Grip Structure

☐ 1. Head upright, eyes on small point

☐ 2. Shoulders relaxed, not rolled

☐ 3. Forearm tension from elbow to wrist

☐ 4. Wrist tendons locked forward, equally engaged

☐ 5. Thumbs high on frame, non-interfering

☐ 6. Palms pressing inward; support dominant

☐ 7. Finger tension unchanged

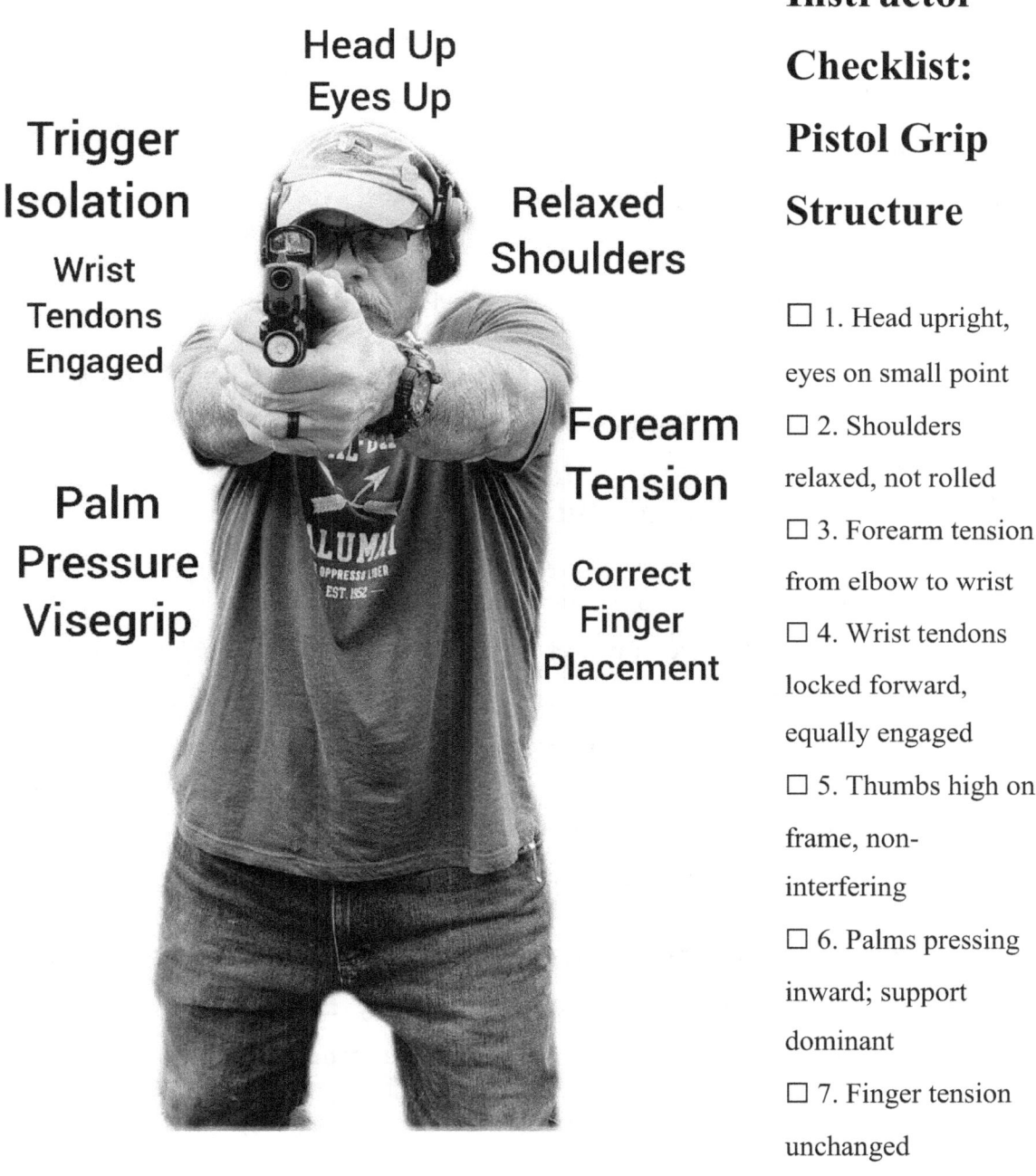

☐ 8. Support index under trigger guard

☐ 9. Support fingers in strong-hand knuckles

☐ 10. Strong fingers rearward

☐ 11. Strong thumb/palm forward

☐ 12. Trigger finger independent

☐ 13. Full 360° vise-like tension

A robust, uniform grip neutralizes trigger flaws at operational distances.

The essence: A high two-handed grip maximizing surface contact, gripped firmly and consistently for predictable recoil and enduring performance.

Dispelling Grip Myths of Old

Evolutions in pedagogy mirror those in martial arts—refinements in articulation. Early queries on grip intensity elicited responses like Fairbairn and Sykes' "hold till it shakes, then back off a wee bit" for the Colt 1911. Subsequent ratios (90/10 to 70/30) underscored support-hand emphasis for recoil, though unquantifiable.

Special Forces' wrist-rolling and thumb-pointing locked tendons, amplifying efficacy. "Aim small, miss small" and augmented support pressure endure as validated tenets.

A solid well-formed grip will mitigate most trigger manipulation issues. A solid well-formed grip that is consistent and predicable will apply the proper tension and friction will mitigate trigger issues at pistol fighting distances!

The bottom line is that a two-handed grip must be as high up on the pistol as possible and still allow the slide to function, the two hands should utilize as much of the gripping surface as possible, grip the pistol as hard as possible.

Be **consistent**. Grab the pistol the same way every time. This will allow the pistol to perform and recoil in a **predictable** manner. The grip should remain **durable** for the number of rounds being fired.

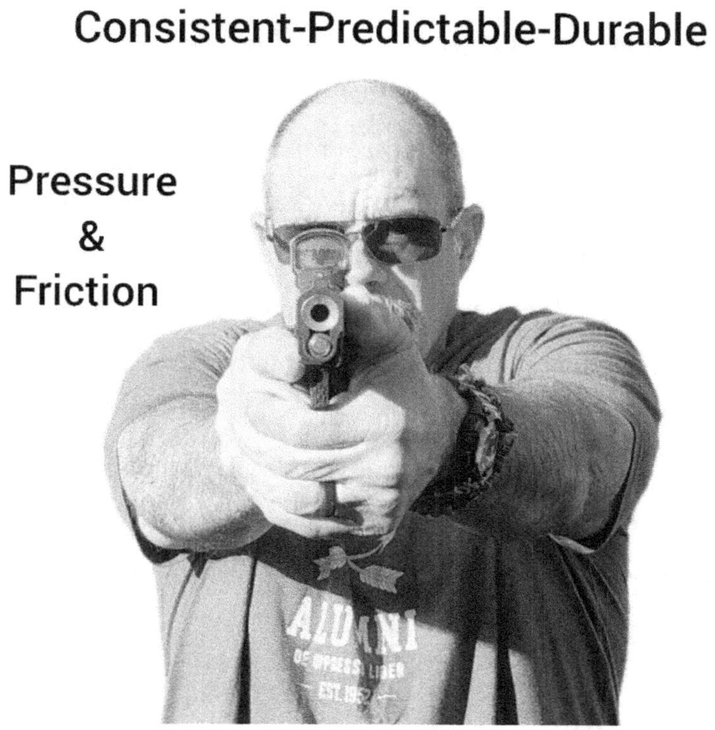

I firmly assert that a solid, well-formed grip stands as the unbreakable foundation for resolving most trigger manipulation issues in pistol shooting, leaving no room for debate on its primacy. Vision always dictates the precise moment to shoot, yet shooters who master a consistent, predictable hold—applying unyielding tension and friction—directly mitigate the majority of trigger problems, especially at pistol fighting distances where hesitation proves fatal. In lethal kinetic encounters under extreme stress, this grip elevates survivability by transforming the pistol into a seamless extension of the body: grip it two-handed as high as possible while allowing flawless slide function, cover every inch of the gripping surface for maximum contact, and squeeze with unrelenting force short of tremor to deliver instinctive, life-saving accuracy.

Trigger Control

The Importance of a Well-Formed Grip in Trigger Control

A well-formed, consistent, predictable, and durable grip serves as the bedrock of effective trigger control, profoundly impacting the performance of individuals who conceal carry a pistol. This foundational element ensures that the firearm remains stable and aligned during the recoil cycle, mitigating common trigger manipulation errors that can compromise accuracy and speed in high-pressure defensive scenarios. For concealed carriers, mastering a reliable grip translates to enhanced confidence, precision, and control, enabling rapid and accurate shot delivery when seconds matter most. Instructors must possess a comprehensive understanding of grip dynamics and their interplay with trigger control, as this knowledge allows them to teach students how to establish and maintain a robust grip that minimizes disruptions to sight alignment. By emphasizing this critical skill, instructors empower shooters to execute responsible and effective self-defense, fostering both technical proficiency and psychological resilience in life-threatening encounters.

Trigger control as a foundational skill

In the discipline of marksmanship, particularly within the context of concealed carry and defensive pistol use, trigger control emerges as a foundational skill that bridges the gap between intention and impact. It encompasses the deliberate and precise manipulation of the trigger to discharge the firearm with minimal disruption to sight alignment, ensuring shots are both rapid and accurate. This control is not merely a mechanical action but a synthesis of mental discipline and physical execution, influenced by factors such as target distance, size, and the inherent characteristics of the pistol. Mastering trigger control demands consistent practice, as it must remain reliable under the duress of high-stress encounters, where rhythm and predictability become vital allies in maintaining composure.

Regardless of a shooter's proficiency, the ability to press and release the trigger at a uniform speed fosters rhythm, which serves as a stabilizing force during adrenaline-fueled situations. Trigger control integrates seamlessly with other shooting fundamentals—grip, stance, sight alignment, and breath control—forming a cohesive system that optimizes performance. The physical application of pressure on the trigger varies by individual physiology and firearm design, yet through disciplined training, it converges toward a standardized technique that prioritizes stability and precision.

At its essence, trigger control involves manipulating the trigger to facilitate swift, accurate shooting while preserving sight alignment on the target. The speed and method of manipulation are dictated by the target's distance, dimensions, associated risks, and the shooter's skill level. A key rule of thumb governs this process: vision dictates trigger speed. As the shooter refines the sight picture, they should progressively engage the trigger's "wall" or resistance point. Once the sights achieve the necessary alignment for the given target, the press completes without hesitation. Efficiency demands that trigger manipulation not impede visual processing; rather, the aligned sights signal the culmination of the press.

Trigger control comprises two interdependent components: mental control and physical manipulation. Mentally, it requires managing emotions and arousal levels to sustain focus—cultivating a state of "calm aggression" where determination and confidence prevail without escalating into panic. This arousal threshold for precise shooting is notably lower than that required for physical altercations, emphasizing the need for emotional regulation. Physically, proficient trigger handling ensures control even at elevated firing rates, preventing deviations that could compromise accuracy.

Types of Triggers

Firearms triggers vary in design, each demanding tailored manipulation techniques.

Double Action: When initiating double-action trigger control, the shooter should momentarily pause upon settling into the aiming area, minimizing the arc of movement. In double-action mode, trigger pull weights typically range from 9.5 to 16.5 pounds. The shooter acquires a sight picture and applies smooth, consistent rearward pressure until the shot breaks, avoiding abrupt jerks that could disturb alignment.

Single Action: For single-action triggers, slack removal begins as the weapon rises toward the target, with initial pressure applied early. Pull weights generally fall between 4.0 and 6.5 pounds. Upon entering the aiming area, the shooter secures the sight picture and executes a steady, uninterrupted increase in pressure to the rear. Post-shot, the trigger is released without disengaging the finger, slack is taken up anew, and focus remains fixed on the front sight throughout the sequence.

Trigger Finger Placement and Isolation

Effective trigger manipulation hinges on a stable grip and balanced stance, which unify the hands and pistol into a single recoiling unit. Proper balance positions the center of gravity slightly forward, allowing the body to absorb recoil naturally without unnecessary tension.

Trigger finger placement is paramount for isolating its movement and preventing sight disturbance. The finger must press the trigger straight rearward, maintaining constant grip tension once established—only the trigger finger articulates. Under stress, trigger control often deteriorates first, underscoring the challenge of mastering it during timed drills or real-world scenarios.

No universal finger placement exists; it must feel natural and enable a fluid pull, accommodating variations in hand size and pistol ergonomics. Typically, the pad centers between the fingertip and first knuckle. Excessive finger insertion pulls impacts toward the strong hand, while insufficient contact pushes them away. The goal: a straight-back press at consistent speed, undisturbed sights.

Trigger Manipulation Concepts

Isolation of the trigger finger remains the cornerstone of manipulation, blending mental fortitude with physical precision. Challenges arise from anticipating recoil and noise, which provoke flinching, and from sympathetic finger movements at higher speeds. Dry fire practice—conducting drills with an unloaded firearm, airsoft replica, or training tool—proves invaluable for honing these skills without ammunition expenditure. It reveals subtleties obscured during live fire, particularly in aligning sights with trigger presses.

Two primary dry fire variants exist, with "dead trigger press" offering superior feedback by simulating post-discharge conditions (detailed further in discussions linking grip to trigger). This method exposes hand inputs affecting the pistol, enabling inductive learning: slap the trigger aggressively in dry fire, observe sight deviations, and apply corrections.

Follow-Through and Recovery

Follow-through entails sustaining focus on sight alignment beyond the shot's discharge, encompassing the ignition, bullet launch, recoil cycle, and slide return. This surprise break mitigates anticipatory reflexes, allowing the shooter to "call" their shot pre-impact. Instructors emphasize follow-through's role in enabling rapid, multiple accurate shots.

Recovery swiftly restores the pistol to its original aiming position and natural point of aim, absorbing recoil directly rearward. Fundamentals resume immediately for subsequent shots, prioritizing speed without sacrificing precision.

Achieving Accurate Hits at Speed

Training begins with perfecting sight pictures in basic presentations, evolving to rapid alignments during speed drills. With practice, shooters discern essential visual cues for fight-stopping hits, accountable for every round. The objective: deliver multiple rounds into vital zones swiftly to neutralize threats.

Instructor Note: A consistent, solid grip mitigates most trigger issues at close-range engagements, providing tension and friction to counteract deviations.

Types of Trigger Manipulation

Prep and Press: Remove pre-travel (slack) initially, then complete the press upon sight confirmation. Ideal for reactive shooting at moderate distances or obscured targets, it aligns with "Confirmation Three" (clear sight/dot return post-recoil). Prep occurs during sight refinement, culminating in a press on alignment.

Rolling Trigger Press: Execute a continuous, smooth rearward motion, akin to revolver firing, resetting promptly for repetition. Suited for mid-to-close ranges and some obscured targets with "Confirmation Two" (color/shape verification). A firm grip minimizes pistol movement.

Slapping: Despite controversy, this technique accelerates firing on close, low-risk targets by pulling through the entire trigger without staging. Proper grip eliminates recoil anticipation inputs, achieving speed and acceptable accuracy in fast, violent encounters.

Low impacts often stem from pre-ignition pushes, not slapping itself. Employed in "Confirmation One" scenarios (spatial orientation recognition), it supports predictive shooting sans per-shot sight confirmation.

For all methods, monitor pistol feel, isolate the trigger finger, and avoid firing-hand curling from excess tension. Observe sight lift and return in recoil for grip and press adjustments.

Trigger Control at Speed

Ensure straight-rearward presses, with hand tension influencing finger efficiency. Heightened tension risks sympathetic movements, often causing low-opposite impacts. Anticipation—pushing downward against expected recoil—exacerbates errors. Isolate the finger to counteract.

Concepts reiterate: manage recoil/noise anticipation and multi-finger sympathy via "dead trigger" dry fire, simulating live inputs for corrective feedback.

Trigger Freeze

This phenomenon halts trigger reset for follow-ups, typically from excessive firing-hand tension. Training emphasizes relaxation and isolation to prevent it.

A robust, unwavering grip empowers concealed carriers to execute precise, rapid shots, anchoring their defense against threats with steadfast control. Shooters actively refine a consistent, predictable grip to stabilize the firearm, neutralizing trigger manipulation errors and preserving sight alignment under duress. This disciplined foundation, paired with rhythmic trigger presses, drives effective responses across diverse target scenarios. Instructors, armed with deep expertise, instill this critical skill, guiding students to master grip mechanics and mental fortitude. Such mastery proves vital, enabling shooters to neutralize dangers decisively while underscoring the instructor's role in forging resilient, proficient defenders.

FYI. A structured instructor-level comparison and contrast of

Trigger Reset vs. Trigger Pinning

Including the **pros, cons, and instructional considerations** for teaching both.

Definitions:

Trigger Pinning

The shooter holds the trigger fully to the rear during and after the shot, then only releases it forward until the reset is felt/clicks before taking the next shot. This isolates reset but **prevents full trigger travel during recoil**.

Trigger Reset (Dynamic Reset or Floating Reset)

The shooter allows the trigger to travel forward naturally during recoil recovery, resetting the trigger as part of the recoil-to-realignment process. The shooter does **not consciously pin or "ride" the reset** but stays in contact with the trigger surface.

Comparison Chart: Instructor-Level

Aspect	Trigger Pinning	Trigger Reset (Floating Reset)
Trigger Control	Emphasizes feel and awareness of mechanical reset	Emphasizes continuous movement and flow
Speed	Slower due to extra time holding/resetting	Faster; more efficient under pressure
Mechanical Familiarization	Teaches students where reset is	Builds intuitive, kinesthetic awareness
Recoil Management	Can hinder natural recoil recovery	Allows full recoil management cycle
Training Benefit	Good for initial trigger education	Ideal for advanced performance under stress
Risk in Real-World Use	Can train a "pause" into shooting cadence	Promotes continuous shooting flow
Diagnostic Use	Useful for diagnosing anticipation or flinch	Better for performance shooting refinement
Under Stress (SNS Activation)	Fine motor skill reliance may fail	Better suited to stress performance dynamics
Common Errors	Reset riding, jerking from reset, excessive pause	Slapping trigger if reset isn't trained

Trigger Pinning

Pros:

- Helps new shooters understand where the reset is.
- Slows the process down for diagnostic purposes.
- Aids in isolating trigger-related issues (flinch, anticipation).

Cons:

- Teaches unnatural cadence and rhythm.
- Can result in "stalling" the trigger during recoil.
- Creates training scars—slower follow-up shots under stress.
- Fails under stress due to reliance on fine motor skills.

Trigger Reset (Dynamic Reset)

Pros:

- More efficient and natural.
- Allows reset to occur during recoil—faster cadence.
- Matches how the brain and body perform under stress (OODA loop efficiency).
- Better long-term performance and durability under pressure.

Cons:

- Requires more skill to teach correctly.
- New shooters may revert to slapping or losing contact with the trigger.
- Lacks the clear tactile feedback that helps some students early on.

Instructional Framework: Layered Teaching Progression

Student Level	Recommended Focus	Key Points to Teach
Beginner	Introduce **trigger pinning** to isolate reset	Teach feel of wall, break, and reset; avoid fast shooting
Intermediate	Transition to **dynamic reset**	Combine recoil recovery with trigger prep/reset; introduce cadence
Advanced	Refine **dynamic reset under time/stress**	Train for efficiency, speed, and consistency under pressure
Instructor	Use both as diagnostic/teaching tools	Understand biomechanical response and stress inoculation principles

Summary Analogy

Think of **trigger pinning** like **training wheels**—they help early on, but keeping them too long inhibits real performance.
Trigger reset (floating reset) is like learning to ride naturally—fast, efficient, and stress-resilient.

Sight Picture + Trigger Control: A Symbiotic Pair

The **symbiotic relationship between vision (sight picture) and trigger control** lies at the heart of precision and speed in pistol shooting. These two elements—**what the shooter sees** and **how the shooter reacts to what they see**—must work in harmony for every shot to land as intended. One guides decision-making; the other executes it.

Remember that to be truly effective at Lethal kinetic engagement speed the entire Trinity of pistol marksmanship must be incorporated.

Definition of the Relationship

Sight picture and trigger control are **mutually dependent**.

- **Vision (sight picture)** provides **feedback** that guides when and how to press the trigger.
- **Trigger control** acts on that feedback — either **respecting** it with discipline or **violating** it with haste, anticipation, or hesitation.

When both systems function in sync, the shooter achieves **accuracy at speed** when the grip is providing a solid platform to operate from. When either breaks down, the shot suffers — regardless of how perfect the other is. Without the addition of speed or rapid timed events (such as untimed Bullseye Shooting) Vision and Trigger control will provide adequate results without the need for a 360 degree viselike grip.

What is Sight Picture?

- A visual input that includes **alignment of the sights** (irons or dot) and **the target**.
- Varies based on **required precision**, i.e., the **Confirmation Level** (1–3).
    - **Confirmation 1**: Minimal visual input; dot orientation or flash of color.
    - **Confirmation 2**: General sight alignment; dot in window or front sight in notch.
    - **Confirmation 3**: Refined, precise sight picture; dot or sights stabilized in the desired aiming area.

What is Trigger Control?

- The ability to press the trigger **without disrupting the sight picture**.
- Involves **isolation of the trigger finger**, a **smooth rearward press**, and **timing** that matches what the shooter sees.

How They Work Together – In Detail

Vision Provides	Trigger Control Does
Visual **clarity or confirmation** of the target and sight alignment	Presses or preps the trigger **with appropriate urgency or patience**
Information about **movement in recoil** (e.g., dot rise/fall)	Adjusts cadence and pressure to **match the dot's return**
Real-time feedback on **stability vs motion**	Delays or finishes the press based on **visual timing**
Confirmation of **sight picture quality**	Determines whether to use **slap, roll, or prep-and-press**

When They Are in Sync (Proper Symbiosis)

- The shooter **preps the trigger** as the dot or front sight is returning to the aiming point. This must be a sub second task.
- The press **finishes smoothly** at the moment the sights stabilize (Confirmation 3).
- In faster shooting, the shooter can **roll or slap the trigger** predictively *because they recognize* the dot's position and trajectory in motion (Confirmation 1 or 2).
- **No visual override** — the shooter doesn't rush the shot when the sight isn't confirmed, nor do they hesitate when it is.

When They Are Out of Sync (Disrupted Symbiosis)

Vision Breakdown	Trigger Consequence
Sights not stabilized, but shooter presses anyway	**Anticipation or jerking** — shots thrown low, wide, or off-target
Shooter sees a perfect sight picture and panics to fire	**Flinch, snatch, or slap** — shot is disrupted by emotional urgency
Shooter waits too long watching the dot/sight	**Trigger freeze** or missed opportunity
Poor grip or recoil control obscures dot/sight movement	**Mistimed trigger press** — press occurs at the wrong moment in the sight cycle

Instructor Cue and Diagnostic Tools

"If the **dot jumps** before the shot — the trigger beat the sight.
If the **dot is stable and it still missed** — the trigger moved it."

Tools:

- **Slow dry fire with visual focus:** Watch the sight package through the entire press.
- **Dead trigger reps:** See what the gun does without the distraction of a click or recoil.
- **Target confirmation drills:** Practice confirmation 1–2–3 with matching trigger techniques.

Why This Matters in Real Shooting

- In **defensive shooting**, you'll often need to press the trigger **before perfect visual confirmation** — requiring extreme trust between what you're seeing and how you're pressing.
- In **competition**, this relationship is the key to shooting **fast with control** — balancing speed and precision.
- In **teaching**, building this link helps new shooters understand **when to press** and **when to wait** — avoiding rushed, flinched, or frozen shots.

Train the Relationship – Practical Drills

1. **Prep on Movement, Press on Stability (Dry or Live)**
   - Begin prepping as the sight picture is returning.
   - Press only when it's acceptable based on confirmation level.
2. **Sight Picture Cue Drill**
   - Instructor calls "press!" only when the shooter visually confirms proper alignment.
   - Teaches shooter to recognize and trust their own visual threshold.
3. **Cadence Ladder Drill (Live Fire)**
   - Increase tempo shot-by-shot while maintaining control of dot/sight behavior.
   - Teaches how to **adjust trigger timing based on sight speed**.

The eye is the navigator; the finger is the executioner.
Without good trigger control, sight picture is meaningless. Without good visual information, trigger control is blind. Together, they form the **bridge between perception and performance** — between what the shooter **sees** and what the shot **does**.

Instructor Note: Understand that **VISION** will always tell shooter when they can shoot, but remember the Trinity of Pistol Marksmanship and that the proper **STRUCTURE** must be in place to provide the required platform for proper trigger manipulation.

Refer to the following chapters of Grip and Trigger Control to enhance the understanding of the total integration at speed. When teaching novice or journeyman shooters at relatively close ranges sights and trigger manipulation alone may provide the desired results, also when teaching Confirmation Three(3) without the burden of time, sights and trigger alone may allow the shooter to gain a better understanding of a slow and methodical trigger press.

As an experienced firearms instructor, and one who does view shooting as a martial art, I can attest that there are not really many advanced skills, sometimes we just find new ways to present ideas. Calling your shot is one of those things that is an advanced skill and once learned the learning curve of the shooter will take off!

Calling Your Shot – Layered Breakdown

Definition: Calling your shot is the ability to know where your bullet impacted based solely on your observation of the sights and weapon movement at the precise moment the trigger breaks—without relying on looking at the target.

Beginner Level

Focus: Awareness & Observation

- **Concept:** At this stage, shooters are learning that the *sights tell the truth.* If the sights were aligned on the target when the shot broke, that's where the bullet went.
- **Drills:**

- **Slow Fire Bullseye:** Fire one round at a time on a large, clean target. Before lowering the pistol, the shooter verbally "calls" the impact (e.g., "9 o'clock in the 8-ring").
- **Dry Fire Sight Hold:** Observe sight stability through the trigger press. Note if the sights dip, lift, or twitch.

- **Objective:** Build a habit of watching the sights through the shot, instead of blinking, flinching, or focusing on the target.

Intermediate Level

Focus: Consistency & Accountability

- **Concept:** Shooters now learn that every shot must be paired with an immediate self-assessment. Targets confirm their accuracy—but only after the shooter has already called it.
- **Drills:**
  - **Ball & Dummy Drill:** Load dummy rounds randomly. When a dummy chambers, shooter must "call the shot." If the gun moves dramatically, it reveals anticipation.
  - **Dot Targets:** Use 2–3 inch dots at 7–10 yards. Shooter fires 5-shot strings, calling each impact before checking.
- **Objective:** Develop the ability to trust the sights and refine grip/trigger control to reduce unwanted sight movement.

Advanced Level

Focus: Predictive Tracking & Real-Time Correction

- **Concept:** The shooter isn't just calling past impacts but also predicting *shot placement in real time* and adjusting instantly for follow-up shots. This is where "calling" evolves into "tracking."
- **Drills:**
    - **Multiple Round Strings:** Fire 3–5 rounds rapidly. Call where each broke. Learn to *see* sight lift and recoil pattern to know where rounds landed.
    - **25-Yard Bulls (B8 Drill):** 10 rounds in 10 seconds. Shooter calls the group placement before scoring.
- **Objective:** Build confidence in shot placement at speed and distance, with minimal reliance on the target for feedback.

Instructor / Mastery Level

Focus: Teaching, Diagnosing, and Coaching Others

- **Concept:** Instructors must not only call their own shots but also read their students' sights, muzzle movement, and body mechanics to identify what caused a miss—even before looking at the target.
- **Instructor Cues:**
    - Watch for sight dip → anticipation/flinch.
    - Watch for high-left/right movement (for right-handed shooters) → grip pressure imbalance.
    - Ask students to call their shot before looking at target—hold them accountable.
- **Advanced Integration:**
    - With RDS pistols, use dot *lift pattern* for tracking shots.
    - With irons, demand front sight awareness at all times.
- **Objective:** Create shooters who are independent learners, able to self-diagnose and self-correct without external feedback.

Key Takeaway

I have come to the conclusion after a great deal of range time that calling your shot is not just about accuracy—it is about **honest accountability**. It transforms shooting from *guesswork* into a *closed feedback loop*, where every round fired produces learning. Mastery of this skill is a clear separator between a marksman who merely shoots and one who truly understands the process.

Shooter Progression in Calling Your Shot

Stage 1: Novice – Awareness

- **Shooter's Mindset:** "I don't know where my rounds go until I look."
- **Behaviors:**
  - Eyes blink or flinch at shot break.
  - Attention shifts from sights to target after the shot.
  - Round placement is a surprise.
- **Training Goals:**
  - Learn to keep visual focus on sights through the break.
  - Build awareness of sight movement during trigger press.
- **Drills:**
  - Slow fire at 5–7 yards.
  - After each shot, shooter must *verbally call* impact before lowering pistol.

Stage 2: Developing – Recognition

- **Shooter's Mindset:** "Sometimes I know where it hit, but not always."
- **Behaviors:**
  - Can sometimes predict misses.
  - Beginning to identify when sights dip, lift, or twitch.
  - Still relies on target feedback for confirmation.

- **Training Goals:**
  - Strengthen accountability—no shot without a call.
  - Introduce ball & dummy drills to expose anticipation.
- **Drills:**
  - Dot drills at 7–10 yards.
  - Ball & dummy with verbal shot calls.

Stage 3: Proficient – Consistency

- **Shooter's Mindset:** "I know where my shots land before I check the target."
- **Behaviors:**
  - Accurately calls most hits and misses.
  - Understands correlation between sight lift and round placement.
  - Rarely "surprised" by impacts.
- **Training Goals:**
  - Build consistency across speed and distance.
  - Transition from single-shot calling to strings of fire.
- **Drills:**
  - 5-shot strings, calling each round.
  - 25-yard bullseye calls with written annotations.

Stage 4: Advanced – Tracking

- **Shooter's Mindset:** "I see every shot break and know where the group is forming."
- **Behaviors:**
  - Calls impacts *and* tracks the recoil pattern.
  - Adjusts grip/trigger mechanics in real time.
  - Develops group predictions (calling clusters instead of single holes).

- **Training Goals:**
  - Call and track impacts during rapid fire.
  - Build predictive adjustments for follow-ups.
- **Drills:**
  - Bill Drill (6 rounds, 7 yards) → call each hit.
  - 10 in 10 at 25 yards on B8 → call group before scoring.

Stage 5: Mastery – Instructor Level

- **Shooter's Mindset:** "I don't just call my shots—I can diagnose yours."
- **Behaviors:**
  - Reads sight picture and recoil in others.
  - Calls misses before student looks at target.
  - Uses student shot calls to identify deficiencies in grip, trigger, or visual focus.
- **Training Goals:**
  - Build ability to coach others using shot-calling principles.
  - Teach accountability culture—every student must call their shot.
- **Drills:**
  - Instructor calls student's shots by watching their gun movement.
  - Force-on-timer drills (fast strings under pressure) → instructor confirms or corrects student calls.

Progression Summary

- **Novice → Awareness**: "I don't know until I look."
- **Developing → Recognition**: "Sometimes I know."
- **Proficient → Consistency**: "I know where every shot went."
- **Advanced → Tracking**: "I see where groups are forming and can adjust on the fly."

- **Mastery → Diagnostic**: "I can read and call my own shots and my students' shots."

You've tied **shot calling** directly to the **diagnostic process**, which is the *real reason* it's such a powerful skill. Let me expand this into a **professional-level breakdown** you can use with students or in instructor modules.

Calling Your Shot: Diagnostic Progression

When done correctly, calling your shot is not just about knowing where the bullet hit—it's about knowing when something went wrong, understanding how and why it went wrong, and applying the correction immediately.

This makes every shot **a feedback loop**, not just a data point.

1. Knowing *When* Something Went Wrong

- **Observation:** The shooter sees the sights deviate *at the moment of the break.*
- **Indicators:**
    - Sight dips low-left → anticipation or heeling.
    - Sight streaks high-right → too much finger pressure.
    - Sight blur from blink → visual interruption.
- **Shooter's Role:** Acknowledge the issue instantly instead of waiting for the target to reveal it.

2. Learning *How* It Went Wrong

- **Analysis of Mechanics:** Identify the physical action that caused the error.
    - Example: "My support hand lost tension."
    - Example: "I slapped the trigger instead of pressing."

- **Sight/Grip Feedback:** The sights don't lie—they reveal the mechanical breakdown.

3. Understanding *Why* It Went Wrong

- **Root Cause:** Move beyond mechanics into the underlying driver.
  - Anticipation = fear of recoil / desire for control.
  - Poor grip = fatigue or improper setup.
  - Blink = visual startle response.
- **Shooter's Role:** Develop self-awareness: is it stress, speed, distance, or mindset causing the breakdown?

4. Applying the Fix

- **Correction Strategy:**
  - Adjust grip, trigger finger placement, or visual focus.
  - Slow down for accountability, then rebuild speed.
  - Reinforce proper reps through dry fire or ball & dummy until correction holds under live fire.
- **Real-Time Integration:** A proficient shooter doesn't wait until after the drill—they correct on the *next shot*.

Practical Example

Shooter breaks a shot at 25 yards, sees the front sight dip low-left.

1. **When:** "I saw it dip as the trigger broke."
2. **How:** "I pushed the gun forward and down in anticipation."
3. **Why:** "I was worried about controlling recoil on a long shot."
4. **Fix:** "I'll refocus on pressing the trigger straight to the rear, letting recoil happen naturally."

The next shot confirms the correction.

Instructor-Level Application

- Hold students accountable to **call, diagnose, explain, and fix** before ever looking at the target.
- Ask:
  - "Where was the sight when it broke?"
  - "What did you do to cause that?"
  - "Why do you think you did that?"
  - "What's your plan for the next shot?"
- This transforms calling the shot from a passive observation into an **active problem-solving cycle.**

Key Takeaway

Calling your shot is not just about prediction—it is about **self-diagnosis and correction**.

- **When** = Recognizing the error in real time.
- **How** = Identifying the mechanical failure.
- **Why** = Understanding the underlying cause.
- **Fix** = Applying the correction immediately.

This loop is the hallmark of a shooter moving from **basic accuracy** to **self-sustaining proficiency**.

Sight Package: Essential Visual Confirmations and Timing in Pistol Shooting

In the pursuit of enhanced pistol shooting proficiency, mastering the sight package—the visual alignment between the shooter, sights, and target—is paramount. This chapter, drawn from foundational principles in tactical firearms training, elucidates what shooters must see and when, emphasizing a progressive refinement of the sight picture across successive shots. Shooters should continually strive to elevate their sight picture, transitioning fluidly to more precise alignments as follow-up shots demand.

Note: The intricacies of Confirmations 1, 2, and 3, along with associated trigger manipulations, will be elaborated further in subsequent discussions on targets, engagements, and the overall shooting process.

Core Visual Confirmations and Trigger Integration

The sight package evolves dynamically based on target distance, size, and risk factors. Three levels of visual confirmation guide this progression, each paired with tailored trigger manipulation to optimize speed, accuracy, and control.

1. **Spatial Orientation (Confirmation 1)**: This involves the holistic alignment of the pistol—ensuring it is oriented toward the target zone—coupled with rapid trigger "slapping" for high-speed engagements.
    - **Confirmation One**: The pistol slide is presented parallel to the ground, with the front sights or red dot optic housing grossly overlaying the target. This suffices for quick acquisitions on large, proximate targets.
    - **Slapping the Trigger**: Execute a swift rearward motion without preparatory staging, prioritizing velocity over finesse.
2. **Color Confirmation (Confirmation 2)**: Visual verification of the sights' or dot's color presence within the target zone, synchronized with trigger prepping to at least the first wall of resistance.
    - **Confirmation Two**: Present the sight package with minimal oscillation. Iron sights achieve loose alignment over medium-range targets; the red dot

remains within an acceptable target boundary. This enables rapid yet accurate engagements.

  - **Prepping the Trigger**: Gradually compress the trigger through resistance stages, completing the press upon acceptable sight verification.

3. **Clean Sight Package (Confirmation 3)**: A stabilized, motionless sight alignment within the target zone, aligned with deep trigger preparation for precision shots.
   - **Confirmation Three**: Attain an unwavering sight picture for high-risk or distant targets, demanding exceptional stability.
   - **Deep Prep of the Trigger**: Initiate trigger movement during presentation, achieving full extension with a stable sight package. As stability is confirmed, continue seamless rearward pressure until discharge.

Shooters must recognize that sight refinement precedes the initial shot, with trigger depth increasing accordingly. Once initiated, rearward trigger motion should remain uninterrupted. The sights' relationship to the target dictates engagement tempo and feasibility.

Instructor-Level Insights: Nuanced Breakdowns

At the instructional level, a profound grasp of these confirmations is essential for effective coaching. Below are detailed analyses, emphasizing anatomical, neuromechanical, and practical elements to equip instructors in conveying these concepts.

Confirmation 1: Spatial Orientation and Trigger Manipulation in Engagements

Overview: Confirmation 1 facilitates high-confidence, close-range shots on large targets, leveraging gross references for maximal speed while maintaining combat-effective accuracy.

Spatial Orientation Defined: This entails intuitive alignment of the pistol's entirety—slide, muzzle, and bore axis—with the impact zone, bypassing precise sight verification. Reliance falls on:

- Kinesthetic proprioception (hand-eye coordination).
- Consistent grip and draw mechanics for predictable presentation.
- Peripheral indexing via blurred sights or red dot.
- Drilled repetitions to engrain spatial positioning.

Neuromechanics:

- **Eyes**: Locked on the target, not sights.
- **Arms and Wrists**: Form a rigid scaffold for alignment amid recoil.
- **Visual Field**: Perceives the pistol as a softened overlay on the target.
- **Muscle Memory**: Cultivated through repetitive draws and dry-fire.

For red dot users, this manifests as a streaking or blurred dot traversing the zone; for iron sights, a fleeting front post glimpse sans rear notch perfection.

Gun Alignment:

- Direct the pistol predictively toward high-value areas (e.g., center mass or cranial box).
- Manage recoil tracking via grip and visual cues.
- Prioritize velocity, accepting hits within broad parameters.

Trigger Manipulation: Aggressive Press or "Slapping":

- Execute a forceful jab, ideal for proximity.
- Omit conscious prep or reset; fully release and re-engage rapidly.

- Exploit recoil for natural reset.

Neurological Aspects:

- Minimize cognitive latency: React subcortically to threats.
- Train an automated loop: Threat detection prompts immediate action.

Mechanics:

- Engage trigger mid-pad.
- Complete full stroke swiftly, with complete finger release between shots.
- Demand unyielding grip to mitigate instability.

Far from an error, "slapping" is a calculated method for speed-accuracy equilibrium in Confirmation 1.

Integration Table:

Component	Execution in Confirmation 1
Visual Focus	Target-centric
Gun Orientation	Kinesthetic with gross index
Trigger Behavior	Rapid, assertive slap
Recoil Control	Grip-managed; no pauses
Decision Process	Predictive pre-verification

Training Drills:

1. **One-Shot Draw (3–5 Yards)**: Target-focus alignment with immediate break.
2. **Bill Drill (6 Shots at 7 Yards)**: Sustain awareness sans dot-chasing; analyze splits and groups.

3. **Trigger Isolation (Dry-Fire)**: Rapid presentation and slap while preserving orientation.
4. **Modified Dot Torture**: Larger circles (3–4 inches) at speed with minimal references.

Instructor Tips:

- Vigilantly identify flinching disguised as slapping.
- Verify grip during rapid sequences—recoil reveals flaws.
- Employ high-speed video and timers for diagnostic feedback.

Confirmation Two: Color Confirmation and Trigger Prep

Overview: Bridging raw speed and precision, Confirmation 2 demands visual cues within moderate constraints (e.g., 5–10 yards or partial exposures).

Color Confirmation Explained: A perceptual signal (hue, form, or pattern) affirming sights' placement in the hit zone, tolerating imperfect alignment.

Red Dot Sights:

- Target-focused; dot visible and contained within zone.
- Accept bounded oscillation; cue press via color and position.

Acceptable: Dot arcs within anatomy; streaking over hits.
Unacceptable: Dot absent, paused, or chased.

Iron Sights:

- Primarily target-focused, with brief sight shifts.
- Loose front-rear alignment; front post color overlays center.

Acceptable: Visible, centered post with minor notch variance.

Unacceptable: Obscured sights or off-target persistence.

Trigger Manipulation:

1. Initiate contact during presentation.
2. Prep through slack to first wall amid alignment.
3. Finalize break on confirmation.
4. Reset in recoil for continuity.

Neuromechanical Integration Table:

Process	Visual	Tactile
Target Index	Identified	Grip stabilizes
Presentation	Color enters field	Finger initiates
Confirmation	Enters zone	Reaches wall
Fire	Confirmation signals	Press completes

Training Drills:

1. **Press Prep (Dry-Fire)**: Mount to target; prep to wall, press on cue.
2. **Half-Split Transitions**: Shift from Confirmation 1 to 2 pacing.
3. **3-2-1 Drill**: Descending rounds on shrinking zones to build integration.

Summary Comparison:

Component	Confirmation 1	Confirmation 2
Target	Large, proximate	Medium, moderate
Visual Focus	Fully target	Target with overlay
Iron Sights	Glimpse/flash	Front color visible
Red Dot	Blur/streak	Dot in zone
Trigger	Slap	Prep to wall, cue-break
Time	Maximal speed	Controlled rapidity
Accuracy	Broad A-zone	Refined A-zone

Confirmation Three: Clean Sight Package and Deep Trigger Prep

Overview: Reserved for precision demands (e.g., 10+ yards, minute zones, or high-stakes), subordinating speed to certainty.

Clean Sight Package:

- Stable, immobile alignment pinpointing impact.
- No deviation; clear superposition on target.

Red Dot:

- Stationary dot in narrow zone; flawless eye-dot-target line.

Iron Sights:

- Exact front-rear: Equal height/light; sight-focused.

Visual Summary Table:

System	Visual Focus	Alignment	Movement Tolerance
Red Dot	Target with precise dot	Centered in zone	None
Irons	Front sight	Equal height/light	None

Deep Trigger Prep:

- Early initiation; eliminate slack progressively.
- "Live in the wall": Sustained pressure through aiming.
- Break solely on stability.

Timing:

1. Contact on presentation.
2. Wall attainment at acquisition.
3. Commit on stasis.
4. Clean break.

Sensory Synchronization Table:

Input	Action
Visual: Stop	Final press
Tactile: Tension	Smooth continuation
Auditory: None	Subtle surprise break

Characteristics:

- Seamless prep-break continuum.
- Linear, hitch-free pressure.
- No residual slack on-target.

Training Drills:

1. **B8 Bullseye (25 Yards)**: Deliberate prep; score precision.
2. **3-Inch Dot (10–15 Yards)**: Break on stillness; emphasize patience.
3. **Wall Drill (Dry-Fire)**: Present and press sans movement.

Summary Table:

Element	Description
Target	Small/distant/high-risk
Visual Focus	Precise dot or front sight
Sight Package	Fully stabilized
Trigger	Deep, continuous prep
Time Pressure	Negligible; accuracy first
Movement	None
Mental Cue	Press on stop

Instructor Tips:

- Cultivate patience against premature breaks.
- Enhance irons with colored fronts or outlined rears.
- Insist on isolation: Pure press, no grip interference.

Instructor Talking Points: Explaining Visual Confirmations to Novice Shooters

Introduction: "In pistol shooting, deciding how much to see before firing is key. We use three confirmation levels to match speed and accuracy to the shot's difficulty. Easier shots allow faster action; tougher ones require more control."

Confirmation 1: Speed Over Precision

- **When**: Close (3–5 yards), large targets, low miss risk, urgent needs.
- **Sight**: Gun pointed grossly; sight flash or dot blur. Target-focused.
- **Trigger**: Quick slap on appearance.
- **Why**: Prioritizes velocity for big, easy hits.

Confirmation 2: Balanced Control

- **When**: Mid-range (5–10 yards), partial exposures, moderate risk.
- **Sight**: Dot in zone or loose irons; color/position cue. Target with sight reference.
- **Trigger**: Prep to wall, finish on acceptability.
- **Why**: Merges rapidity with assurance.

Confirmation 3: Precision Over Speed

- **When**: Distant/small/high-risk shots.
- **Sight**: Stable dot or perfect irons. Sight-focused.
- **Trigger**: Deep prep; break on stasis.
- **Why**: Guarantees exact placement.

Student Comparison Table:

Confirmation	Target Type	Distance	Sight Picture	Eye Focus	Trigger Work	Priority
1 (Speed)	Big/close	0–5 yds	Flash/blur	Target	Quick slap	Speed
2 (Balanced)	Medium	5–10 yds	Dot in zone/loose irons	Target w/reference	Prep to wall, cue-press	Speed + Control
3 (Precision)	Small/far	10–25+ yds	Stable dot/irons	Sight	Deep prep, clean break	Accuracy

Reinforcement Strategies:

1. **Analogies**: "Confirmation 1 is punching a balloon; 3 is threading a needle."
2. **Experiential**: Vary distances in drills; query perceptual shifts.
3. **Drill Matching**: Align exercises to confirmations for progressive mastery.

Red Dot Sighting Packages: A Modern Sight Picture for Defensive Shooting

1. What Is a Red Dot Sighting Package?

A Red Dot Sight (RDS) package represents a comprehensive aiming system that empowers the shooter to:

- Maintain focus on the target rather than the sights.
- Minimize visual demands by reducing the number of focal planes required for alignment.

- Accelerate the processing of visual information, facilitating quicker and more precise threat engagement.

Unlike traditional iron sights, which necessitate aligning the front sight, rear sight, and target across multiple focal points, an RDS allows the shooter to peer through the optic, superimpose the dot on the target, and fire—all while maintaining a singular focal point: the target itself.

2. Why Sighting Packages Matter

The sighting package transcends mere optics or iron sights; it embodies a conceptual framework dictating the level of visual precision required for an effective and ethical shot. Shooters employ as much of the package as necessary, calibrated to factors such as distance, target size, and immediacy.

Whether utilizing:

- Iron sights (front and rear),
- Front iron sight alone,
- A red dot optic, or
- A laser aiming device,

The objective remains consistent: to secure an appropriate sight picture tailored to the threat and range, executed swiftly and accurately.

3. Red Dot Optics: Changing the Game

Single Focal Plane

Iron sights demand attention across five distinct focal planes: the rear sight, front sight, target, and the light gaps on either side. In contrast, a red dot optic condenses this to one plane—the target.

- This streamlining expedites visual processing.
- It harmonizes with innate human responses, where eyes instinctively fixate on threats.

No Need to Shift Focus

With iron sights, the shooter must:

- Prioritize the front sight,
- Align it within the rear notch,
- Overlay this alignment onto the target.

A red dot optic enables the shooter to:

- Remain target-focused, with the dot appearing superimposed.
- Preserve situational awareness, essential in defensive scenarios.

Accuracy Enhancement

Contrary to common misconceptions, red dots bolster accuracy—particularly at intermediate and extended ranges—thanks to their precise reticle and unlimited eye relief.

- Alignment errors with iron sights are prevalent and challenging to self-correct.
- Red dots eradicate such errors, provided the optic is properly zeroed and presented.

Choosing the Right Dot: MOA Considerations

The red dot's size, quantified in Minutes of Angle (MOA), dictates the extent of target coverage at 100 yards.

MOA Size	Use Case	Pros	Cons
6 MOA	Self-defense, competition	Easy acquisition, faster shots	Reduced precision at distance
3.5 MOA	General use, balance	Versatile	Slightly slower under stress
2 MOA	Precision shooting, distance	Superior accuracy	Harder to acquire in stress or low light

RDS Training Curriculum

This Red Dot Sight (RDS) training curriculum is segmented into seven structured modules, suitable for defensive pistol instruction and instructor development. Each module progressively builds proficiency, guiding shooters or students toward mastery with RDS-equipped pistols.

Module 1: Introduction to the RDS Sighting Package

Objective: Comprehend the purpose, advantages, and theoretical foundations of Red Dot Sight (RDS) systems.

Key Topics:

- Definition of an RDS sighting package.
- Comparison of RDS to traditional iron sights.
- Benefits: single focal plane, accelerated processing, threat-focused shooting.
- Limitations and common misconceptions.

Instructor Notes:

- Employ visual aids to illustrate focal plane differences between iron sights and RDS.
- Demonstrate sight picture variations using a slide-mounted RDS.

Module 2: Red Dot Optic Selection and Configuration

Objective: Select and comprehend suitable RDS configurations aligned with specific applications.

Key Topics:

- Dot size and MOA considerations (e.g., 2 MOA vs. 6 MOA).
- Window dimensions and optic footprints.
- Zeroing distances (7, 15, 25 yards).
- Tailored selections for everyday carry (EDC), competition, precision shooting, or law enforcement/military use.

Instructor Notes:

- Present various optics (e.g., Holosun, Trijicon, Aimpoint).
- Explore the trade-offs between visibility and precision.

Module 3: Zeroing the RDS

Objective: Achieve proper RDS zeroing and grasp holdovers across distances.

Key Topics:

- Importance of zeroing (distinctions from iron sights).
- Recommended zero distances:
  - EDC: 7–10 yards.
  - Compact pistols: 15 yards.
  - Full-size pistols: 25 yards.
- Ammunition factors (duty vs. training loads).
- Ensuring mechanical stability via bench-resting.
- Targeting: Use B8 bullseye for group confirmation.

Instructor Notes:

- Guide participants through range-based zeroing steps.
- Require multiple groups for verification, avoiding reliance on single shots.

Module 4: Dry Fire: Presentation and Dot Acquisition

Objective: Cultivate presentation techniques to consistently acquire the dot.

Key Topics:

- Addressing "dot hunting" and its root causes.
- Optimal draw stroke and presentation angles.
- Head positioning, eye-target focus, and line of sight.
- Alignment methods: Elevate the gun to the eyes, not vice versa.

Dry Fire Drills:

- Wall drill: Draw and verify centered dot.
- Dot tracking during presentation without corrections.
- Incorporate laser trainers or airsoft for feedback.

Instructor Notes:

- Stress: "Inability to find the dot often mirrors challenges with front sight acquisition."

Module 5: Live Fire: Tracking the Dot and Recoil Control

Objective: Master dot tracking amid recoil while upholding visual consistency.

Key Topics:

- Accepting normal dot movement and managing it.
- Grip essentials: tension, leverage, recoil mitigation.
- Dot return: Ensure it resets to its origin.
- Full recoil cycle observation.

Live Fire Drills:

- Controlled pairs: Emphasize dot return.
- Bill Drill (6 rounds at 7 yards): Monitor dot path and pacing.
- Failure Drill: Observe dot reset between shots.

Instructor Notes:

- Utilize video analysis to depict dot patterns.

- Differentiate between "controlling" and "predicting" the dot.

Module 6: Target-Focused Shooting Under Stress

Objective: Hone target-focused engagement with speed and precision under pressure.

Key Topics:

- Visual discipline: Fixate on exact impact points, not the dot.
- How dot fixation elevates shot placement.
- Sustaining target lock during rapid engagements.
- Visual patience in reactive scenarios.

Live Fire Drills:

- Dot-on-target exercises with varying MOAs.
- Point-of-impact comparisons: Dot vs. target focus.
- Time-compressed drills: Draw and fire from concealment.

Instructor Notes:

- Highlight threat cue processing (e.g., body language, motion).
- Leverage steel or reactive targets for rapid feedback.

Module 7: Situational Application and Problem Solving

Objective: *Fuse RDS skills into realistic defensive contexts.*

Key Topics:

- *Shooting while moving.*

- *Low-light RDS employment (with or without illumination).*
- *Multiple-target engagements.*
- *Firing from cover or unconventional positions.*

Scenario-Based Drills:

- *Shoot/no-shoot decisions.*
- *Movement exercises: Lateral, forward, backward with dot tracking.*
- *Target identification amid occlusion or partial exposure.*

Instructor Notes:

- *Apply timers and scenarios to mimic real-world urgency.*
- *Debrief each exercise, focusing on dot tracking and visual verification.*

Bonus: Instructor & Shooter Development Notes

- **Tracking Progress:** Monitor shot group consistency, first-shot speed, and split times.
- **Common Problems:**
  - "Dot search": Remedy with refined presentation.
  - "Dot jump": Address grip and recoil management.
  - "High impacts": Correct by shifting focus from dot to target.
- **Performance Benchmarks:**
  - 1.5 seconds draw to first shot at 7 yards (A-zone hit).
  - Under 2.0 seconds for Failure Drill with all hits.
  - Less than 3-inch group at 25 yards (RDS zero validation).

Instructor-Level Expansion & Teaching Breakdown: Red Dot Sight (RDS) Sighting Package

Definition (Instructor Framing)

An RDS sighting package constitutes a unified aiming ecosystem integrating hardware (the optic), visual processing (target-centric focus), and cognitive efficiency (diminished focal demands) to yield rapid, precise, and instinctive shooting—particularly in high-stress environments. It redirects visual emphasis from mechanical alignments to threat-oriented engagements.

Comparison: RDS vs. Iron Sights

Aspect	Iron Sights	Red Dot Sight
Focal Planes	3 (rear sight, front sight, target)	1 (target)
Focus Point	Front sight	Target
Sight Picture	Requires sight alignment	Dot superimposed on target
Speed	Slower under stress	Accelerated visual processing
Precision at Distance	Demands greater visual effort	Clear dot simplifies POA/POI
Stress Adaptability	Front sight often overlooked	Target focus aligns with instincts

Key RDS Benefits (Instructor Talking Points)

1. **Target-Focused Shooting**
    - **Relevance:** Stress induces natural fixation on threats.
    - **Iron Sights Contrast:** Requires overriding instincts to prioritize the front sight.

- **RDS Advantage:** Leverages instincts by overlaying the dot on the target.
- **Analogy:** Comparable to a laser pointer on a presentation slide—focus on the content, not the device.

2. **Reduced Visual Workload**
    - **Iron Sights Demand:** Alignment of rear notch, front post, and target, fragmenting attention.
    - **RDS Simplification:** Consolidates to one plane, with the dot appearing parallax-free.
    - **Analogy:** Transitioning from manual to automatic transmission: equivalent control with reduced exertion.
3. **Faster Visual Processing**
    - Enables swifter identification, decision-making, and engagement.
    - Minimizes alignment refinement and hard front-sight focus.
    - Accelerates shooting decisions via rapid visual confirmation.
    - **Instructor Insight:** This enhancement extends beyond speed to superior judgment in dynamic, uncertain encounters.

Visual Behavior Under RDS

Confirmation Level	Visual Description	Trigger Behavior
Confirmation 1	Flash of dot over target (close range)	Predictive trigger press
Confirmation 2	Dot stabilized in target zone	Prep-and-press
Confirmation 3	Stable dot on precise POA	Controlled press

Layered Teaching Progression

Beginner Level

Goal: Master dot acquisition and usage.

- Prioritize eye-target alignment: "Focus on your intended hit."
- Teach: "The dot overlays your gaze."
- Conduct sight picture drills: Dry fire to eliminate "fishing" for the dot.
- Early emphasis: "Present to the dot," not search for it.

Common Issues:

- "Dot chasing" (ocular search for the dot).
- Focusing on the dot over the target.
- Inconsistent presentation leading to absent dot.

Intermediate Level

Goal: Enhance visual efficiency and confirmation mastery.

- Stabilize dot during presentation.
- Introduce confirmation levels.
- Address dot dynamics in motion and transitions.
- Sequence: "See dot → decide → press cleanly."

Drills:

- Bill Drill (confirmation speed).
- Dot Torture (precision).
- Failure to Stop (level transitions).

Advanced Level

Goal: Optimize dot employment in stress, motion, and low light.

- Merge with movement, transitions, and flashlight use.
- Bolster acquisition from atypical angles.
- Timed live fire across confirmation levels.
- Incorporate OODA loop: Observe dot, orient to threat, decide, act.

Instructor Tips for Effective RDS Integration

- Advocate uniform presentation: The dot emerges from solid mechanics.
- Avoid optic overemphasis: "Target primary, dot secondary."
- Use diagnostic targets to link dot behavior with impacts.
- Dry fire fosters discipline: Repetitive presentations for instant dot appearance.
- Discourage "dot hunting": Indicates flawed index, grip, or wrist alignment.

Symbiotic Relationship between Grip and Trigger Control

One cannot function optimally without the other

In pistol shooting, **grip and trigger control** are two of the most critical fundamentals. When executed properly and consistently, they **support and reinforce each other**, leading to faster, more accurate, and repeatable shooting — even under stress, fatigue, or speed.

GRIP – The Structural Foundation of Pistol Shooting

A **consistent, predictable, and durable grip** provides the physical *anchor* for the gun's movement and your visual reference (the sight or dot). It controls recoil, keeps the gun indexed to the eye line, and enables **repetition under pressure**.

Key Grip Elements:

- **Consistent Placement**: Both hands must meet the pistol in exactly the same location and orientation every time.
- **Predictable Pressure**: 360° pressure applied by the support hand and firing hand must be balanced and repeatable.
- **Durable Under Recoil**: The structure must not collapse, shift, or fatigue under recoil, multiple shots, or time.

An effective grip **minimizes muzzle movement** during trigger manipulation — meaning the sights stay aligned with the shooter's intended point of impact *while the trigger is being moved.*

TRIGGER CONTROL – The Precision Input

Trigger control is **the only input that causes the gun to fire**. Even with perfect alignment and stance, if the trigger is pressed incorrectly, the shot will miss.

Essential Aspects of Trigger Control:

- **Isolated Finger Movement**: The trigger finger must move independently of the rest of the firing hand.
- **Straight Rearward Path**: The press must not cause lateral displacement of the gun.

- **Timing with Visual Input**: Trigger press must coincide with the required level of sight confirmation.

The trigger press **has a direct effect on the orientation of the muzzle** at the moment the shot breaks. If done improperly, it undermines even the most solid grip.

How Grip and Trigger Control Reinforce Each Other

Grip Supports Trigger Control	Trigger Control Protects the Grip
A stable grip **anchors the gun**, reducing motion and allowing the trigger finger to **move independently**.	Smooth, straight trigger presses prevent **torque or lateral pressure**, which could **disrupt the grip** or sight alignment.
Proper grip tension allows the shooter to **press the trigger without inducing movement** in the frame.	Clean trigger control minimizes over-travel and sympathetic tension, which **preserves grip structure** and recoil integrity.
A predictable grip **manages recoil**, helping the shooter reset the trigger during recoil and maintain cadence.	Controlled, rhythmic trigger manipulation **avoids grip breakdown**, especially during fast strings.
A durable grip withstands **trigger slapping or aggressive presses** during high-speed engagements.	Trigger control ensures that **rapid shots do not introduce chaos** into the gun-hand interface.

Performance Outcome: When Both Are Working Together

When grip and trigger control are **properly synchronized**:

- The dot or front sight **tracks predictably in recoil**.
- The shooter maintains **sight integrity during the trigger press**.
- The gun **returns to the same place** shot after shot.
- The shooter can transition between **reactive and predictive shooting** without changing grip or technique.

- **Trigger freeze, anticipation, and low-left hits** are dramatically reduced.

When the Relationship Fails

Bad Grip → Poor Trigger Control	Bad Trigger Control → Poor Grip
Inconsistent grip tension causes **gun movement during trigger press**.	Jerking or slapping the trigger distorts the firing hand, which **breaks grip stability**.
Lack of grip structure forces the shooter to **over-control with the trigger finger**, introducing sympathetic movement.	Poor control causes recoil to impact **unevenly**, wearing out grip endurance.
Grip failure forces compensations (e.g., more finger on trigger), leading to **non-isolated movement**.	Abrupt trigger press causes grip to **slip, shift, or open**, especially during rapid fire.

Instructor Tip – Diagnostic Cue:

"If the dot moves **before** the shot, it's your trigger.
If it moves **after** the shot and doesn't return, it's your grip.
If it moves **before, during, and after**, it's both."

REAL-WORLD DIAGNOSTICS & TEACHING CUES

Dot or Front Sight Movement before the Shot:

- Problem: **Trigger control error**
- Cue: "You moved it before it went bang — slow down the press."

Dot Does Not Return to the Same Spot After Recoil:

- Problem: **Grip collapse or asymmetrical tension**
- Cue: "You're losing your grip in recoil — fix your support hand."

Gun Jumps Sideways on Shot Break:

- Problem: **Combined grip and trigger failure**
- Cue: "Relax your firing hand — the finger is fighting the frame."

ANATOMICAL & NEUROMUSCULAR COMPONENTS

Grip:

- Muscular tension comes from **flexors and extensors** in the forearm.
- A strong grip with the **support hand** allows the **firing hand** to relax, preserving finger isolation.

Trigger Finger Isolation:

- The **flexor digitorum profundus** and **superficialis** control the fingers.
- Tension in the palm or pinky/ring fingers of the firing hand creates **sympathetic movement**, causing the **trigger finger to arc or pull sideways**, disrupting alignment.
- Over-gripping or squeezing the entire firing hand during the press causes **"milking"**, collapsing the structure and disrupting the sights.

THE FEEDBACK LOOP IN SHOOTING

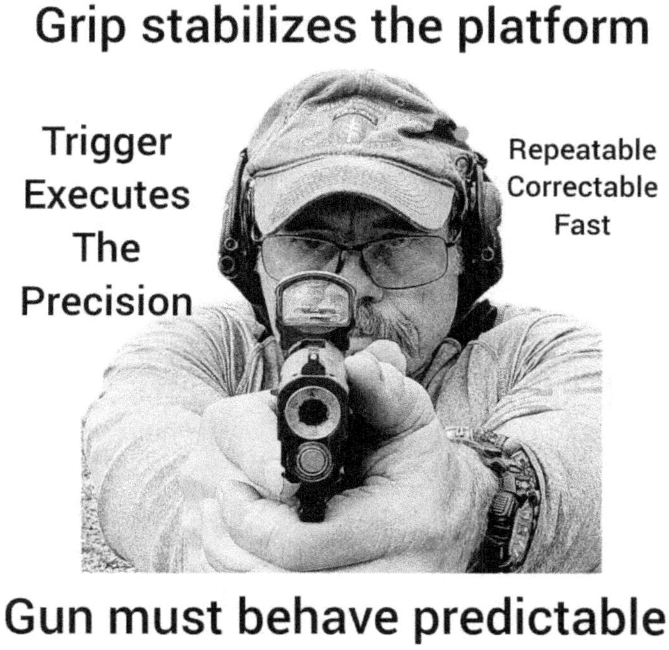

- A good grip **reduces the visual and mechanical penalty** of minor trigger errors.
- Good trigger control **maximizes the benefit** of a stable grip.
- The shooter can then **learn from the visual feedback of the sight package** — seeing exactly what their mechanics produced.
- Over time, this allows for **inductive learning** and **intuitive correction**.

“You won’t see what matters in recoil unless your trigger press and grip let you.”

How to Train the Symbiosis

- **Dry Fire with Live Trigger Press**
  – Watch for dot or sight movement during the press.

    - Watch the dot or front sight for *pre-ignition movement*.
    - Focus on maintaining grip pressure while pressing cleanly.

- **"Dot Bounce" Recoil Observation Drill**
  – Watch how the dot lifts and returns under recoil to analyze grip recovery.

- Fire multiple shots and **observe dot lift and return**.
- If it doesn't return to the same point, it's a grip failure.
- If it jitters before the shot, it's a trigger failure.

- **Trigger Isolation + Grip Endurance**
  – Conduct cadence drills at different paces (Bill Drill, 1-2-3-4 Drill).
- **Ball and Dummy Live Fire**
  – Isolate unexpected shot breaks and grip collapse moments.

  - Mix dummy rounds into mags.
  - When the dummy round is encountered, *observe sight movement on trigger press.*
  - Was it the grip or the finger?

- **"Dead Trigger" Follow-Through Drill**
  – Press the trigger on an empty chamber and **observe what moved** when recoil doesn't distract.

  - After a dry fire press, the trigger goes dead.
  - Attempt a second press to observe *what the hand does* without the "click" or distraction.
  - This reveals true grip vs. trigger separation.

The **grip stabilizes the platform**; the **trigger executes the precision**.
A durable grip allows you to press the trigger **without disturbing** the gun.
Good trigger control allows the gun to **behave predictably** under recoil — protecting your grip.
Together, they produce a shooting experience that is **repeatable, correctable, and fast**.

Shooter Performance Objective Triangle

Core Elements: Speed – Accuracy – Consistency

Beginner Level – Learning to Control the Gun

Key Objective: Build foundational ability to hit what you're aiming at safely and predictably.

- **Speed:** Introduced only after safe, consistent weapon handling is achieved. Emphasis is on **deliberate mechanics**, not rapid fire.
- **Accuracy:** Priority #1. Shooters must learn to achieve reliable hits using proper grip, sight alignment, and trigger control.
- **Consistency:** Introduced through **repetitive dry fire**, focusing on stance, draw, and follow-through.

Technique Integration at this level:

- Isolated drills (dry fire, single shot live fire)
- High repetition with **low complexity**
- Reinforce gross motor patterns (grip, presentation, trigger press)

Stress Response Consideration:

- Begin teaching about stress effects on fine motor skills.
- Emphasize relaxed performance. No stress inoculation needed yet.

Intermediate Level – Beginning to Perform Under Pressure

Key Objective: Blend skills and begin to manage cognitive load (e.g., decision-making, transitions, shot cadence).

- **Speed:** Introduced in bursts. Par times and drills like draw-to-first-shot start to matter.
- **Accuracy:** Must still be maintained as speed increases. Hits on zone-specific targets (A-zone or 4" circles).
- **Consistency:** Focus on reproducibility under slight fatigue or movement (multiple reps, compressed time, etc.)

Technique Integration:

- Shooters begin to combine learned techniques (e.g., movement + draw + multiple rounds)
- Performance **may dip temporarily** (Model Baseline 2–3) as new skill layers are added.
- Instructor must help student push through frustration.

Stress Concepts Introduced:

- Gross vs. fine motor skill degradation
- Performance under elevated heart rate (drills w/ burpees, timers)
- Teach visual narrowing and auditory exclusion effects

Advanced Level – Subconscious Execution and Efficiency Under Duress

Key Objective: Execute tasks with unconscious competence and transition seamlessly across complex demands.

- **Speed:** Becomes reactive and natural. Visual processing drives shooting tempo.
- **Accuracy:** Maintained even during transitions, movement, and compressed timelines. *"Fast is fine, but accurate is final."*
- **Consistency:** Bullet performance reflects training depth. Hits are no longer lucky; they're *expected.*

Technique Integration:

- Technique is now subconsciously integrated (Model Baseline 3–4).
- Drills include low-light, stress, simulated injury, decision-making.
- Focus shifts from mechanics to **problem-solving under stress**.

Stress Mitigation & Motor Skills:

- Train under **elevated heart rate** (>140 bpm) to preserve performance
- Practice complex motor tasks (e.g., reloads, transitions) during SNS activation drills
- Visualization and self-talk actively coached ("breathe, see it, say it, do it")

Instructor-Level Understanding – Teaching Under Pressure and Across Progressions

Key Objective: Understand the science of stress, performance, and motor learning so you can build shooters, not just pass quals.

1. Teaching Through the Triangle

- **Speed, Accuracy, and Consistency** are *not* separate goals — they are interdependent.

Speed, Accuracy, and Consistency
Are Not Separate Goals
Balance
Target
Threat
Time

- Instructors must show shooters how to balance the triangle based on target type, threat, and time.
- Example:
    - *Close threat, low risk = Speed & Predictive Shooting (Confirmation 1 / Slap trigger).*
    - *Partially obscured target = Accuracy + Deep Trigger Prep(Confirmation 3)*

2. Technique Integration Curve

- **Model Baseline 1–2:** Early wins when student focuses on one thing (e.g., grip refinement).

- **Model Baseline 2–3:** Dip in performance as new technique is integrated into real drills. *Instructor MUST push student past frustration here.*
- **Model Baseline 3–4:** True subconscious competence. "I don't think about it anymore — I just do it right."

Instructor Note: Don't overload new shooters with technique stacking too early. Introduce new layers only once the previous is consistent under mild pressure.

3. Managing the Stress Curve (SNS Activation)

- Teach how the **Autonomic Nervous System** influences decision-making and performance:
  - Fine motor degradation (~115 bpm)
  - Complex motor loss (~145 bpm)
  - Auditory exclusion, tunnel vision, and depth perception loss (>150 bpm)
- **Goal:** Train students to operate in the 115–145 bpm window — the "performance zone."

Instructor Objective*:* Use drills (e.g., time pressure, physical stress, unexpected commands) to raise heart rate while preserving *form under fire*.

4. Inoculate to Stress Through Repetition and Simulation

- Use **Simunitions / Airsoft / Role-Play** to introduce real consequences
- Short drills → Complex strings → Decision drills
- **Repetition builds prediction** → Prediction builds confidence → Confidence reduces panic

Example:

"Tap-Rack-Ready" becomes automatic only when:

- The movement is rehearsed under **controlled and stressed conditions**,
- The shooter **understands the context** (malfunction vs. dry gun),
- The instructor has reinforced correct movement with **corrective feedback at speed**.

5. Build the Warrior Mindset, Not Just the Skillset

- Teach visualization, mental rehearsal, and performance scripting
- Use instructor-led "talk-throughs" to reinforce self-coaching
- Encourage aggressive, proactive posture in drills (*Dominate weapon → Dominate opponent → Dominate environment*)

Instructor Cue:
"Don't let the fight surprise you. You've already been there a hundred times — in your reps, in your mind, in your training."

Summary Table: Progressive Triangle Breakdown

Level	Speed	Accuracy	Consistency	Technique Focus	Stress Handling
Beginner	Slow/Measured	High Priority	Repetitive Form	Isolated reps	Intro to fine motor control
Intermediate	Controlled	Sustained	Timed drills	Skill stacking begins	Elevated heart rate exposure
Advanced	Reactive	Maintained	Subconscious	Real-world application	Inoculated via realistic sims

Level	Speed	Accuracy	Consistency	Technique Focus	Stress Handling
Instructor	Diagnostic	Target-specific	Taught to others	Teaching + performance	Teaches stress inoculation

Shooter Performance Objective Triangle Instructor Framework

Goal: Train shooters through the progressive development of **Speed, Accuracy, and Consistency**, while integrating techniques, inoculating to stress, and building mindset.

Phase 1: Establish the Foundation (Beginner to Early Intermediate)

Objective: Build safe, repeatable mechanics with strong fundamentals under low/no pressure.

Step 1: Introduce the Triangle Concept

- Use visual aids or draw the triangle: Speed – Accuracy – Consistency.
- Explain the relationship: **Speed without Accuracy is irrelevant**, **Accuracy without Speed is insufficient**, **and Consistency makes both reliable**.

Step 2: Drill Basic Marksmanship

- Teach grip, stance, sight picture, and trigger press.
- Run basic drills (e.g., single-shot accuracy from ready and from holster).
- Emphasize **repeatable grip** and **sight tracking** over time.

Step 3: Dry Fire & Diagnostic Reinforcement

- Introduce *Live Trigger Dry Fire* with wall drills, trigger preps, and reset training.
- Begin dry-fire **trigger isolation** under your supervision.

Step 4: Teach Technique Integration Model (Baseline 1–2)

- Introduce one performance-enhancing technique at a time (e.g., prepping the trigger, high thumbs-forward grip).
- Let shooters experience the **initial performance bump** from focused execution.

Phase 2: Controlled Complexity (Mid-Level Intermediate)

Objective: Begin stacking techniques and introducing pressure/decision-making.

Step 5: Reinforce Triangle Under Pressure

- Use **simple timer-based drills** (e.g., draw-to-first-shot with par times).
- Add *accountability* through scoring zones or pass/fail standards.

Step 6: Apply Technique Integration (Baseline 2–3)

- Add movement, multiple targets, or transitions.
- Expect a **temporary dip in performance**—coach through frustration.
- Teach that **this dip is a normal and necessary step** in learning.

Step 7: Introduce Stress Physiology

- Use basic physical stressors: e.g., jumping jacks before drills, loud commands, short time limits.

- Teach students how **fine/complex motor skills degrade under SNS activation** (visual narrowing, trigger errors, misreads).

Step 8: Start Building Stress Inoculation

- Use controlled scenario training or SimFX/Airsoft.
- Observe changes in form under pressure and debrief student perception vs. performance.
- Encourage brief instructor-led **post-drill self-assessment** ("What did you see? What worked? What didn't?").

Phase 3: Advanced Integration (Advanced Shooters)

Objective: Perform with subconscious competence under increasing levels of stress and complexity.

Step 9: Push for High-Speed Accuracy

- Use confirmation-based shooting drills (e.g., 1-dot = speed only, 2-dot = color confirmation, 3-dot = full visual confirmation).
- Run timed headshot drills, obscured targets, or hostage offset drills under time pressure.

Step 10: Reinforce Baseline 3–4 Performance

- Coach students into subconscious integration:
    - "You don't think about your grip anymore—you just fix it before the beep."
    - "Your body's doing it. Now your eyes and brain need to lead it."

Step 11: Apply Realistic, Tactical Context

- Run multi-phase problem-solving drills (e.g., move to cover, verbal commands, threat ID).
- Start teaching *in-structure stress*—unknown start commands, light/noise changes, judgment calls.
- Push cognitive decision-making inside complex motor tasks.

Step 12: Teach Visualization and Self-Coaching

- Assign *daily mental rehearsal* exercises.
- Guide them to use *positive task-oriented self-talk* before and during complex drills.
- Encourage reflection: "What do I need to see next time? What do I fix next run?"

Phase 4: Instructor-Level Concepts

Objective: Prepare instructors to diagnose performance, manage stress inoculation, and teach skill progression across all levels.

Step 13: Teach the Triangle from a Coaching Lens

- Show instructors how to **evaluate performance breakdowns**:
  - Misses? = Accuracy
  - Hesitation? = Confidence or technique confusion
  - Sloppy performance? = Inconsistent execution or lack of integration

Step 14: Teach the Technique Integration Curve

- Help instructors spot where students are in the curve:

- Excited (new skill, working well)
- Frustrated (too many moving parts)
- Confident (subconscious control returning)

Step 15: Plan Training Based on Motor Skill Science

- Apply **SNS heart rate zones** (115–145 bpm) when planning intensity.
- Teach instructors to use **gross motor drills under high stress**, **complex motor skills under controlled conditions**.
- Train them to "scale" drills: task complexity + stressor = desired skill exposure.

Step 16: Reinforce Warrior Mindset Building

- Embed visualization, mindset lectures, and mental walk-throughs in every advanced course.
- Use layered scenario immersion to build **emotional and physiological inoculation**.
- Teach instructors to lead not just technical development, but **mental performance preparation**.

INSTRUCTOR MODULE: SHOOTER PERFORMANCE OBJECTIVE TRIANGLE

Module Title: Shooter Performance Objective Triangle and Integrated Performance Training

Training Level: Beginner to Instructor

Objective: Equip instructors with a structured method for developing shooter performance through the triad of Speed, Accuracy, and Consistency, integrated with technique adoption, stress exposure, and cognitive preparation.

OVERVIEW

The Shooter Performance Objective Triangle consists of three critical elements:

- **Speed:** The shooter's ability to deliver rounds rapidly from a ready or holstered position.
- **Accuracy:** The shooter's ability to place rounds in vital zones under varying conditions.
- **Consistency:** The shooter's ability to repeatedly demonstrate both speed and accuracy across multiple reps, scenarios, and environments.

This model works in conjunction with the Technique Integration Curve, Stress Performance Science, and the shooter's physical/mental capacity to deliver under pressure.

PHASED DEVELOPMENT MODEL

Phase 1: Foundational Control (Beginner to Early Intermediate)

Instructor Goals:

- Instill safe weapon handling and mechanical repetition.
- Emphasize deliberate accuracy over speed.

Key Concepts:

- Dry fire fundamentals (grip, trigger press, sight alignment).

- Simple live fire accuracy drills.
- Repetition under low stress.

Drills:

- Wall Drill (Trigger Isolation)
- One-Round Accuracy from Ready
- 5-Round B8 Slow Fire (7yd)

Phase 2: Controlled Complexity (Mid-Level Intermediate)

Instructor Goals:

- Introduce the interplay of the triangle elements.
- Begin integration of multiple techniques.
- Train under mild stress or time.

Key Concepts:

- Technique stacking: movement, reloads, transitions.
- Performance dip awareness (Baseline 2–3).
- Heart-rate elevation and basic stress response.

Drills:

- Draw to First Shot (Par Time)
- 1–2–3 Target Transition
- Tap-Rack-Ready under Timer

Phase 3: Advanced Integration (Advanced Shooters)

Instructor Goals:

- Solidify unconscious competence under dynamic stress.
- Maintain triangle balance under time and environmental pressure.

Key Concepts:

- Complex scenarios with movement, decision, and stress.
- Performance consistency under time and fatigue.
- Transition to confirmation-based shooting (1-2-3 visual confirmation levels).

Drills:

- Shoot/No-Shoot Visual ID Drills
- Movement to Cover + Fire
- 2-Round Headbox Timed Standards

INSTRUCTOR APPLICATION

Teaching Through the Triangle:

- Diagnose breakdowns via triangle imbalance.
- Reinforce triangle adjustments depending on target, distance, and scenario.

Technique Integration Curve:

1. Initial Performance Boost
2. Temporary Dip (Due to Conscious Integration)
3. Subconscious Mastery

Performance Under Stress:

- Teach ANS response: SNS/PNS roles
- Motor skills: Fine (degrades ~115 bpm), Complex (~145 bpm), Gross (>150 bpm)
- Use stress inoculation tools (Simunitions, Airsoft, timer, elevated HR drills)

MENTAL PERFORMANCE

Visualization & Self-Talk:

- Coach shooters to mentally rehearse drills, visualize success, and use instructional self-talk.
- Integrate warrior mindset: aggressive, prepared, and deliberate.

Mindset Goals:

- Dominate the weapon.
- Dominate the situation.
- Dominate the visual field.

Instructor Note: This module is designed to be scalable. Increase or decrease complexity and pressure based on shooter maturity and course duration. Always link technical training back to

Instructor Module Expansion: OODA Loop – Boyd's Cycle

The **OODA Loop** is a decision-making and action-execution cycle developed by U.S. Air Force Colonel John Boyd. Originally designed for air-to-air combat, its principles now widely apply to **tactical, competitive, and combative shooting** and **defensive decision-making**.

The acronym stands for:

1. **Observe**
2. **Orient**
3. **Decide**
4. **Act**

This is not a linear process—it's a **cyclical, recursive model** that helps shooters process and dominate rapidly changing situations.

Breakdown of the OODA Loop in a Shooting Context

1. **Observe**

- **Gather information through all sensory channels**: eyes, ears, touch, and proprioception.
- Environmental scan: Identify threats, positions, lighting, bystanders, and cover.
- On the range: Identify target type, distance, position, and movement.

Instructor Focus:

- Train students to see more than just the target (target ID, environment, and movement).
- Reinforce scanning before and after engagements.
- Use multiple stimulus inputs in drills (visual, audible cues).

2. **Orient**

- **Process and analyze the data** gathered in the Observe phase.
- Involves interpretation based on:
  - Past experience
  - Training and doctrine
  - Cultural and psychological factors
  - Physical ability
  - Gear and weapon setup

Instructor Focus:

- Teach shooters how **bias and expectation** can delay this step.
- Use scenario drills to challenge assumptions.
- Emphasize the importance of proper gear setup and muscle memory to minimize *processing time.*

3. **Decide**

- Choose a course of action based on orientation.
- Example decisions: Engage or not, single shot or controlled pair, move to cover or hold position.

Instructor Focus:

- Develop decisiveness under pressure.
- Use drills that create **micro-decisions**: target priority, type of engagement, movement choice.
- Teach decision-making under compressed time with visual/mental stress.

4. **Act**

- Execute the decided course of action with **speed and precision**.
- This is where **motor programs and muscle memory** play a major role.

Instructor Focus:

- Actions must be trained until subconscious.
- Use repetitions that are high quality, consistent, and correct.
- Emphasize **execution without hesitation** once a decision is made.

Loop Restarts

Every action causes a new change in the environment. That change feeds back into **new observation**, and the cycle begins again.

Train students to **loop faster and more effectively** than their opponent or the situation—this is known as "**getting inside the enemy's OODA Loop**."

OODA Loop & Shooter Performance Triangle Integration

- **Speed** applies to **Act** and the loop time itself.
- **Accuracy** is critical during the **Act** phase—ineffective or errant actions must be avoided.
- **Consistency** is developed through drilling the loop—until action selection and execution are reliable under stress.

Practical Instructor Drills

OODA Stimulus Reaction Drill

- Targets face away. Instructor gives a visual or verbal cue.
- Shooter must observe, orient to target type (threat/no threat), decide and act accordingly.
- Use multiple target types (handgun drawn, no weapon, hostage, etc.).

OODA Loop Walk-Through Scenarios

- Use shoot/no-shoot drills with added complexity: environmental audio, moving targets, low light.
- Force students to walk through their loop afterward in AAR (After Action Review).

Instructor Takeaway

"The goal is not just to shoot fast. It's to **decide and act faster** than the threat—**without compromising judgment or control.** That's the difference between reacting and dominating."

The 3Ps of Pistol Presentation

1. Presentation

This refers to the **mechanics of bringing the pistol from the holster to the target** in a controlled and consistent manner.

- **Biomechanical efficiency**: The movement should be straight, minimizing wasted motion. The pistol should travel on a predictable line, not an arcing or scooping path.
- **Consistency**: Every repetition must look the same—whether in training or under stress. Presentation is not just about speed, but about delivering the pistol to the eye-target line with repeatable precision.
- **Grip integrity**: Proper grip must be established in the holster and maintained through the presentation. A poor initial grip compromises everything that follows.

Instructor Point: Stress that shooters "fight from the holster they train with." Presentation is only as good as the grip, stance, and indexing built at the start.

2. Pressure

Pressure refers to the **applied grip force and trigger control** during the draw and extension.

- **Grip Pressure**: Must be firm enough to manage recoil but not so tense that it causes tremors or anticipatory movement. The support hand applies inward and forward pressure, locking the pistol into the shooter's frame.
- **Trigger Pressure**: As the pistol joins the eye-target line, pressure on the trigger should be **staged and controlled**. The shooter must avoid "snatching" the trigger at full extension. Instead, pressure is applied smoothly as the sights settle.
- **Mental Pressure**: This also extends to the psychological component—keeping composure under time stress, close-distance threat, or high heart rate.

Instructor Point: Pressure is not just physical. It is the balance between **controlling the pistol and controlling yourself.**

3. Pathway

Pathway is the **trajectory of the pistol to the target**—the invisible line along which the pistol travels.

- **Straight-line Pathway**: The pistol should travel in a direct line from the holster to the target, moving efficiently into the shooter's line of sight. Scooping, fishing, or lateral "wandering" of the muzzle wastes time and consistency.
- **Visual Pathway**: The eyes lead the pathway. The shooter must pick up the sight picture early and bring the gun to the line of vision—not dip their head to the gun.
- **Retractable Pathway**: Pathway works both ways. Just as the pistol travels outward efficiently, it must be retracted smoothly for reholstering, reloads, or post-engagement scanning.

Instructor Point: Emphasize that pathway is about **economy of motion**. The shortest, cleanest path reduces decision time (Hick's Law) and improves speed without loss of accuracy

Pulling It Together

The **3Ps—Presentation, Pressure, Pathway—work as a system**:

- **Presentation** ensures the pistol is delivered correctly.
- **Pressure** ensures control of both the firearm and the shooter.
- **Pathway** ensures efficiency and repeatability of movement.

When trained together, these Ps create a biomechanically sound, stress-proof draw stroke that holds under both competition and combat conditions.

Training Module: The 3Ps of Pistol Presentation

(Presentation · Pressure · Pathway)

Beginner Level (Fundamentals)

Objective: Build awareness of the 3Ps and establish consistent mechanics.

Key Points

1. **Presentation**
   - Establish a correct grip in the holster.
   - Draw the pistol directly toward the eye-target line.
   - Keep movements smooth and consistent—speed comes later.
2. **Pressure**
   - Apply a firm, even grip with both hands (no gaps or uneven tension).
   - Avoid "crushing" the grip—use consistent forward and inward pressure.
   - Trigger finger indexed until the pistol is on target.
3. **Pathway**
   - Move the pistol in a straight, efficient line from holster to target.
   - Lead with the eyes: lock onto the target first, then bring pistol to line of sight.
   - Avoid "scooping" or over-extending.

Drills

- **Dry Fire Presentation Drill**: 10–20 slow reps focusing on grip and straight-line draw.

- **Wall Drill**: Stand close to a wall, present the pistol without the muzzle drifting sideways—teaches clean pathway.
- **3P Verbal Reinforcement**: Instructor calls "Presentation / Pressure / Pathway" as students execute each step.

Intermediate Level (Performance)

Objective: Apply the 3Ps at speed under realistic conditions.

Key Points

1. **Presentation**
   - Consistency at speed—draw stroke looks the same every time.
   - Focus on first-round hit accuracy while increasing pace.
2. **Pressure**
   - Adjust grip pressure dynamically: tight enough for recoil control, relaxed enough for precision.
   - Begin applying trigger pressure ("prep") as sights approach target.
3. **Pathway**
   - Efficient movement at speed—no wasted arcs or scoops.
   - Pathway consistency during multiple target transitions.

Drills

- **Draw to First Shot Drill**: Timed draws at 3–7 yards with strict accuracy requirement.
- **Trigger Prep Drill**: Present the pistol and stage the trigger smoothly—breaking only when sight picture stabilizes.

- **Target Transition Drill**: Engage two targets using the same clean pathway each time.

Advanced Level (Stress-Proofing)

Objective: Harden the 3Ps against stress, movement, and adverse conditions.

Key Points

1. **Presentation**
   - Adapt presentation from seated, moving, or compromised positions.
   - Maintain mechanics even when using concealment or barriers.
2. **Pressure**
   - Manage grip and trigger under stress (shot timer, low light, heart rate).
   - Emphasize mental pressure management: breathing, calm execution.
3. **Pathway**
   - Maintain pathway efficiency when moving off-line or using lateral footwork.
   - Retract pathway into low ready or compressed ready as needed for multiple threats.

Drills

- **Stress Timer Drill**: Students draw and fire under par times to test mechanics.
- **Movement Presentation Drill**: Draw while moving laterally or stepping off line.
- **Low-Light 3Ps Drill**: Apply same principles using handheld or WML illumination.

Instructor Level (Teaching & Diagnostics)

Objective: Teach instructors how to evaluate, correct, and refine the 3Ps in students.

Instructor Checklist

- **Presentation**:
  - Is the grip correct before the pistol leaves the holster?
  - Is the pistol delivered to the eye-target line without wasted motion?
- **Pressure**:
  - Is grip pressure balanced between hands?
  - Is trigger press staged smoothly instead of snapped?
  - Is student showing mental control under pressure?
- **Pathway**:
  - Does the pistol move in a straight line, or is there scooping/curving?
  - Are eyes leading the pistol to the target?
  - Is the pathway retractable and repeatable?

Instructor Drills

- **Error Identification Drill**: Students deliberately exaggerate poor Presentation, Pressure, or Pathway; instructors diagnose and correct.
- **3P Breakdown Teaching**: Instructors explain and demo each P separately, then integrate them for the full draw stroke.
- **Progressive Overload Drill**: Add variables (timer, multiple targets, concealment) while ensuring students maintain the 3Ps.

Summary

The **3Ps—Presentation, Pressure, Pathway—create a biomechanical and mental framework for a stress-proof pistol draw.**

- Beginners learn clean fundamentals.
- Intermediate shooters build speed and accuracy.
- Advanced shooters stress-proof mechanics in real-world conditions.
- Instructors use the 3Ps as diagnostic tools to correct errors and reinforce consistency.

The 3Ps of Pistol Presentation

Presentation · Pressure · Pathway

Beginner Level: Foundation

Goal: Build consistent mechanics and awareness of the 3Ps.

1. **Presentation**
   - Grip formed in the holster.
   - Pistol lifted and driven in a straight line toward the eyes.
   - Movement is smooth, not rushed.
2. **Pressure**
   - Firm, balanced grip from both hands.
   - No over-crushing—just enough to manage recoil.
   - Trigger finger straight until the pistol is on target.
3. **Pathway**
   - Pistol moves on a straight track—no fishing, scooping, or arcing.

- Eyes lock on the target first; pistol follows into vision.
- Return path (reholstering) mirrors the draw.

Drill: *Dry-fire presentation.* 10 slow reps, calling out each P as you move.

Intermediate Level: Performance

Goal: Execute the 3Ps with speed and accuracy.

1. **Presentation**
    - Draw is identical every time, regardless of speed.
    - First-round hit accuracy is non-negotiable.
2. **Pressure**
    - Grip is consistent across multiple strings of fire.
    - Trigger is prepped during extension—breaking only as sights settle.
3. **Pathway**
    - Pathway remains straight at full speed.
    - Efficient transitions—muzzle tracks cleanly between targets.

Drill: *Draw to First Shot on timer.* Must balance accuracy and speed while maintaining 3Ps.

Advanced Level: Stress-Proofing

Goal: Maintain the 3Ps under stress, movement, and real-world variables.

1. **Presentation**
    - Works from concealment, seated, or moving positions.

    - Same mechanics regardless of starting point.
2. **Pressure**
    - Grip and trigger control hold under timer, low light, and elevated heart rate.
    - Mental pressure is managed—shooter executes, not overthinks.
3. **Pathway**
    - Muzzle stays efficient even when stepping off-line or engaging multiple threats.
    - Retraction pathway is just as clean for scanning, reloading, or reholstering.

Drill: *Movement + Timer Drill.* Step laterally, draw, and engage. Check for clean 3Ps under stress.

Instructor Level: Teaching & Diagnostics

Goal: Use the 3Ps to evaluate, coach, and correct.

- **Presentation** → Look for wasted motion, scooping draw, or poor initial grip.
- **Pressure** → Check hand tension balance; watch for trigger snatch or grip collapse.
- **Pathway** → Observe muzzle travel; correct "fishing" or inconsistent lines.

Instructor Drill: *Error Demo.* Have students exaggerate mistakes in each P. Diagnose and correct using the 3Ps as the framework.

Summary

The **3Ps** create a framework for a **biomechanically efficient, stress-resistant draw stroke**:

- **Presentation** delivers the pistol consistently.
- **Pressure** controls the pistol and the shooter.
- **Pathway** keeps the draw efficient and repeatable.

Train slow, build consistent 3Ps, then add speed and stress.

The 3Ps of Pistol Presentation

Presentation · Pressure · Pathway

Instructor Quick Reference

1. Presentation

- Grip formed correctly in holster.
- Draw stroke is direct, efficient, and repeatable.
- Pistol delivered to eye–target line (eyes lead, pistol follows).

Common Errors:

- Scooping or arcing draw.
- Poor grip established in holster.
- Head drops to meet pistol.

2. Pressure

- Firm, balanced grip pressure (support hand drives inward/forward).
- Trigger prep during extension—smooth press as sights settle.
- Control **both** pistol and mental pressure.

Common Errors:

- Over-crushing grip, causing tremor.
- Trigger slap/snatch at full extension.
- Grip collapse after first shot.

3. Pathway

- Straight-line draw, no wasted motion.
- Muzzle tracks cleanly between targets on transitions.
- Retract pathway is controlled (low ready, reholster, reload).

Common Errors:

- "Fishing" or scooping upward.
- Muzzle wandering during transitions.
- Sloppy reholstering pathway.

Instructor Diagnostic Checklist

- Grip correct before pistol leaves holster.
- Pistol moves on straight pathway to eye–target line.
- Trigger press staged smoothly, not snapped.
- Grip and pressure remain consistent under speed/stress.
- Pathway is clean both outward (draw) and inward (reholster/retract).

Key Teaching Points

- **Slow is smooth. Smooth becomes fast.**
- Speed builds only after consistent 3Ps.

- Use the 3Ps to diagnose and correct any draw error.

The Difference between
Reacting and Dominating
Decide and Act
Faster. Without
Compromising
Judgment or control

The Pistol Draw-stroke: A Layered, Instructor-Level Breakdown

Objective:

The goal of the pistol draw-stroke is to present the pistol from the holster to the target with **maximum efficiency, consistency, and alignment**, ensuring the shooter is able to fire accurately and rapidly under stress—whether in a controlled environment or in a defensive encounter.

Core Instructional Concepts

Economy of motion
Indexing and body contact points
Symmetry and natural biomechanics
Readiness for threat engagement at any stage
Consistency under stress via gross motor programming

Position-by-Position Breakdown

Position 1 – Grip Establishment & Access

Cue: "Grip and clear."

Action:

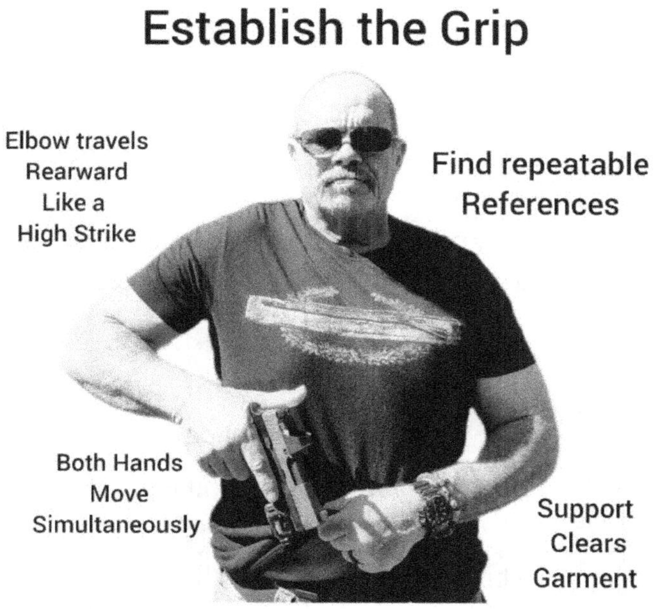

Both hands begin moving **simultaneously**:

Strong hand (dominant) moves back along the ribcage, establishing contact with the torso (creating a proprioceptive reference point under stress).

Elbow travels rearward like a high rearward strike, then the hand drops **vertically** down to the holster (no lateral fishing).

Defeat holster retention while achieving a **high tang grip** immediately.

Strong-hand **thumb stays high and horizontal**, not clamped down—this **preserves space** for the support hand and sets up thumb-index tendon tension for recoil control.

Support hand travels to the sternum, fingers open, palm out, **ready to accept the pistol** at Position 3.

Instructor Emphasis:

- Teach **body contact** (ribcage, pectoral stretch) as a **repeatable reference**.
- Reinforce **thumb position** for optimal support-hand integration later.
- Ensure **no early grip adjustments**—build the correct grip in the holster.

Position 2 – Draw and Orientation

Cue: "Lift and rotate."

Action:

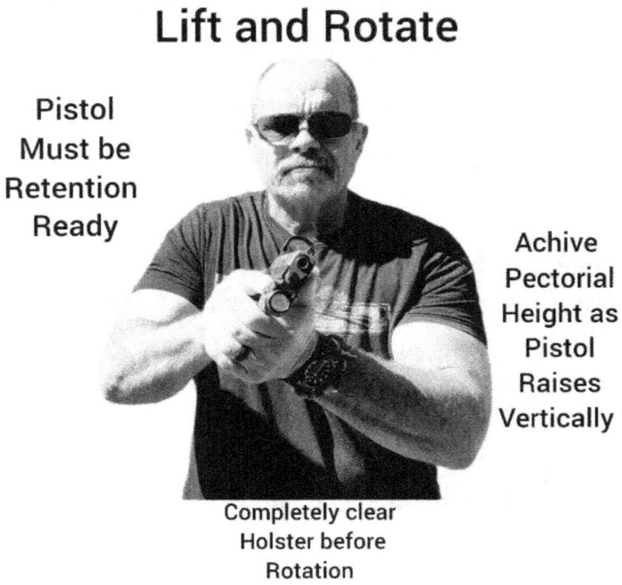
Lift and Rotate
Pistol Must be Retention Ready
Achive Pectorial Height as Pistol Raises Vertically
Completely clear Holster before Rotation

Weapon lifts vertically, staying tight to the body—up to the pectoral/armpit region.

Only after lifting does the shooter **rotate the muzzle toward the target**.

This rotation should ideally happen at **pectoral height**, so the muzzle can enter the **sight plane early**.

Safety (if present) is disengaged during this motion using the strong-hand thumb.

- The gun is now in a **retention-ready orientation**, muzzle forward, slide parallel to the ground.

Instructor Emphasis:

- **Do not rotate immediately** after clearing holster—this results in an arcing path and lost visual alignment.
- Weapon orientation here allows:
    - Immediate defensive fire (CQB)
    - Transition to extreme close quarters techniques (indexing pistol to rib cage)
- Teach **vertical extraction** with high pectoral indexing as a cornerstone of consistency.

Position 3 – Close Quarters / Grip Completion

Cue: "Meet and drive."

Action:

The **support hand meets the pistol** at or near the body's midline.

Establish a **two-handed grip**:

Support thumb wraps under the high-position strong-hand thumb.

Avoid downward pressure from strong-hand thumb—this defeats the tension needed in the support hand for recoil management.

- At this point, the shooter may:
  - Fire from retention
  - Transition to full presentation (Position 4)
- If the safety hasn't been disengaged yet, the **support hand** can do so here.
- **Trigger prep begins** as sights start to rise.

Instructor Emphasis:

- Stress importance of **early grip formation**—not waiting too long.
- Adjust for individual biomechanics (eye dominance, shoulder width, holster position).
- Practice **dry fire Position 3 shooting** for close quarter accuracy training.

Position 4 – Presentation to Target

Cue: "Press and break."

Action: Weapon is **driven straight forward** into the target line—**not arced upward**.

Arms extend naturally, aligning sights with the dominant eye.

Trigger prep completes—slack removed en route, final press happens at full extension as the **sight picture stabilizes**.

- Bodyweight shifts slightly forward (fighting stance).
- After firing, shooter **immediately resets trigger** and reacquires **sight picture** for follow-up shots.

Instructor Emphasis:

- Emphasize **straight-line extension**—no scoop or arc.
- Use of **target-focused presentation drills** to teach press-and-break cadence.
- Integrate **visual verification drills** (Confirmations 1, 2, 3) into this position.

Step-by-Step Framework for *Teaching the Draw-stroke*

Step	*Instructional Focus*	*Drills / Key Points*
1. Introduce the Four Positions	Explain biomechanical reasoning	Dry practice each position slowly and in isolation
2. Position 1 to 2	Focus on consistent grip and high draw	Wall drill, mirror drill, slow reps with eyes closed
3. Position 2 to 3	Train high orientation and meeting of hands	Partner mirror work, step-by-step verbal callouts
4. Position 3 to 4	Work on press out, sight acquisition, trigger press	Presentation drills to different ranges (3/7/15 yd)
5. Full Drawstroke Reps	Combine all into fluid draw	1/4 speed, 1/2 speed, then full speed (dry/live)
6. Add Stress and Variability	Introduce time pressure and movement	Shot timer drills, CQB retention shooting, target transitions
7. Diagnose & Refine	Evaluate grip formation, hand timing, angle	Video feedback, grip audits, hand isolation drills

From Range To Reality

Instructor-Level Tips for Effective Draw-stroke Instruction

- **Drill to Isolate**: Use part-task training (e.g., 1 → 2 reps only) to build consistent motion.
- **Eyes Lead Hands**: Ensure the shooter's **vision transitions** ahead of muzzle.
- **Holster Access**: For duty/CCW users, simulate clearing garments and retention work.
- **Incorporate Confirmations**: Sight confirmation levels 1–3 help pair target engagement to presentation quality.
- **Safety Considerations**: Strict adherence to **trigger discipline** until Position 3 or 4 depending on context.
- **Dry Fire Before Live Fire**: Master mechanical pathway before introducing recoil or timers.

A detailed **instructor-level breakdown** of **drawing from concealment with an OWB holster covered by an over garment**, tailored specifically for **Law Enforcement (LE)** and **Concealed Carry (CCW)** contexts. This expansion includes **biomechanics, garment clearing techniques, and training considerations**, and integrates seamlessly into the 4-position draw-stroke provided earlier.

OWB Concealed Drawstroke (Covered by Overgarment)

For LE & CCW Applications

Context-Specific Considerations

LE	CCW
Duty belt w/ retention, OWB holster covered by a softshell, windbreaker, or raid jacket	OWB concealment holster under flannel shirt, jacket, or vest
May transition from uniformed to plainclothes role	Must blend concealment with rapid access in reactive self-defense
Training must simulate both overt draw and concealed access	Speed of access under pressure is critical due to defensive posture

Core Instructional Objectives

- Enable the shooter to defeat the garment efficiently **under duress**
- Maintain **body mechanics** and high-quality grip during garment clearance
- Ensure the shooter can fire from **any point in the draw** if needed (CQB context)
- Preserve concealment techniques **without sacrificing access time**

Modified 4-Position Drawstroke with Garment Clearance

Pre-Draw – Garment Management Setup

Before Position 1, the shooter must **clear the garment** to access the weapon.

Garment Clearing Techniques:

1. **Strong-Side Rip (Standard Method)**
   - Shooter uses strong hand to sweep the outer garment **up and rearward**, clearing it above the holster line.
   - **Elbow flares out** slightly as hand grabs fabric around the hip or hemline.
   - **Anchor the garment** high on the rib cage or armpit momentarily.
   - Then continue into **Position 1** (grip establishment).
2. **Two-Handed Sweep (Alternate or Tucked Garment)**
   - Both hands rip the shirt/jacket hem **upward** simultaneously.
   - Support hand **holds the garment high on the sternum or chest** while the strong hand transitions to the holster.
3. **Breakaway or Tearaway Access (for LE raid vests or specialized jackets)**
   - Emphasis on using **one gross motor motion** to open jacket and immediately access weapon.
   - Practice this **one-handed or in movement**.

Position 1 (Grip Establishment under Concealment)

- **Critical point**: Ensure the shooter doesn't compromise grip in haste after clearing the garment.
- Many shooters develop the bad habit of **gripping too low or angled** when rushing from concealment.

Instructor Cues:

- "Clear high, grip high."
- "Anchor the garment, don't fight it on the draw."
- "The garment clearance is part of the drawstroke, not before it."

Position 2 (Vertical Lift & Orientation)

- Same principles apply: lift to armpit/pectoral area before rotating.
- **Common mistake** from concealment: rotating the gun **too early** due to rushing.

Instructor Adjustments:

- Drill vertical lift as a standalone component: "Lift first, rotate second."
- Use mirrored dry fire or camera feedback to spot premature muzzle orientation.

Position 3 (Grip Completion & Retention Ready)

- Especially relevant in **close-contact civilian self-defense** or **LE CQB** scenarios.
- At this stage:
  - Jacket may be bunched or flared—ensure shooter keeps **garment out of ejection port and slide path**.
  - **Muzzle awareness** is paramount during movement.

Instructor Drills:

- Dry reps in front of mirror or partner to build garment control muscle memory.
- "Garment up, gun out" cadence training.

Position 4 (Full Presentation & Fire)

- Ensure support-hand thumb is properly placed after garment clearance.
- Many shooters will "rush" into extension without stabilizing the grip—especially after garment delay.

Instructor Cue:

- "Grip and drive, not slap and extend."

Teaching Framework for OWB Concealed Drawstroke

Step	Focus Area	Key Drill	Instructor Notes
1	Garment Clearing Mechanics	Garment Rip Drill (5 reps per method)	Use timer to compare strong-hand rip vs. two-handed
2	Grip Integrity	Dry Draw to Position 1 w/ garment	Check for grip slippage or angle misalignment
3	Full 4-Count Drawstroke	Step-by-step draw with par timer	Add verbal cues for each position
4	Movement Integration	Draw while stepping offline	Reinforces reactive CCW/LE movement
5	Retention Fire Drills	Fire from Position 3 (1-handed)	Integrate safety disengagement timing
6	Concealment to Fire Under Stress	Timer, concealment garment, lateral targets	Introduce "failure to clear" problem solving

LE & CCW Specific Training Adjustments

For LE:

- Train with full gear, jacket/raid vest **buttoned/zipped** as in patrol/undercover mode.

- Practice **weapon retention scenarios** after draw from OWB under concealment.
- Conduct **weapon access in vehicle/seatbelted** positions (common for surveillance, off-duty work).

For CCW:

- Reps from **typical everyday clothing** (hoodies, flannels, windbreakers).
- Emphasize **garment management in public (e.g., seated at restaurant, driving, carrying bags)**.
- Dry practice in **mirrored environments** to see garment-handling mechanics.

Summary: Key Teaching Cues

- "Clear High, Grip High"
- "Vertical First, Rotate Second"
- "Meet and Greet for Control"
- "Drive Straight, Break Clean"
- "Grip Before Go"

Drawing from an **Inside the Waistband (IWB)** or **Appendix Inside the Waistband (AIWB)** holster requires **adjustments in technique, biomechanics, and safety protocols** compared to OWB carry. The fundamentals of the four-position drawstroke still apply, but **access mechanics, garment clearance, angles of draw, and muzzle management** must be tailored for these concealment-specific carry positions.

Instructor-Level Overview: Differences in IWB & AIWB Drawstrokes

Aspect	IWB (Strong Side Hip/4–5 o'clock)	AIWB (12–1 o'clock)
Holster Position	Behind the hip bone, under belt line	In front of pelvis, under navel/hip
Draw Angle	Rearward and vertical	Forward and vertical
Garment Clearance	Requires rear sweep or lift	Straight vertical lift
Grip Access	Limited by elbow angle and torso twist	Faster access, shorter motion
Safety Considerations	Muzzle crosses leg/hip during draw	Muzzle crosses **femoral artery/genital area**
Reholstering Risk	Less acute, but still serious	**Highest risk** – must be deliberate and conscious
Advantages	Deep concealment, comfort when seated	Fastest draw time from concealment
Challenges	Slower access, arm entanglement	High reholster danger, must train for safe draw angle

1. Pre-Draw: Garment Clearance

IWB at 4–5 o'clock

- **Garment Rip Style:**
  - Strong hand performs a **rearward sweep** or upward rip of outer garment (shirt, jacket).
  - Support hand may anchor the shirt high on the chest.
- **Watchpoints:**
  - Ensure garment clears **over the hip**—instructors must emphasize **not catching the pistol butt** on the way up.
  - Arm must **rotate rearward** to access the grip—requires torso movement.

AIWB (12–1 o'clock)

- **Garment Rip Style:**
  - Strong or support hand grabs **the front hem** and lifts the garment **straight up**, high over the beltline.
  - Often done with **support hand anchoring** garment on the chest while strong hand draws.
- **Watchpoints:**
  - Ensure **strong hand stays vertical**; no fishing under shirt.
  - Create a **clear visual pathway** to the grip to reduce chance of ND.

2. Position 1: Grip Establishment

IWB:

- Arm may need to **flare slightly** to reach rearward holster position.

- Ensure **full grip** is achieved before drawing—many shooters compromise grip under pressure due to concealment.

Instructor Emphasis:

- “Rotate, reach, and lock the grip.”
- “No fishing, no adjusting mid-draw.”

AIWB:

- Grip is acquired by **driving hand straight down** from high chest to belt line.
- Shorter travel makes this **faster**, but must maintain **trigger discipline** even more strictly.

Instructor Emphasis:

- “Grip high, thumb high, elbow to rear.”
- "No trigger contact until gun clears belt line and is rotated."

3. Position 2: Lift & Orientation

IWB:

- Weapon is lifted **up and out**, clearing any belt tension or holster retention.
- Rotate muzzle toward target at chest/armpit level to avoid **"muzzle sweep of the hip/thigh."**

Instructor Adjustment:

- Teach a **deliberate upward draw path**, don’t let student arc forward immediately.

AIWB:

- Weapon is lifted **vertically** to the sternum line.
- Muzzle must rotate **forward and away from the body**, never angling backward or downward.

Instructor Warning:

- AIWB draws are **fast** but require absolute control and discipline.
- Use **dry fire reps** extensively to prevent premature muzzle rotation or poor indexing.

4. Position 3: Close Quarters Grip Completion

IWB & AIWB:

- Both techniques converge here:
    - **Hands meet at the midline**
    - Establish a two-handed grip
    - Begin prepping the trigger if threat engagement is imminent

Instructor Note:

- With IWB, there may be **more delay** in getting the support hand on due to garment tangle.
- With AIWB, this happens **faster**, but ensure full support-hand purchase before extending.

5. Position 4: Presentation & Fire

- This is largely **identical** across all carry types.
- Weapon is pressed to eye level, with final sight picture and trigger press occurring in sync.

Instructor Cue:

- "Don't race to full extension before building the shot platform."

Reholstering Specifics – Critical for AIWB and IWB

This is the **most dangerous moment** of the entire process due to **muzzle proximity to the body**.

Safe Reholstering Protocols:

1. **Remove distractions** – no multitasking or movement.
2. **Scan, breathe, and slow down.**
3. **Visually confirm** the reholster path is clear.
4. **Index the trigger finger high**, well away from trigger guard.
5. **Reholster deliberately**—never force the gun into the holster.

For AIWB:

- **Lean the hips backward** while reholstering to create space between muzzle and femoral triangle.
- Optionally, **remove the holster from waistband**, holster the gun outside of pants, then replace holster (common safety step in training).

Instructor Mandate:

- Reholster slowly, always with visual confirmation.
- **"Speed on the draw, caution on the holster."**

Instructor-Level Training Progression

Level	Skill	Focus	Drills
Beginner	IWB/AIWB draw isolation	Garment clearing, grip indexing	Dry draw with mirror feedback
Intermediate	4-position integration	Timing, grip integrity, muzzle orientation	Live fire draw to shot (par timer)
Advanced	Movement & stress	Off-line movement, contact shots	AIWB retention fire, IWB lateral draws
Instructor	Diagnostics & safety	Error correction, reholster protocol	Video feedback, emergency stoppage drills

Final Key Teaching Cues

- "Grip deep, clear clean."
- "Lift vertical before you rotate."
- "Eyes lead, muzzle follows."
- "Holster slow, eyes on."
- "AIWB is fast—but only with discipline."

Weapon Reloads: A Layered Breakdown

Foundational Principles (Applicable to All Reloads)

- **Control Zone**: Perform all reloads in front of the upper chest and chin, maintaining an "eye-muzzle-threat" alignment.
- **Two Hands in Motion**: Ensure both hands move simultaneously to minimize time.
- **Visual Discipline**: Shift eyes to the magwell only as necessary, then immediately return focus to the threat.
- **Finger off Trigger**: Keep the trigger finger indexed outside the trigger guard throughout the manipulation.
- **Efficiency under Pressure**: Prioritize consistent, simple, and resilient movements that withstand stress.

Emergency Reload (Slide-Lock Reload)

An emergency reload addresses a shooter-induced malfunction, such as running out of ammunition. Concealed carry permit holders should always carry at least one spare magazine for potential tactical reloads following expended rounds.

"The slide is locked to the rear. The pistol is empty. You are out of ammunition—this is an emergency."

Step-by-Step Instructor Breakdown

1. **Stoppage Recognition**
    - The shooter presses the trigger, experiences no discharge, feels a dead trigger, and observes the locked slide.

- Remove finger from trigger and bring the weapon to the control zone.

2. **Magazine Ejection**
    - Keep the pistol vertical.
    - Depress the magazine release using the strong-hand thumb or support-hand thumb.
    - Allow the empty magazine to drop freely (no retention).
    - *Instructor Note*: Position the strong-hand thumb above the slide stop lever to prevent premature activation if employing the slide release method.
3. **Index and Insert New Magazine**
    - The support hand draws a fresh magazine from the pouch using proper indexing.
    - Shift visual focus to the magwell as required.
    - Insert the magazine firmly and deliberately.
4. **Chamber a Round**
    - Select one of the following techniques:
        - Slingshot method.
        - Overhand/power stroke.
        - Slide release (only if trained and the slide stop is accessible).
    - Release the slide fully—do not ride it forward.
5. **Rebuild Grip and Reassess Threat**
    - Reestablish a two-handed grip.
    - Extend the pistol and acquire a fresh sight picture.
    - Continue engagement or reassess the situation.

Layered Learning Progression

Level	Focus	Instructor Cues	Common Errors
Beginner	Simple topping off	"Mag in, grip on, back out."	Watching mag fall; fumbled draw.
Intermediate	Smooth transitions	"Eyes threat → eyes magwell → eyes threat."	Poor grip re-establishment.
Advanced	Speed and awareness	"Topped off and back in the fight."	Premature ejection of magazine; incorrect mag selection.

Magazine Exchange (Tactical Reload with Retention)

Ammunition remains in the firearm, but a reload is necessary while retaining the partially spent magazine.

Two Primary Methods

Method 1: Catch First, Then Insert

1. Bring the pistol to the control zone.
2. Kant inboard to view the magwell.
3. Eject the magazine into the support hand.
4. Secure the magazine in a pocket or pouch.
5. Index a fresh magazine and insert it.
6. Reacquire the grip and reassess.

Method 2: Fresh Mag First (Preferred for Speed)

1. The support hand draws a fresh magazine.
2. Position it at the base of the pistol.

3. Eject the old magazine while retaining it between the index finger and thumb.
4. Insert the new magazine immediately.
5. Secure the retained magazine in a pocket.
6. Reacquire the grip and reassess.

Reloads: Philosophy, Efficiency, and Training Methodology

In tactical and defensive contexts, it is always preferable for the shooter to proactively choose to reload, rather than being forced to do so under duress. Voluntary reloads offer control, timing, and efficiency—factors that are critical in dynamic environments where time and attention are limited.

From this philosophy arises a critical assertion: unless mandated by training protocols or competition rules, an emergency reload resulting from a completely empty magazine should be considered a **shooter-induced malfunction**. Running the gun dry unnecessarily introduces risk and removes control from the shooter.

All reloads—emergency, tactical (with or without retention), administrative, or magazine exchanges—serve a singular purpose: **to add ammunition to the pistol.** How this is done, and under what conditions, determines efficiency, speed, and survivability.

Reload Efficiency: Key Concepts

Reloading speed and consistency improve significantly by adjusting the positioning of the pistol, the magazine, or both. Above all, the shooter must remember: **the most important task is reloading the pistol**. In that moment, nothing takes precedence.

Law enforcement and military training traditionally teaches shooters to bring the pistol into the **high visual working space**—close to the face and within the field of vision. This technique enables the shooter to maintain visual awareness of the threat while managing the reload. The pistol may be observed over the slide, through the trigger guard, or past the magazine well. The core principle remains the same: **see the threat, and see the reload.**

While this method maximizes situational awareness, it often sacrifices speed. The magazine's path from pouch to pistol is rarely straight, and many shooters fumble the insertion when the pathway lacks alignment or consistency.

A key point of contention arises here: **should the shooter look at the magazine well?** In reality, glancing at the magwell to ensure proper alignment and insertion is often not only acceptable—it's essential. Precision matters. The shooter should glance, seat the magazine firmly, and return their eyes to the threat.

Optimizing the Reload Pathway

To streamline the reload, many instructors teach a slight cant of the pistol. This maintains the pistol in the working space while angling the magazine well toward the magazine pouch, creating a more direct, linear path. Shooters may fix their gaze on a specific point on the grip—some focus on the far interior of the magazine well, others on the edge of the grip itself.

The objective is to **build a direct, repeatable pathway** from the magazine pouch to the magazine well, keeping the pistol in the high workspace while maximizing efficiency.

Alternative Methods: Sport vs. Tactical Priorities

Some faster reload methods, while common in competition shooting, are less accepted in tactical environments. One method brings the pistol to the magazine rather than the other way around. When the support hand retrieves the magazine, the natural bend of the elbow places the magazine in a fixed position. The shooter then moves the pistol quickly to the magazine, allowing the magwell to "swallow" it efficiently. While the eyes may or may not leave the threat, the pistol must return to the line of sight afterward.

Another variation, popular among competitive shooters, moves the pistol entirely downward toward the magazine pouch. While this can increase speed with aggressive movement, it sacrifices pistol positioning and requires a longer recovery to presentation.

In tactical training, we often ask, **"How much time do you have for a reload?"** The answer: **the rest of your life.** In a gunfight, failing to reload effectively can be fatal. An unloaded pistol is nothing more than a paperweight.

Micro-Drills: Isolating Skill Components

Every reload can be broken into component parts and trained individually in dry fire. A highly effective micro-drill is the **Burkett Reload**, which isolates the motion of bringing the magazine to the pistol without seating it fully. It focuses on the accuracy and alignment of the initial magazine insertion—**"just the tip."**

Begin this drill with the pistol already in the working position, canted slightly to receive the magazine. Quickly retrieve the magazine with the support hand, ensuring proper finger placement. Drive the magazine directly to the pistol and stop just short of seating. This variation can be practiced with the slide forward, allowing high-volume repetitions.

Drill Progression Breakdown

1. **Magazine Snatch Drill**
   Begin by simply forming a proper grip and rapidly removing the magazine from the pouch. The goal is to clear the pouch with speed and consistency.
2. **Partial Insertion Drill**
   Start with the magazine tip already in the magwell. Practice the firm seating motion repeatedly. With the slide forward, this allows for rapid, consistent reps.

3. **Full Burkett Reload**
   Combine the two above: retrieve the magazine and drive it to the pistol, stopping short of full seating.
4. **Complete Reload (Slide Forward)**
   Begin with the pistol aimed in. Retrieve the magazine, move the pistol into the workspace, and insert and seat the magazine. Reestablish the grip and return to presentation.
5. **Slide-Lock Reload**
   Repeat the full reload with the slide locked to the rear. After seating the magazine, manipulate the slide stop/release or use your chosen technique (scissors or power stroke) to chamber a round. Complete the grip and presentation.
6. **Integrated Reload**
   Perform a full emergency reload: drop the empty magazine as the support hand moves to retrieve the fresh magazine. Insert, seat, chamber, and present.

Slide Manipulation Methods

There are several acceptable methods to release the slide following a reload:

- **Slide Stop**
- **Slide Release**
- **Scissors Technique**
- **Power Stroke**

Each method has advantages and drawbacks, and should be selected based on context, training, and individual capability.

Slide Release Techniques After a Reload

1. Slide Stop

- **Description:** Press the slide stop lever using your **strong-hand thumb** after inserting a fresh magazine.
- **Pros:** Fast, efficient, minimal movement.
- **Cons:** May be difficult under stress or with gloves; slide stop size varies by pistol.

2. Slide Release

- **Description:** Press the slide stop lever using your **support-hand thumb** immediately after seating the magazine.
- **Pros:** Maintains strong-hand grip integrity.
- **Cons:** Requires fine motor skills; some pistols have smaller or stiffer levers.

3. Scissors Technique

- **Description:** Use the **support hand to pinch** the rear of the slide and slide stop lever simultaneously—like a "scissor"—to drop the slide.
- **Pros:** Gross motor movement; works with gloves.
- **Cons:** Slower; requires hand repositioning.

4. Power Stroke

- **Description:** Grasp the rear of the slide with the support hand, pull fully to the rear, then release to allow the slide to chamber a round.
- **Pros:** Gross motor friendly; universal across all pistols.
- **Cons:** Slightly slower; requires strong grip and clear workspace.

Key Considerations

- Train **all four** to build adaptability.
- Choose based on **context**, **stress level**, and **equipment**.
- Ensure consistency in grip and **return to presentation** immediately after.

Final Thoughts

Reloading is more than a mechanical process—it is a critical skill that must be executed under stress, in motion, and without hesitation. Mastery comes from repetition and from isolating the components of the reload into manageable, trainable elements. The more refined and deliberate each micro-skill becomes, the more subconscious and fluid the entire reload will be.

In combat or defense, when lives are on the line, **reloads are not just important—they are life-preserving.**

The Burkett Reload: A Precision Micro-Drill for Speed and Efficiency

Overview

The **Burkett Reload**, named after competitive shooter **Matt Burkett**, is a specialized dry fire and live fire **micro-drill** designed to improve the **speed, efficiency, and accuracy** of pistol reloads. Unlike a full reload drill, the Burkett Reload isolates a specific portion of the reload process: **driving the magazine into the magazine well**, with the pistol held in the high working space.

Burkett Reload

Micro Drill -
speed,efficiency, and accuracy

Slide Foreward- Multiple Repetitions

This micro-drill develops:

- Consistent hand positioning
- Efficient mag pouch access
- A direct pathway from pouch to magwell
- Visual indexing and insertion precision

Purpose

The Burkett Reload focuses on **refining the reload process by breaking it into manageable components**. By isolating the "mag insertion" segment, shooters can:

- Develop muscle memory for rapid and precise reloads

- Identify and correct inefficient movements
- Reduce fumbles and bobbles during high-stress manipulations
- Build subconscious competence for use in defensive and tactical settings

Key Concepts

- **High Working Space**: The pistol remains close to the face, within the shooter's visual field.
- **Efficient Pathway**: The magazine follows a straight, repeatable line from pouch to magwell.
- **Visual Confirmation**: The shooter glances at a fixed visual index point—typically the magwell opening or the grip surface—to guide insertion.
- **Micro-Repetition**: The focus is not on speed initially but on perfect, repeatable motion.

Execution: Dry Fire Setup

Step-by-step Burkett Reload (Slide Forward Variant):

1. **Pistol Positioning**:
    - Hold the pistol in the **dominant hand** in the high ready position.
    - Slightly **cant the pistol** toward the magazine pouch so the magwell points at the incoming magazine.
2. **Support Hand Magazine Snatch**:
    - The support hand reaches down and **grips the magazine** in the pouch using correct finger placement (index finger along the front edge or bullet tip, depending on shooter preference).

3. **Magazine Movement**:
   - Draw the magazine upward and **drive it directly to the magwell** in a linear path.
   - **Stop just before full seating**—the magazine should be aligned and partially inserted (e.g., "just the tip").
4. **Pause and Reset**:
   - Stop, verify alignment, and **reset** by returning the magazine to the pouch or beginning the next repetition.

Progression: From Micro to Full Reload

Once the micro-drill becomes consistent, **build on it progressively**:

1. **Partial Insertions**:
   - Practice seating the magazine from the "just the tip" position.
   - Ensure a firm click into place, verifying consistent seating pressure.
2. **Mag Pouch to Full Insertion**:
   - Combine the magazine snatch with full insertion in one smooth motion.
3. **Pistol in High Ready**:
   - Start with the pistol pointed downrange or canted in the workspace. Retrieve the magazine and insert it as before.
4. **Slide Locked to Rear**:
   - Perform the full reload with the slide locked open.
   - After seating the mag, use the chosen method (slide stop, power stroke, etc.) to release the slide and return to presentation.

◆ Live Fire Integration

In live fire, once the mechanical precision has been drilled:

- Practice the Burkett Reload **with live rounds**, beginning with the pistol slide forward.
- Use **single-round magazines** or **dummy rounds** to simulate reload necessity.
- Emphasize returning to target focus and trigger control **immediately after reload**.

Common Errors to Address

- **Fumbling insertion**: Often due to an indirect path or poor visual indexing.
- **Magazine misses or bobbles**: Caused by poor canting or misaligned grip.
- **Failure to fully seat**: Ensure forceful insertion, especially under stress.
- **Inconsistent hand movement**: Keep the draw path from pouch to magwell direct and repeatable.

Instructional Tips

- Use a shot timer or metronome for paced practice.
- Film drills from multiple angles to evaluate hand movement.
- Pair with the **"reload on command"** dry fire format to simulate decision-based reps.
- Use **dummy mags or weighted practice mags** for more realistic reps

Summary

The **Burkett Reload** is a high-yield, focused training tool that can significantly enhance reload speed and reliability when practiced regularly. By **isolating the reload into subcomponents**, shooters gain greater control over the mechanics, which translates into improved performance under pressure.

"Speed is fine. Precision is final." – The Burkett Reload sharpens both.

Instructor Module: Loading, Press Check, and Unloading Procedures

Core Principle

All firearm handling must occur within the control zone—the area directly in front of the shooter's chest and chin. This approach reinforces alignment among the eyes, firearm, and threat, promoting safe and efficient manipulations even under stress.

Layered Skill Progression

Layer	Focus	Goal	Instructor Note
Beginner	Safety, familiarity, repetition	Develop clean procedural habits	Prioritize clarity and coach each repetition
Intermediate	Efficiency, pressure-tested handling	Improve speed without sacrificing control	Introduce dynamic drills (e.g., timed repetitions)
Advanced	Economy of motion, context adaptation	Perform consistently under simulated stress	Integrate into scenario-based training
Instructor	Diagnose errors, correct technique	Build skills in others, ensure doctrinal consistency	Use demonstration, error induction, and layered feedback

Checklist Framework

Loading (Slide Forward / Slide Locked)

Control Zone Position (Working Area)

- Draw the firearm and position it in the chest-level workspace.
- Orient the muzzle in a safe direction (e.g., toward the range or a downed threat).
- Keep the finger off the trigger, indexed in a high register.

Magazine Indexing and Insertion

- Use the support hand to retrieve the magazine via an indexing method.
- Insert the magazine with deliberate pressure, avoiding aggression.
- Adhere to the Soft Hands Principle: Refrain from slapping the magazine to prevent premature slide release.

Chambering a Round

Power Stroke / Overhand Slide Manipulation Method

Purpose

The Power Stroke, also known as the Overhand Method, is a robust and reliable technique for manipulating the slide of a semi-automatic pistol. It facilitates chambering a round, conducting a press check, clearing malfunctions, or performing slide-lock reloads.

Mechanics of the Power Stroke

This method maximizes leverage and mechanical advantage, ensuring reliability under stress, adverse conditions, or diminished fine motor skills.

Step-by-Step Breakdown

1. **Position the Firearm**:
    - Bring the pistol into the control zone (chest-height workspace in front of the face).
    - Orient the pistol inboard (tilted slightly inward toward the body) or vertically upright (slide facing upward).
2. **Establish Grip**:
    - Strong hand: Maintain the firing grip.
    - Support hand: Reach over the top of the slide with the entire palm—fingers angled forward, palm covering the rear serrations.
    - Grip pressure: Firmly wrap fingers over the top and around the sides, akin to grasping a hammer or heavy tool.
3. **Manipulate the Slide**:
    - Pull the slide straight to the rear with the support hand (avoid upward or diagonal motion).
    - Simultaneously push forward with the strong hand to create push-pull tension for enhanced reliability and control.
    - Release the slide cleanly once it reaches full rearward travel—do not ride it forward.
4. **Recovery**:
    - As the slide drives forward and chambers the round, immediately re-establish a two-handed grip.
    - Extend the pistol and acquire a fresh sight picture.

- Recover to Position 3 (high ready) or compressed ready, with the finger off the trigger.

Why the Power Stroke Is Preferred

Purpose

The Power Stroke, also known as the Overhand Method, is a robust and reliable technique for manipulating the slide of a semi-automatic pistol. It facilitates chambering a round, conducting a press check, clearing malfunctions, or performing slide-lock reloads.

Mechanics of the Power Stroke

This method maximizes leverage and mechanical advantage, ensuring reliability under stress, adverse conditions, or diminished fine motor skills.

Step-by-Step Breakdown

1. **Position the Firearm**:
   - Bring the pistol into the control zone (chest-height workspace in front of the face).
   - Orient the pistol inboard (tilted slightly inward toward the body) or vertically upright (slide facing upward).
2. **Establish Grip**:
   - Strong hand: Maintain the firing grip.
   - Support hand: Reach over the top of the slide with the entire palm—fingers angled forward, palm covering the rear serrations.
   - Grip pressure: Firmly wrap fingers over the top and around the sides, akin to grasping a hammer or heavy tool.

3. **Manipulate the Slide**:
    - Pull the slide straight to the rear with the support hand (avoid upward or diagonal motion).
    - Simultaneously push forward with the strong hand to create push-pull tension for enhanced reliability and control.
    - Release the slide cleanly once it reaches full rearward travel—do not ride it forward.
4. **Recovery**:
    - As the slide drives forward and chambers the round, immediately re-establish a two-handed grip.
    - Extend the pistol and acquire a fresh sight picture.
    - Recover to Position 3 (high ready) or compressed ready, with the finger off the trigger.

Why the Power Stroke Is Preferred

Factor	Benefit
Gross motor skills	Requires less dexterity under stress (sympathetic nervous system-dominant)
Mechanical leverage	Engages large muscle groups in the back and shoulders
Versatility	Effective for clearing malfunctions, press checks, and slide-lock reloads
Symmetry	Easier to teach and perform with either hand or in off-hand scenarios
Tactile consistency	Ideal for gloved hands or wet, bloody, or gritty conditions

Factor	Benefit
Factor	Benefit
Gross motor skills	Requires less dexterity under stress (sympathetic nervous system-dominant)
Mechanical leverage	Engages large muscle groups in the back and shoulders
Versatility	Effective for clearing malfunctions, press checks, and slide-lock reloads
Symmetry	Easier to teach and perform with either hand or in off-hand scenarios
Tactile consistency	Ideal for gloved hands or wet, bloody, or gritty conditions

Slingshot Method (Inboard Rotation) – Detailed Expansion

Purpose

The Slingshot Method is a fundamental technique for chambering a round or clearing malfunctions by pulling the slide fully to the rear and releasing it under spring tension. It is simple, effective, and relies on gross motor skills.

Mechanics of the Slingshot Method

This method enhances tactile feedback, ensures consistent chambering, and minimizes the need for fine motor skills—making it ideal under stress.

Step-by-Step Breakdown

1. **Bring the Firearm to the Control Zone**

- Draw or return the pistol to the working area (chest-high, in front of the face).

- Rotate the firearm slightly inboard (about 30–45 degrees inward) so the ejection port faces outward and the top of the slide is exposed to the support hand.

2. Grip the Slide:

- Strong hand: Maintain the firing grip, finger off the trigger.
- Support hand: Reach up and grasp the rear of the slide from both sides using the thumb and fingers, like pinching the back of a slingshot.
- Grip placement: Use the rear serrations or traction area—avoid grabbing over the top of the ejection port.
- Engage all fingers for control, emphasizing the thumb and index/middle fingers for strength.

3. Rack the Slide:

- Push forward with the strong hand while pulling back firmly with the support hand.
- This simultaneous motion generates the push-pull tension required for a full slide cycle.
- Release the slide cleanly at full rearward travel—do not ride it forward.
- Allow the recoil spring to chamber the round under full tension.

4. Post-Action Grip Recovery:

- Immediately re-establish a two-handed grip.
- Extend the pistol.
- Acquire a fresh sight picture or return to Position 3 (close-quarters ready), depending on context.

Technical Benefits of the Slingshot Method

Attribute	Value
Gross motor based	Easy to retain under stress
No reliance on slide stop	Ideal if motor skills deteriorate or the slide stop malfunctions
Ambidextrous	Works for left- or right-handed shooters without hardware dependence
Consistent slide velocity	Enhances reliability for chambering a round
Clean mechanical operation	No interference with internal parts or ejection port

Slide Release Method (Slide Locked Only)

(Also known as: Slide Lock Lever, Slide Stop, Slide Catch)

Purpose
The Slide Release Method chambers a round from slide lock by depressing the slide stop lever, allowing the slide to drive forward under full spring tension. It is fast and efficient but demands greater dexterity, hand strength, and platform familiarity.

Mechanics of the Slide Release Method
Slide release is the quickest way to restore functionality after slide lock—if executed correctly, deliberately, and under control.

Step-by-Step Breakdown

1. **Position the Firearm in the Working Area**:

- Bring the pistol into the control zone (chest-level, in front of the face).
- Maintain alignment among eyes, muzzle, and threat.

2. **Confirm Slide Locked to the Rear**:

- Verify the slide is held open, typically after emptying the magazine or manual locking during administrative handling.

3. **Insert Magazine**:

- Support hand indexes and inserts a fresh magazine firmly into the mag well.
- Avoid over-slamming the magazine, which may cause premature slide drop (inconsistent across platforms and users).

4. **Depress the Slide Release Lever**:

- • Use the strong-hand thumb to press down firmly on the slide release lever.
- Alternatively, use the support-hand thumb (common with Glock-style pistols or shorter thumbs) immediately after seating the magazine.
- The slide will advance, chambering a round.

5. **Grip and Recover**:

- Establish a proper two-handed grip.
- Extend the pistol and acquire a fresh sight picture.
- Keep the finger off the trigger until the decision to fire is made.

Technical Notes

Factor	Explanation
Spring tension	Modern pistols feature stiff recoil springs—requires strong, deliberate thumb pressure
Platform-specific	Lever size, position, and mechanical advantage vary (e.g., Glock, SIG, Smith & Wesson)
Ambidexterity	Many levers are non-ambidextrous—left-handed shooters may encounter challenges
Fine vs. gross motor	A fine motor action, less reliable under stress compared to overhand or slingshot methods

Post-Load Actions

- Reacquire a solid two-handed grip.
- Extend the firearm and obtain a sight picture.
- Keep the finger indexed.
- Recover to Position 3 or close-quarters ready.

Neurological Imprinting Concept

1. Repetition within the same spatial context accelerates recall under stress.
2. Maintaining eye-muzzle-threat alignment keeps the shooter head-up and aware of threats.

Press Check (Verifying a Chambered Round)

Grip and Control

- Maintain the strong-hand grip; position the thumb high on the tang or slide.
- Use the support hand to manipulate the slide—index and middle fingers in front of the rear sight.
- Pull the slide just enough to observe the casing or feel it with the pinky (in low-light conditions).

Confirm Battery

- Allow the slide to return forward under tension.
- Tap the rear of the slide to verify full battery.
- Never rely solely on loaded chamber indicators.

Post-Check Actions

- De-cock if using a double-action/single-action pistol (where applicable).
- Return to the holster only after a full control check.

Unloading Procedure

- Draw the firearm to the control zone.
- Point the muzzle downrange or in a safe direction.
- Keep the finger off the trigger.

Magazine Removal

- Remove the magazine and retain it.

Clear the Chamber

- Rack the slide three times—observe the ejection of any round.
- Lock the slide to the rear.
- Visually and physically inspect the chamber and mag well.
- Check it twice: Look away and re-confirm (Check It Twice principle).

Final Actions

- Release the slide (if transitioning to dry-fire training).
- De-cock (if applicable).
- Holster safely, performing a thumb check to verify battery or de-cocked status.

Instructor Tips for Delivery

Phase	Cue Words	Corrections
Loading	"Two hands in motion," "Soft hands," "Control zone"	Correct over-forceful magazine insertions or failure to use slingshot
Press Check	"Verify visually or by touch," "Battery check"	Address over-racking or failure to verify slide closure
Unloading	"CIT: Check It Twice"	Reinforce visual and tactile confirmation

Weapons Malfunction Clearance: Type 1 & Type 2

"Stoppages are fought and cleared from the chest, not the waist. All manipulations occur in the control zone—eye, muzzle, threat."

INSTRUCTOR OVERVIEW: Understanding Stoppages

- A **malfunction** or **stoppage** is an unintended interruption in the pistol's cycle of operation.
- All shooters must be able to:
    1. **Identify** what the weapon is doing (or not doing),
    2. **Diagnose** the likely cause based on visual and tactile feedback,
    3. **Apply the correct corrective action** in the fewest steps necessary.

TYPE 1 MALFUNCTION

AKA: ***Failure to Fire / Click No Bang***

Symptoms:

- "Dead trigger" — you press the trigger, and nothing happens
- Slide is in **battery** (fully forward)
- No felt recoil
- Possible failure to seat magazine, bad primer, or misfeed

CLEARING A TYPE 1 MALFUNCTION: IMMEDIATE ACTION DRILL

"Tap – Rack – Reassess"

Step-by-Step Process

1. **Stoppage Stimulus Detected**
    - Pistol is in the aimed-in position
    - Trigger pressed → **No bang**

- Shooter senses a “dead trigger” (no resistance or audible reset)
- Shooter **removes finger from trigger**

2. **Weapon Diagnosis**
    - Shooter **breaks the wrist up** (elbows remain in)
    - Looks at the ejection port without coming off target
    - Slide appears fully forward → Type 1 likely
3. **Immediate Action**
    - **TAP**
        - Strike the base of the magazine with support hand palm to ensure its fully seated
        - Use enough pressure to lock it in but not enough to damage feed lips
    - **RACK**
        - Use slingshot or power stroke method to rack the slide
        - Ejects any bad round and loads a new one
    - **REASSESS**
        - Reacquire grip and push back out
        - Obtain sight picture and evaluate the threat condition

Instructor Teaching Notes: Type 1

Area	Insight
Control zone	Ensure manipulations happen chest-high for visibility and consistency
Trigger discipline	Reinforce immediate trigger finger removal

Area	Insight
Pressure	Too little tap may not seat mag; too hard may misalign feed lips
Corrections	Don't allow students to tilt gun too far or sweep others while racking
Cue Words	"Tap it, rack it, send it." or "Fix it like you mean it."

Drills for Type 1 Training

Drill	Purpose
Induced Type 1 (dummy round)	Insert inert round in mag to simulate failure to fire
Dry Fire Tap-Rack	Repetition of proper hand movement
1-Round + Dummy Reps	Builds recognition of click/no bang reaction

AKA: ***Failure to Eject / "Stovepipe" / Slide Out of Battery***

Symptoms:

- Slide is slightly out of battery (not fully forward)
- Brass visible in ejection port, often sticking out at an angle
- "Soft click" or mushy trigger
- Caused by limp-wristing, dirty extractor, or faulty ejection

CLEARING A TYPE 2 MALFUNCTION: AGGRESSIVE RACKING

"Don't pick the brass out—violence of action clears it faster."

Step-by-Step Process

1. **Stoppage Stimulus Detected**
    - Dead trigger or weak trigger pull
    - Pistol in the aimed-in position
    - Shooter removes finger from trigger
2. **Weapon Diagnosis**
    - Shooter breaks the wrist up
    - **Brass is visibly stuck in the ejection port**
    - Slide is visibly **out of battery**
    - Shooter **identifies a Type 2 malfunction**
3. **Immediate Action**
    - **Support hand performs aggressive rack** using:
        - **Overhand power stroke**
        - OR **slingshot method**
    - Do not try to pick the brass out; force it out via full slide cycle
    - **Do not induce double-feed** by short-stroking
4. **Reassess and Fire**
    - Rebuild grip
    - Push back out
    - Acquire sight picture
    - Decide to re-engage threat or scan

Instructor Teaching Notes: Type 2

Area	Insight
Action = Aggression	Clearing must be **fast and violent**, not finessed

Area	Insight
Control zone = visibility	Keep manipulations at chest level for rapid feedback
Cue Words	"See brass? Rack fast." or "Don't baby the slide—send it flying."
Training Aid	Use spent brass to simulate stovepipe manually for reps
Common Mistakes	Picking brass, riding the slide, weak rack, or pressing trigger before resolving issue

DIFFERENTIATING TYPE 1 VS TYPE 2 – INSTRUCTOR GUIDE

Feature	Type 1	Type 2
Slide position	Fully in battery	Slightly out of battery
Brass visible	No	Yes – in ejection port
Trigger feel	Dead trigger	Soft or no reset
Correction	Tap-Rack-Reassess	Immediate aggressive rack
Primary cause	Mag not seated, bad primer	Failure to eject, limp wristing

Three Consistencies of Pistol Operation

When working with a pistol, consistency is king. In moments of stress—whether in training, competition, or a real defensive encounter—the shooter will not rise to the occasion but will default to the level of ingrained habit. For this reason, there are three operational actions that must remain absolutely consistent:

1. Operating the Slide (Loading, Malfunctions, Manipulations)

The slide is the heart of the pistol's cycling system. Any interaction with it—whether chambering a round, clearing a malfunction, or performing administrative tasks—should be done the same way, every time.

- **Loading the Pistol:** Always use a firm, overhand grip on the rear of the slide, pulling it fully to the rear and releasing it to allow maximum spring tension to chamber a round. Avoid riding the slide forward or "slingshotting" inconsistently, which can induce failures to feed.
- **Clearing Malfunctions:** Whether a stovepipe, double feed, or out-of-battery issue, the shooter should employ a uniform clearing method. For example, a tap-rack procedure (tap the magazine, rack the slide aggressively) must be performed identically regardless of the scenario. Consistency reduces decision-making time and ensures immediate corrective action.
- **Consistency Benefit:** By operating the slide the same way in every context, the shooter builds automaticity. When stress, fatigue, or injury are factors, there is no hesitation or wasted motion—just one ingrained, reliable method.

2. Presentation from the Draw (Draw-stroke, Reloads, Malfunctions)

The draw and presentation to the target form the backbone of pistol employment. This movement must remain identical whether drawing from concealment, performing a reload, or recovering from a malfunction.

- **Draw-stroke Mechanics:** A consistent four-step draw—establishing a master grip, clearing the holster, orienting the pistol toward the target line, and extending into the shooting position—ensures smoothness and efficiency.
- **Reloads:** The pistol always returns to the same "workspace" (usually chest-height, close to the shooter's line of sight) during reloads. This ensures the shooter maintains situational awareness and doesn't "hunt" for the magazine well at inconsistent angles.
- **Malfunction Clearance:** The pistol should also return to this same workspace for malfunction procedures. This standardization makes it so whether you are reloading, conducting a tap-rack, or assessing a stoppage, your eyes, hands, and gun always move to the same place.
- **Consistency Benefit:** By anchoring all critical actions to the same presentation point, the shooter eliminates hesitation, improves efficiency, and increases the likelihood of success under duress.

3. Magazine Manipulation (Loading, Unloading, Malfunctions)

The way the shooter handles magazines is just as important as the way the pistol itself is manipulated. Every interaction with a magazine must be identical.

- **Loading the Magazine into the Pistol:** Always seat the magazine with a firm upward push, followed by a slight tug to ensure it is locked in place. This prevents failures to feed due to incomplete seating.
- **Unloading the Magazine:** Whether administratively or tactically, the release of a magazine should always be done the same way. The support hand should move immediately to retrieve or stow a fresh magazine when appropriate, eliminating guesswork.

- **Clearing Malfunctions:** In cases such as double feeds, the magazine must be stripped out decisively and consistently before reloading. Training to perform this movement the same way every time reduces wasted effort.
- **Consistency Benefit:** Proper magazine handling keeps the pistol fed and ready. More importantly, a shooter who always treats the magazine the same way will not fumble during a critical reload or malfunction clearance.

Conclusion

Consistency in these three operational areas—slide manipulation, draw/presentation, and magazine handling—builds reliability and confidence. When stress levels rise and fine motor skills deteriorate, the body will revert to trained patterns. If those patterns are inconsistent, failures and delays are likely. But if they are standardized and reinforced, the shooter will perform fluidly and effectively.

This framework provides the foundation for pistol proficiency. All other skills—marksmanship, movement, and tactics—depend on these core consistencies being executed without hesitation or error.

Would you like me to also **break this into a layered version** (beginner, intermediate, advanced, instructor) so you can use it for training modules, or keep it as a single professional-level publication piece?

Pistol Engagement Strategies

In my experience, I have found that shooters determine pistol engagement strategies deciding when and how to initiate lethal kinetic encounters based on their accumulated experiences from training sessions and real-world engagements. We systematically break down these strategies by integrating diverse shooting methods, such as single shots for precision targeting, controlled pairs for balanced follow-up accuracy, and hammer pairs for rapid threat neutralization, while aligning them with attack/control engagement models that emphasize offensive dominance or defensive restraint. We further weigh reactive strategies, which respond to immediate threats, against predictive ones that anticipate adversary actions, all while applying three levels of visual confirmation: Confirmation 1 for initial target acquisition, Confirmation 2 for threat validation, and Confirmation 3 for post-engagement assessment. This comprehensive framework serves instructional purposes, fostering progressive skill development that guides novices through foundational techniques, intermediates toward refined decision-making, and advanced practitioners to expert-level adaptability in high-stakes scenarios.

This chapter provides a systematic breakdown of pistol engagement strategies, integrating various shooting methods (such as single shots, controlled pairs, and hammer pairs) with attack/control engagement models, reactive versus predictive strategies, and the three levels of visual confirmation (Confirmation 1, 2, and 3). This framework is designed for instructional use and supports progressive skill development across novice, intermediate, and advanced shooter levels.

Core Engagement Concepts

Foundational Concepts

Concept	Definition
Attack Method	A proactive, aggressive shooting approach designed to seize the initiative and drive performance. It prioritizes speed, movement, and dominance over the threat.

Concept	Definition
Control Method	A reactive, deliberate approach that emphasizes accountability, precision, and target discrimination to ensure accurate and justified shots.
Predictive Engagement	The shooter predetermines the firing moment based on confidence in sight acquisition and an acceptable hit zone, firing as the sights "flash" into alignment without full settling.
Reactive Engagement	The shooter delays firing until visual confirmation is achieved, validating sight alignment both visually and cognitively before committing to the shot.

Visual Confirmation Levels

Visual confirmation levels represent escalating degrees of sight verification, balancing speed and precision based on the tactical context.

Confirmation Level	Visual Reference	Purpose	Tempo	Accuracy Demanded
Confirmation 1	Flash sight picture or red dot sight (RDS) over target	Speed over Precision	Fastest	High center mass hit zone
Confirmation 2	Front sight or dot briefly settles	Balance of Speed & Accuracy	Moderate	A-zone or upper thoracic cavity
Confirmation 3	Full sight alignment or stopped red dot	Precision over Speed	Slowest	Headshots, partial exposures, or distant targets

Cross-Matrix: Matching Engagement Strategy with Visual Confirmation

This matrix integrates engagement strategies with visual confirmation levels, providing a quick reference for selecting the appropriate method.

Strategy	Attack/Control	Method	Visual Confirmation	Round Type	Typical Use
Hammer Pairs	Attack	Predictive	Confirmation 1	2 fast shots, 1 sight picture	Close threat, fast entry
Controlled Pairs	Control	Reactive	Confirmation 2 or 3	2 shots, 2 sight pictures	Accountability, known distance
Single Shot	Control	Reactive	Confirmation 3	1 round	Headshot, hostage, partial target
Multi-Round Engagements	Attack → Control	Predictive → Reactive	Confirmation 1 → 2 → 3	Burst, adaptive cadence	Transitioning targets, active threat
Failure Drill (2+1)	Attack → Control	Predictive → Reactive	Body: Confirmation 1 or 2; Head: 3	2 hammers + 1 precision shot	Escalation, armor, close quarters (CQB)

Engagement Types and Their Tactical Contexts

Engagement Type	Round Count	Description	Best Used With	Visual Confirmation	Attack/Control	Method (Predictive/Reactive)
Single Shot	1	Deliberate,single round fired.	Known precision threats, target ID required	Confirmation 3 or 2	Control	Reactive
Controlled Pair	2	Two deliberate shots with two sight pictures.	Threats requiring accountability (e.g., law enforcement or concealed carry)	Confirmation 2 to 3	Control	Predictive or Reactive
Hammer Pair	2	Two rapid shots, one sight picture, recoil drives second shot.	Close threat, time-critical	Confirmation 1	Attack	Predictive
Multi-Round Strings (Bursts)	3–5+	Volume fire with recoil mitigation, sight tracking optional.	CQB, high-threat targets, rapid neutralization	Confirmation 1, transitioning to 2	Attack	Predictive
Failure Drill / Failure-to-Stop	2 to body + 1 to head	Combines hammer or controlled pair + precision shot.	Body shot ineffective or armored threat	Body: Confirmation 1 or 2; Head: 3	Attack → Control	Predictive or Reactive

Integration with Shooter Decision-Making

Reactive Shooting Flow (e.g., Ambushed or Surprised Scenarios)

1. **Recognition**: Identify the threat and present the gun while moving off the line of attack ("Get off the X").
2. **Initial Engagement**: Employ a flash sight picture (Confirmation 1).
3. **Strategy Selection**: Use hammer pairs or multi-round bursts.
4. **Visual Transition**: If the threat persists, refine to Confirmation 2 or 3.
5. **Method Shift**: Transition from Attack to Control based on target feedback.

Reactive Shooting Definition: Firing only after visual confirmation occurs, reacting to the alignment of sights or dot with the intended hit zone. This is accuracy-driven and used when precision is paramount or the shooter's subconscious requires validation.

Predictive Engagement Flow (e.g., Clearing a Room or Approaching a Known Threat)

1. **Anticipation**: Prepare for contact.
2. **Platform Establishment**: Achieve a stable stance with visual readiness.
3. **Engagement**: Use controlled pairs or single shots (Confirmation 2 or 3).
4. **Method Maintenance**: Stay in Control, shifting to Attack if sudden aggression is detected.

Predictive Shooting Definition: Firing based on the prediction of acceptable sight alignment. This is speed-driven and applied when target difficulty is low and outcomes are foreseeable (e.g., an open A-zone at close range).

Shooter Decision-Making with Reactive/Predictive Model

When to Shoot Predictively

- The target is close, large, and does not require precise sights.
- The layout has been processed, ensuring hits will land acceptably (e.g., 7-yard A-zone).
- The gun is in motion, firing as it enters the zone rather than when stopped.

Example: Engaging a full torso at 5 yards during a fast draw. Employ a hammer pair with Confirmation 1.

When to Shoot Reactively

- The target is small, distant, or partially obscured.
- Uncertainty exists about the hit without visual confirmation of sight settling.
- Sights dictate the timing, overriding predictive cadence.

Example: Executing a headshot at 15 yards. Use a single shot or controlled pair with Confirmation 3.

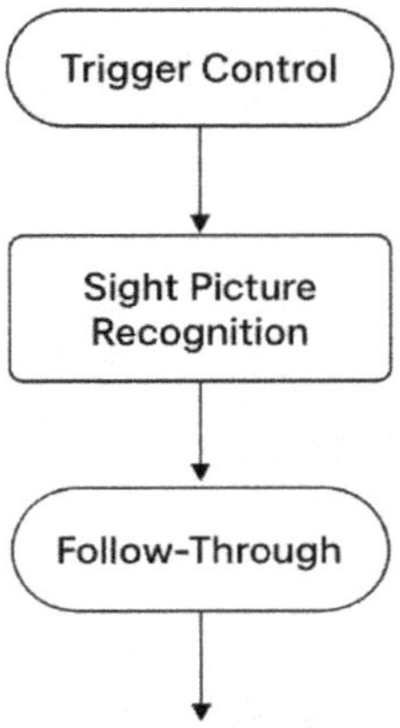

Combining Methods into Dynamic Engagements: Adaptive Shooting Loop

This loop reflects real-world gunfights or competitive stages.

1. **Initial Contact**: Threat appears suddenly → Predictive shots with Confirmation 1 or 2.
2. **Assessment**: Threat remains active or requires correction → Shift to Reactive shooting, escalating to Confirmation 3 if needed.
3. **Finish or Transition**: For multiple threats, revert to Predictive as appropriate → Rapid target acquisition.

Layered Shooter Development Model

Beginner Level

- **Focus**: Trigger control, sight picture recognition, and follow-through.

Drills:

    - Single shot with Confirmation 3.
    - Controlled pair with full recovery.
- **Concepts Introduced**: Control method, basic predictive engagements.

Intermediate Level

- **Focus**: Engagement speed, recoil management, and transitions between confirmation levels.
- **Drills**:
    - Controlled pairs versus hammer pairs (targets at 3–7 yards).
    - Movement and engagement (draw to hammer).
- **Concepts Introduced**: Attack versus Control methods, flash sight picture, reactive engagement flow.

Advanced Level

- **Focus**: Real-time transitions between confirmation levels, adapting fire based on target feedback.
- **Drills**:
    - Reactive target engagement (e.g., turning paper targets or visual signals).
    - Multiple target transitions using varied engagement types.
    - Failure-to-stop drills incorporating movement and cover.
- **Concepts Introduced**: Rapid visual processing, recoil-timed shooting, initiative-based tactics.

Instructor Considerations

- Teach the rationale for each method: balancing speed versus control, and accountability versus decisiveness.

- Reinforce cue recognition: Identify when a target demands precision over speed.
- Provide immediate feedback using shot timers and hit zone analysis.
- Employ progressive drills:
  - 1R1 (draw, fire one, reload, fire one).
  - Hammer versus controlled pair identification drill (based on distance).
  - Multiple threat drills with varying confirmation levels.

Advanced Shooter Layer

Skill	Objective	Drills	Key Teaching Point
Predictive Cadence	Fire as sights flash into zone	Bill Drill, 1-5-1 Drill	Trust timing; avoid overconfirmation

Skill	Objective	Drills	Key Teaching Point
Reactive Discipline	Fire only when sights are confirmed	Dot Torture, Headbox shots	Patience under pressure
Predictive→Reactive Switch	Fire rapidly, then slow for precision	Failure drill, Split-target sizes	Mindset shift mid-engagement
Confirmation Mapping	Match level to target	"Confirmation Ladder" (5–15 yds)	Visual judgment under stress

Instructor Tips

- Have students verbalize "Predictive" or "Reactive" before drills.
- Designate confirmation zones on targets:
  - Large center mass = Confirmation 1.
  - A-zone = Confirmation 2.
  - Head/small box = Confirmation 3.
- Begin drills at predictive distances (5–7 yards), then increase range or reduce target size to prompt reactive shifts.
- Use instructional language:
- Send it when the sights flash in" → Predictive.
- "Wait for confirmation" → Reactive.

Emphasize: "Let the sight picture dictate the method."

Summary Table: Method Matrix

Distance	Target Size	Visual Confirmation	Engagement Type	Predictive or Reactive
< 5 yds	Large (C-zone)	1	Hammers / Bursts	Predictive
5–10 yds	A-zone	2	Controlled Pairs	Predictive or Reactive
> 10 yds	Head / Small zone	3	Single Shot / Failure Drill	Reactive

Instructors must diligently study and master this pistol engagement framework to effectively teach it, as their expertise directly shapes shooters' ability to make life-or-death decisions in lethal encounters. By immersing themselves in the accumulated insights from training and real-world scenarios, instructors empower students to integrate shooting methods like single shots, controlled pairs, and hammer pairs with attack/control models, reactive and predictive strategies, and the three levels of visual confirmation. This commitment not only accelerates progressive skill development—from novices building basics to advanced shooters achieving seamless adaptability—but also ensures that future generations of practitioners respond with precision, confidence, and ethical restraint in the chaos of high-stakes confrontations.

Concept Overview: "Getting Off the X"

Definition:

"Getting off the X" refers to immediately moving off the attack line (the "X") to avoid being a static target during a threat or ambush. The "X" symbolizes your last known position—where incoming rounds or attacks are directed. Remaining on the X can be fatal. Movement—directional, purposeful, and trained—is essential to survivability.

Purpose:

- Avoid being a static, predictable target.
- Force the adversary to react.
- Create space, angles, and opportunity for effective counter-engagement.
- Disrupt the threat's OODA loop (Observe–Orient–Decide–Act).

Instructor-Level Breakdown: Three Primary Timing Strategies

1. Draw, Then Move

Sequence:

- Establish grip on the pistol.
- Complete the draw process (clear, rotate, join, extend, prep trigger).
- THEN move off the X.

When to Teach:

- **Beginner shooters** during initial drawstroke training.
- Ensures foundational mechanics are intact before layering complexity.
- Emphasizes **safe muzzle orientation**, **trigger discipline**, and **grip formation**.

Pros:

- Cleaner mechanics for newer shooters.
- Reduces risk of safety violations while developing good habits.

- Easier to diagnose errors.

Cons:

- Delays movement under threat.
- Not tactically optimal under fire or ambush.

Instructor Cues:

- "Establish mastery of the gun before adding complexity."
- "Slow is smooth; smooth becomes fast with consistency."

2. Move, Then Draw

Sequence:

- Initiate lateral or angular movement off the X.
- Simultaneously establish grip during movement.
- Complete the draw during or immediately after moving.

When to Teach:

- **Intermediate shooters** who demonstrate safe and consistent drawstroke.
- Start integrating combat-realistic responses.

Pros:

- Movement begins immediately—more tactically relevant.
- Allows visual assessment of environment before engagement.
- Builds muscle memory for reaction under duress.

Cons:

- May cause rushed or incomplete grip if poorly trained.
- Movement can introduce instability during draw.

Instructor Cues:

- "Move first to deny the threat an easy shot."
- "Your grip is your control—don't sacrifice control for speed."

3. Draw While Moving

Sequence:

- Initiate movement and draw simultaneously.
- Gun is presented *as movement occurs*, stabilizing into extension.
- Sight package and trigger prep occur during controlled footwork.

When to Teach:

- **Advanced students** with proven safety, control, and spatial awareness.
- Reinforces realistic application during live-threat simulations.

Pros:

- Closest to real-world defensive engagement.
- Maximizes time and movement efficiency.
- Keeps shooter unpredictable.

Cons:

- High potential for poor muzzle control if not trained properly.
- Difficult for instructors to observe and diagnose breakdowns.
- May degrade fundamentals if rushed into.

Instructor Cues:

- "Your gun must arrive ready to fight—not just be out of the holster."
- "Footwork drives the fight; don't outrun your ability to shoot."

Additional Instructor Notes: Tailoring by Skill Level

Beginner:

- Focus on clean draw mechanics and directional movement separately.
- Introduce *Draw-Then-Move* in static-to-dynamic progression.
- Emphasize 360-degree spatial awareness and safe gun handling.

Intermediate:

- Blend movement into the draw (Move-Then-Draw).
- Introduce step-and-draw drills (e.g., L-step, V-step, lateral bursts).
- Use shot timers to build urgency and real-world pacing.

Advanced:

- Pressure-based drills (e.g., force-on-force, visual stimulus starts).
- Draw while moving backward, laterally, or off-angle under stress.
- Integrate decision-making under movement (e.g., threat vs. no-threat).

Key Movement Types to Train

- Lateral sidestep (off-line)
- Diagonal (V or triangle step)
- Rearward angular movement (to create distance/space)
- Forward oblique (to close distance or flank)

Conclusion for Instructors

"Getting off the X" is not just a movement—it's a mindset. Survival is linked to the ability to displace and engage with purpose. As instructors, your role is to ensure that students internalize movement as part of their draw and response—not as an afterthought. The method must fit their skill level, and progression must be layered with feedback, repetition, and correction.

INSTRUCTOR MODULE: GETTING OFF THE X AND DRAWING UNDER MOVEMENT

MODULE TITLE: Getting Off the X: Drawing and Engaging While Moving

INTENDED AUDIENCE: Intermediate to Advanced Shooters / Law Enforcement / CCW Permit Holders / Instructor Development

INSTRUCTOR OBJECTIVES:

- Define the concept of "Getting Off the X" within the context of threat avoidance and defensive shooting.

- Break down the differences between Draw-Then-Move, Move-Then-Draw, and Draw-While-Moving.
- Provide scalable drills and cue-based language to build progression in students.
- Emphasize biomechanical efficiency, visual processing, and safety under stress.

KEY TERMS:

- X (threat axis or point of attack)
- Drawstroke
- Visual Processing
- Lateral Movement / Oblique Angles / V-Step
- OODA Loop Disruption

I. CONCEPTUAL FRAMEWORK

What is "The X"?

- The "X" is the shooter's last known position—the point where a threat anticipates or targets their presence.
- Staying static on the X invites attack. Movement creates uncertainty and survivability.

Purpose of Movement:

- Disrupts threat targeting and OODA loop.
- Creates angles and space.
- Forces the threat to reacquire.

II. THREE TIMING STRATEGIES

1. Draw Then Move

- **Used With:** Beginners / Foundation Building
- **Sequence:** Establish grip → Clear and extend weapon → THEN displace.
- **Focus Points:**
  - Clean draw mechanics.
  - Safe muzzle direction.
  - Visual focus on target.
- **Instructor Cues:**
  - "Grip it with intention before you move."
  - "Sight picture before footwork."

2. Move Then Draw

- **Used With:** Intermediate Students
- **Sequence:** Initiate lateral/oblique movement → Establish master grip during movement → Complete draw.
- **Focus Points:**
  - Movement first to break line of attack.
  - Grip formation and draw during locomotion.
- **Instructor Cues:**
  - "Step off the X before you're shot on it."
  - "Your hands can multitask."

3. Draw While Moving

- **Used With:** Advanced / Force-on-Force Contexts

- **Sequence:** Simultaneous movement and drawstroke → Controlled extension → Sights arrive on target while moving.
- **Focus Points:**
  - Control under motion.
  - Sight package acquisition during displacement.
- **Instructor Cues:**
  - "Let your feet buy you time."
  - "Gun and body must arrive ready together."

III. DRILL PROGRESSION

Drill 1: Static Draw, Move After Shot (Foundational)

- Fire 1-2 rounds from holster.
- Step laterally or obliquely after shot.
- Focus on timing and muzzle control.

Drill 2: Movement First, Draw Mid-Stride (Intermediate)

- Begin with a quick lateral burst.
- Draw during movement.
- Engage target once stable or while finishing step.

Drill 3: Continuous Motion & Engagement (Advanced)

- Initiate movement and draw at same time.
- Engage target from movement.
- Add threat/no-threat visual stimuli.

IV. SAFETY CONSIDERATIONS

- Always confirm holster is secure and compatible.
- Ensure range space supports lateral/oblique movement.
- Enforce strict trigger discipline during all phases.
- Observe muzzle orientation during transitional movement.

V. COMMON ERRORS TO CORRECT

- Drawing before establishing master grip under pressure.
- Crossing feet or stumbling due to poor footwork.
- Rushing the trigger before visual confirmation.
- Breaking 180-degree line during movement.

VI. EVALUATION & PROGRESSION CRITERIA

- Shooter demonstrates safe muzzle control.
- Drawstroke is consistent regardless of movement.
- Shot placement remains accurate during motion.
- Ability to explain rationale behind each method.

VII. INSTRUCTOR DEVELOPMENT NOTES

- Teach in layers: Static → Dynamic → Pressure.
- Use video playback for diagnostics.
- Focus on decision-making under stress.
- Reinforce context: Self-defense, LEO ambush response, vehicle egress, etc.

CLOSING THOUGHTS

Getting off the X isn't just a technique—it's a survival principle. Movement must be trained, contextualized, and instinctive. The ability to draw and fight while displacing is a critical skill for anyone who carries a firearm for defense. Teach it with discipline. Build it with purpose. Refine it with pressure.

Advancing, Retreating, and Lateral Movement

A Comparative Analysis of Movement Under Threat for the Armed Professional

I. Purpose of Movement in a Gunfight

Movement is not arbitrary. It serves specific combat purposes:

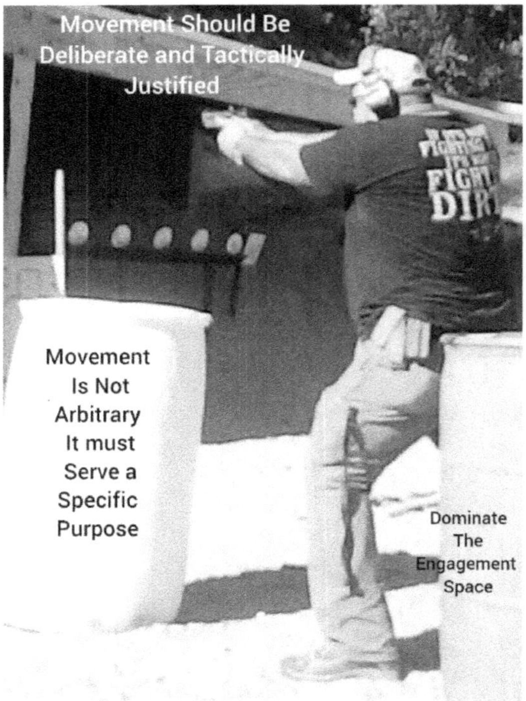

- Gaining positional advantage
- Disrupting the threat's engagement plan
- Creating time and distance
- Accessing cover
- Improving field of fire

When teaching movement, instructors must emphasize that movement should be **deliberate, purposeful, and tactically justified**.

II. Definitions

Advancing (Forward Movement)

Purposeful movement *toward* the threat to close distance, seize initiative, or dominate the engagement space.

Retreating (Rearward Movement)

Purposeful movement *away* from the threat to create space, break contact, or reposition to a more advantageous or defensible location.

Lateral Movement (Side-to-Side)

Movement *perpendicular* to the threat axis (left or right), used to disrupt the threat's aim, change angles, or gain access to cover.

III. Tactical Comparison Chart

Aspect	Advancing	Retreating	Lateral Movement
Direction Relative to Threat	Toward	Away	Sideways (90° offset)
Primary Purpose	Gain control, apply pressure, close distance	Break contact, buy time, reach cover	Disrupt aim, gain angle, improve positioning
Posture & Mindset	Offensive, aggressive	Defensive, reactive	Angular, deceptive

Aspect	Advancing	Retreating	Lateral Movement
Exposure to Threat	High if uncontrolled	Moderate; risk of tripping	Lowest if timed with threat's OODA disruption
Accuracy Under Movement	Generally stable platform if controlled	Less stable; prone to backward sway	Varies: challenging at speed; requires skill
Common Application	CQB, bounding overwatch, counterattack	Civilian self-defense, tactical withdrawal	Immediate action drill, flanking, team tactics
Integration with Cover	Often moving *to* cover	Often moving *from* threat *to* cover	Often moving *between* cover or to gain angle on cover

IV. Pros and Cons of Each Movement Type

Advancing

Pros	Cons
Maintains or seizes initiative	Increases risk if done without control
Closes distance for higher accuracy	Reduces reaction time if threat counters
Can dominate or overwhelm unprepared threats	Over-committing may compromise cover options

Retreating

Pros	Cons
Creates space and time to react	Prone to tripping, falling, or poor footing
Enables disengagement or access to cover	Difficult to maintain shot accuracy under stress
De-escalates legal and tactical liability (CCW)	Risk of being flanked or exposed from behind

Lateral Movement

Pros	Cons
Breaks the opponent's aim and disrupts OODA loop	Harder to shoot while moving smoothly
Gains angles and exposes blind spots	Can expose the shooter to unseen threats
Often requires less ground to be tactically useful	Can overrun cover or expose to crossfire

V. Teaching Context: Layered Skill Development

Beginner Level

- Teach **basic controlled movement** (step, plant, shoot).
- Start with forward and rearward movement **without shooting**.
- Introduce **lateral movement with pivot** drills for postural awareness.
- Emphasize **visual orientation**

Intermediate Level

- Introduce **shooting on the move**: forward and backward at slow pace.

- Introduce **lateral movement drills with live fire**, focusing on shot placement under motion.
- Start **decision-making**: "When do I move, and why?"

Advanced Level

- Combine **multi-directional movement under fire**.
- Add **threat-based problem-solving** (e.g., react to threat from unknown direction).
- Introduce **terrain and structure** (use of cover, navigating hallways, vehicles).
- Emphasize **timing**: when lateral movement breaks visual lock, when retreating invites chase, when advancing closes the decision window.

VI. Common Shooter Errors by Movement Type

Movement Type	Typical Error	Instructor Cue
Advancing	Overrunning cover or muzzle bounce	"Move with control. Close space deliberately."
Retreating	Crossing feet or leaning backward	"Step, plant, balance. Keep weight centered."
Lateral	Hips square to target (inefficient movement)	"Turn hips slightly—athletic posture."

VII. Integrated Instructor Talking Points

- "Every step you take changes the geometry of the fight. Move with intent."
- "Movement must serve a purpose—buy time, gain ground, break their rhythm."

- “You’re not moving to look cool. You’re moving to win the fight.”

VIII. Summary Comparison Table

Tactical Movement	Purpose	Best When...
Advancing	Gain control, dominate space	You have initiative and visual/positional advantage
Retreating	Create time, space, reposition	You are overwhelmed, unready, or outgunned
Lateral Movement	Disrupt, flank, reposition	You need a better angle or to avoid direct fire

The following is an **expanded, professionally refined breakdown of lateral movement** in the context of pistol use under threat. It is structured for **instructor-level delivery** with layered explanations, tactical application, student development guidance, and common shooter errors.

Lateral Movement with a Pistol: An Instructor-Level Expansion

Definition and Purpose

Lateral movement refers to **side-to-side movement perpendicular to the line of threat** (left or right), executed while maintaining threat orientation. It is employed to disrupt the opponent’s ability to accurately engage, create angular advantage, and access cover or positional superiority.

II. Tactical Purpose and Value

Lateral movement is not just footwork—it is **tactical decision-making expressed through movement**. It has value in every application: military, law enforcement, and civilian self-defense.

Key Tactical Advantages:

1. **Breaks the Threat's Sight Alignment:**
    - Human aim is primarily built on predictive tracking. A lateral shift breaks that prediction.
2. **Disrupts the Threat's OODA Loop:**
    - Sudden movement causes a delay in decision-making: Observe–Orient–Decide–Act must restart.
3. **Creates Angles of Advantage:**
    - Movement opens up flank angles, exposes threats behind concealment, or repositions the shooter for cleaner lines of fire.
4. **Access to Cover:**
    - Often the fastest route to usable cover is not backward—but sideways.
5. **Improves Multi-threat Management:**
    - Lateral movement expands peripheral awareness and sets up better engagement sequencing.

II. Types of Lateral Movement

Type	Description	Use Case
Step and Plant	Controlled lateral step followed by a stable shooting stance	Beginner drills, live fire accuracy

Type	Description	Use Case
Lateral Glide (Combat Shuffle)	Smooth, small-footed side-step maintaining muzzle and balance	CQB, close-quarters, bounding
Hard Lateral Break	Aggressive, quick lateral move off the X to evade or reposition	Ambush response, point-blank defense
Angular Displacement (45°)	Moving at a diagonal to change angle while maintaining offensive posture	Room entry, cover-to-cover movement
Shooting While Moving Laterally	Maintaining rounds on target during side movement	Advanced engagement, suppressive fire

Layered Skill Development: Teaching Lateral Movement

Beginner Level

- Start with **dry practice**: step, plant, present.
- Emphasize **foot order**: lead footsteps first, trail foot follows to re-establish base.
- Ensure the shooter maintains **muzzle orientation and eye-target focus**.
- Teach **balance over speed**.

Drill:

Step-Shoot-Step

– From ready: Step left, plant, fire 1 round; step right, plant, fire 1 round.

– Emphasize timing and recovery.

Intermediate Level

- Introduce **lateral movement while maintaining fire** (controlled cadence).
- Add **dynamic targets or lateral transitions**.
- Emphasize **trigger discipline and sight tracking** during motion.
- Reinforce **“move to solve, not to survive”**—only move when it serves the engagement.

Drill:

Lateral Traverse Drill

– Move 3 yards left/right while engaging 3 targets.

– Focus: muzzle tracking, trigger prep during movement, eyes-first transition.

Advanced Level

- Combine **lateral movement with verbal commands, decision-making**, and **non-linear footwork**.
- Use **force-on-force** or **cognitive shooting** to test real-time lateral evasion and engagement.
- Incorporate **low-light, confined-space, and bounding exercises**.

Drill:

Contact Left/Right Reaction

– Shooter receives a call ("Threat left!")

– Performs hard lateral break 3–5 feet, draws, and fires from offset angle.

– Used to simulate ambush or crowd-based movement.

V. Common Shooter Errors and Corrections

Error	Cause	Instructor Correction
Crossing feet	Poor footwork discipline	“Slide, don’t cross. Stay grounded.”

Error	Cause	Instructor Correction
Bouncing or vertical movement	Over-striding or upright posture	"Bend your knees. Glide like you're on rails."
Failing to maintain muzzle orientation	Losing threat focus during movement	"Eyes and muzzle stay locked—your body moves around them."
Jerky or abrupt stops	Inconsistent step size or over-committing	"Smooth is fast. Control the deceleration."
Losing balance under recoil	Feet too close or too far, poor core control	"Rebuild the base every two steps—stance supports your shot."

VI. Tactical Integration Scenarios

Scenario	Lateral Movement Application
Civilian CCW – Parking Lot Ambush	Quick break right to draw from concealment behind parked vehicle
Law Enforcement – Hallway Encounter	Side-step to "cut the corner" and avoid direct hallway engagement
Military – Exterior Contact Left	Lateral break and bounding to establish flank fire superiority
Competition – Stage Entry	Lateral step into a shooting box to engage three targets around a barricade

VII. Instructor Talking Points

- "Lateral movement isn't just about dodging—it's about taking space the enemy didn't expect you to take."
- "The threat's sight picture is built on stillness. Your movement changes the math."
- "Learn to move like a fighter, not like a target."
- "A lateral step is one of the fastest ways to control distance without giving ground."

VIII. Final Summary: Why Lateral Movement Matters

Tactical Effect	Why It Matters
Breaks line of fire	Reduces probability of being hit
Creates tactical angles	Exposes threat vulnerabilities and weak points
Facilitates movement to cover	Reduces reaction time to access ballistic protection
Enables superior engagements	Enhances control of multiple threats and terrain
Builds dynamic survivability	Makes you harder to target in close, confined encounters

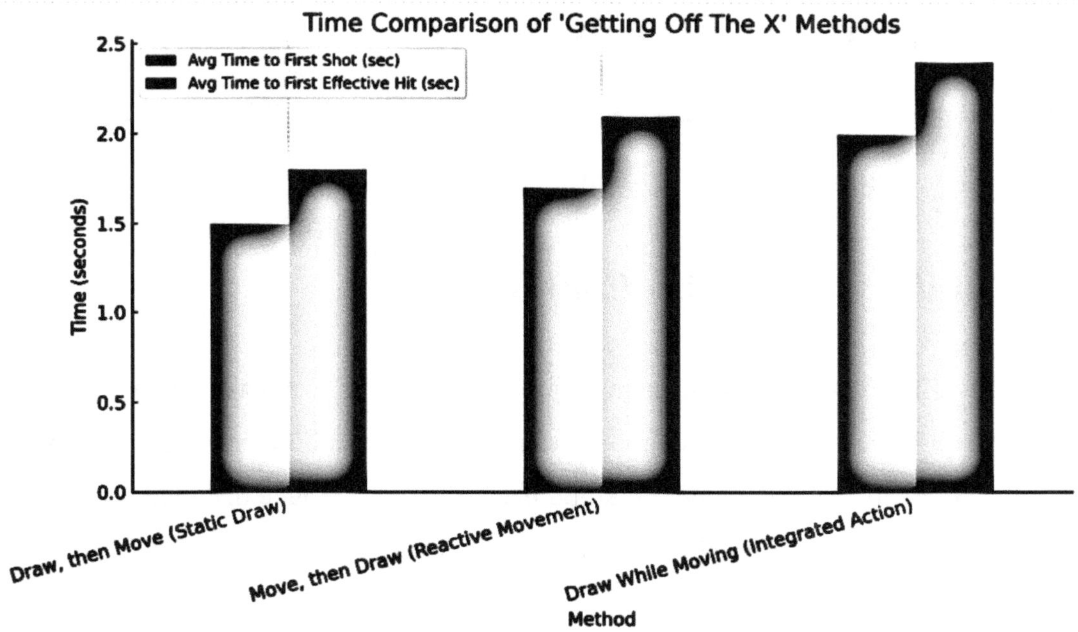

Here's a visual comparison of the time requirements for three different methods of "Getting Off the X":

- **Draw, then Move** is fastest but most static.
- **Move, then Draw** introduces a slight delay but adds survivability.
- **Draw While Moving** requires the most time and training but offers the greatest real-world utility under threat.

Pistol Shooting While Advancing

Professional Analysis, Pros/Cons, and Instructor-Level Teaching Framework

I. Definition and Tactical Context

Shooting while advancing entails engaging threats with live fire while progressing forward toward the adversary, as opposed to firing from a stationary or lateral stance. This mobility-oriented engagement method is employed to reduce distance, assert dominance over the operational space, or sustain momentum amid conflict.

It finds frequent application in law enforcement, military operations, and self-defense scenarios where aggressive action, positional superiority, or suppressive fire is essential during forward progression.

II. Pros and Cons of Shooting While Advancing

Pros	Tactical/Technical Advantage
Maintains Pressure on Threat	Forward advancement renders the threat reactive, curtailing their capacity to deliberate, aim, or reposition.
Closes Distance for Accuracy/Control	Proximity enhances pistol precision, particularly under duress or in diminished visibility.
Disrupts Opponent's Decision Cycle	Interrupts the adversary's OODA loop (Observe–Orient–Decide–Act) by depriving them of temporal and spatial resources.

Pros	Tactical/Technical Advantage
Dominates the Engagement Space	Seizing terrain imparts psychological and tactical supremacy.
Supports Team Tactics	In bounding overwatch or close-quarters battle (CQB), advancing fire can immobilize or suppress threats.

Cons Tactical **Technical Disadvantage**

Cons	Tactical/Technical Disadvantage
Reduced Stability and Accuracy	Movement introduces platform instability, compromising sight alignment and trigger control.
Increased Exposure to Return Fire	Forward motion may heighten vulnerability without adequate cover or suppression.
Potential for Collateral Damage	Diminished precision elevates risks in populated or dynamic environments.
Physical and Cognitive Strain	Balancing locomotion and marksmanship demands heightened focus, potentially leading to fatigue.
Legal and Ethical Implications	Aggressive advancement may complicate post-incident justification in civilian or law enforcement contexts.

III. Movement vs. Speed of Engagement

(Refining the Distinction)

Movement = Physical Locomotion

- Directional control: forward, lateral, oblique.
- Gait: walk vs. bound vs. sprint.

- Stability during motion.

Speed of Engagement = Time to Fire an Effective Shot

- Draw to first shot time.
- Time between sight acquisition and break.
- Cadence of follow-up shots.

Key Principle: The more rapidly one attempts to engage while in motion, the greater the compromise to visual and physical control. Accuracy and accountability diminish when the speed of engagement surpasses the shooter's capacity to verify the sight picture and execute a clean trigger press.

V. How Speed Affects Accuracy During Movement

Speed Level	Movement Impact	Accuracy Implication
Slow, deliberate walk	Stable platform with minimal bounce or sway	High potential for precision and control
Moderate speed (tactical advance)	Controlled locomotion, with some upper-body instability	Accuracy degrades without compensatory techniques (e.g., grip, timing)
Running or bounding	Severe disruption to shooting platform	Suitable only for reactive or suppressive fire; precision markedly impaired

Instructional Note:
Instruct shooters to "advance as swiftly as they can maintain accurate fire",not merely to discharge rounds as rapidly as possible during movement. This nuance is pivotal in

fostering target accountability, especially within law enforcement and civilian defensive frameworks.

V. Instructor-Level Teaching Framework

Beginner Level

- Establish foundational proficiency with static firing to ensure shot accountability.
- Introduce walk-and-fire exercises along linear paths.
- Emphasize stability of the sight picture and a controlled firing cadence.
- Reinforce the mantra: "Prioritize accuracy over velocity; control over unbridled aggression."

Intermediate Level

- Incorporate oblique and lateral movement drills.
- Concentrate on sustaining visual tracking of sights amid motion.
- Implement timed exercises with defined hit thresholds (e.g., IDPA scoring zones, requiring confirmation of two impacts).
- Conduct debriefings to analyze the loci and causes of accuracy degradation.

Advanced Level

- Integrate shoot/no-shoot decision-making during dynamic movement.
- Diversify terrain: uneven ground, barricades, angled firing lanes.
- Employ moving targets and force-on-force simulations to evaluate performance under stress.
- Merge with bounding maneuvers, team coordination, or CQB entries.

VI. Key Instructor Cautions and Corrections

Observed Error	Correction
Stomping gait or bouncing head	"Soften the knees. Glide smoothly, avoiding bounces."
Loss of sight picture during movement	"Fire only upon visual confirmation. Await a momentary sight alignment."
Outrunning their ability to shoot	"Do not advance beyond your capacity to process and execute the shot."
Failure to scan or assess threat cues	"Lead with your eyes. Observe before engaging."
Over-aggressive advance into danger area	"Motion devoid of strategy merely amplifies exposure."

VII. Final Professional Takeaways

- Shooting while advancing constitutes an advanced tactical proficiency, not a routine default.
- Deploy it solely when it confers a clear tactical edge, rather than as an incidental byproduct of movement.
- Train practitioners to appreciate that mobility does not supersede accuracy—the optimal equilibrium is governed by the threat's nature, range, and surrounding conditions.

When Instructors teach movement it generally progresses from side steps to moving forward and backwards or Advancing or Retreating. Remember there is a difference between teaching a shooter movement and employing sound tactics. The movements are similar but distinct.

Advancing vs. Retreating with a Pistol: A Professional Comparison with Tactical Context and Instructional Guidance

In the high-stakes realm of armed encounters—spanning law enforcement, military operations, and civilian self-defense—the capacity to maneuver effectively while wielding a pistol can determine the outcome between survival and peril. Mastering advancing and retreating techniques is crucial, as static shooting drills fail to replicate the fluid dynamics of real-world threats, where mobility directly impacts initiative, survivability, and legal ramifications. By internalizing these movements, practitioners cultivate tactical acuity that sharpens decision-making under duress, mitigates pitfalls such as instability or excessive exposure, and harmonizes with complementary skills like cover exploitation and threat evaluation. This expertise enables professionals and civilians to adapt fluidly, transforming vulnerabilities into strategic assets amid unpredictable confrontations.

I. Conceptual Overview

In armed engagements, every movement must align with a tactical objective: to secure an edge, establish separation, thwart adversarial opportunities, or reposition for optimal engagement. Forward and rearward locomotion transcend mere directional shifts; they encapsulate intent, stance, and risk mitigation within the engagement's framework.

II. Definitions

Advancing (Moving Forward)

The intentional progression toward a threat or objective while armed, designed to assert dominance, optimize firing angles, exert pressure, or resolve the confrontation.

- **Common Applications**: Law enforcement close-quarters battle (CQB), bounding overwatch, room clearing, and counter-ambush tactics.
- **Mindset**: Offensive and assertive.

Retreating (Moving Rearward)

The methodical withdrawal while preserving orientation toward the threat, utilized to generate distance, disengage, access weaponry, or relocate to cover.

- **Common Applications**: Defensive shooting situations, civilian self-defense, and tactical withdrawal.
- **Mindset**: Defensive and distance-oriented.

III. Comparative Analysis

Factor	Advancing (Forward Movement)	Retreating (Rearward Movement)
Primary Purpose	Close distance, secure advantage, pressure adversary	Create distance, evade close-quarters, access cover
Posture	Aggressive, offensive, commanding	Defensive, responsive, evasion-focused
Visual Control	Stable; forward gaze, intuitive engagement posture	Essential to sustain threat observation during motion
Footwork Dynamics	Heel-to-toe, flexed knees, measured strides	Toe-to-heel, intentional steps to avert stumbling

Factor	Advancing (Forward Movement)	Retreating (Rearward Movement)
Stability Under Fire	Superior base for recoil management and firing rhythm	Reduced stability; susceptible to rearward imbalance and interrupted rhythm
Engagement Readiness	Supports rapid and voluminous fire	Prioritizes accuracy and judicious shot selection
Risk Exposure	Heightened if overextended	Hazards include falls, footing issues, or diminished awareness
Use of Cover	Frequently advancing toward cover	Typically retreating from threat toward cover

IV. Tactical Considerations and Applications

When to Advance

- Initiative has been or must be captured.
- As part of a coordinated team effort to control an area.
- When the adversary is impaired, suppressed, or vulnerable, necessitating neutralization.
- To attain positional superiority (e.g., enhanced cover, flanking positions, or separation from non-combatants).

Key Instructional Insight: Advancing absent a clear objective verges on imprudence. Employ it solely when it yields a definitive benefit.

When to Retreat

- Facing superior firepower, ambush, or inadequate readiness.
- Where greater separation bolsters survival (e.g., against edged weapons or multiple assailants).
- To access cover or disrupt line-of-sight.
- In civilian contexts, to strengthen legal defensibility.

Key Instructional Insight: Retreat signifies neither capitulation nor defeat—it embodies strategic repositioning to dictate engagement pace or diminish hazards.

V. Common Shooter Errors and Coaching Strategies

Movement Type	Common Errors	Corrective Strategy
Advancing	Overexposure (protruding excessively from cover)	Promote brief, purposeful advances with predefined cover transitions
	Excessive firing rate sans sight alignment	Instill rhythm tied to verification (e.g., 1–2–3 rounds per confirmation)
	Muzzle oscillation from forceful steps	Encourage knee flexion and minimized step elevation
Retreating	Rearward motion without environmental scanning	Advocate threat-focused gaze paired with deliberate toe-to-heel technique
	Foot entanglement or stumbling	Stress equilibrium: "Step, stabilize, then engage"
	Inaccurate shots amid instability	Commence with "engage, then relocate" sequences in foundational drills

VI. Teaching Progression: Layered Skill Development

Beginner Level

- Isolate movement from shooting, practicing sequentially.
- Commence rearward drills with dry-fire over minimal distances.
- Introduce forward progression via static-to-dynamic exercises (1–2 yards).

Intermediate Level

- Merge movement with live fire, focusing on disciplined rhythm and accountability.
- Incorporate judgment calls: Advance or retreat per threat cues.
- Integrate oblique movements to hone footwork coordination.

Advanced Level

- Embed maneuvers in simulated adversarial scenarios, including role-based or cognitive exercises.
- Highlight rhythm mastery: When to maintain position, converge, or withdraw.
- Execute relocation-to-cover drills under pressure, with embedded decision nodes.

VII. Instructor Talking Points

- "Distance affords time, yet time devoid of purpose yields naught."
- "Advance to prevail; retreat to endure."
- "Cover and mobility are indispensable instruments—deploy the appropriate one at the pivotal juncture."
- "The confrontation heeds not your trajectory; it exacts only your resolve."

VIII. Final Professional Summary

Advancing	Retreating
Offensive orientation	Defensive orientation
Contracts space to command	Expands space to persevere
Demands regulated assertiveness	Demands poise and restraint
Suited to bold practitioners	Suited to meticulous practitioners
Imperative to apply judiciously	Imperative to apply vigilantly

This curriculum holds profound significance, furnishing individuals with refined proficiencies to traverse mortal perils with acumen, merging biomechanical prowess with psychological fortitude and moral discernment. In an age of escalating unpredictability in armed disputes and protective encounters, proficiency in advancing and retreating not only augments endurance but also champions accountable force application, curbing unwarranted intensifications and favoring de-escalation when feasible. In essence, this erudition preserves lives, amplifies operational prowess, and reinforces tenets of disciplined tactics in a landscape that necessitates vigilance sans alarmism.

Entries and Exits: Mastering Movement Into and Out of Cover

In tactical environments, the adept use of cover can mean the difference between survival and vulnerability. This chapter provides an instructor-ready framework for teaching the principles of entering and exiting cover, emphasizing layered breakdowns suitable for progressive skill development. Drawing on established tactical doctrines, we explore foundational concepts, practical applications, and advanced strategies to equip shooters with the tools for minimizing exposure, optimizing angles, and maintaining offensive or defensive initiative.

I. Introduction: The Principle of Cover Utilization

Cover denotes any object or structure capable of halting or substantially mitigating incoming projectiles, thereby affording ballistic protection. Its effective employment is a cornerstone of survivability in defensive or tactical scenarios. Mastery of entries (moving into cover) and exits (moving out of cover) is essential for reducing exposure, controlling sightlines, and facilitating engagement or disengagement. These maneuvers demand situational awareness, disciplined movement, and seamless integration with weapon handling to preserve tactical advantage.

II. Teaching Framework by Skill Level

Tailor instruction to the learner's proficiency, progressing from basic awareness to sophisticated tactical execution.

Beginner Level: Fundamental Concepts

- **Key Objective**: Instill an understanding of cover's purpose and basic utilization.
- **Core Concepts**:
  - Differentiate cover (ballistic resistance) from concealment (visual obfuscation only).
  - Prioritize cover when available as a default protective measure.
  - Execute deliberate walks or jogs into cover, maintaining muzzle awareness.
  - Avoid "crowding" cover, which restricts mobility and engagement angles.

    - Uphold muzzle discipline with the trigger finger indexed until engagement is warranted.
- **Teaching Tip**: Employ large, unambiguous props such as barrels, vehicles, or walls for drills. Emphasize safety and spatial orientation to build confidence without overwhelming complexity.

Intermediate Level: Practical Application

- **Key Objective**: Foster efficient, secure approaches to and departures from cover, incorporating angle management and engagement opportunities.
- **Entries**:
    - Approach obliquely to sustain threat visibility while curtailing exposure.
    - Keep the weapon at ready, muzzle directed toward potential threats.
    - Decelerate and compact movements prior to contact to prevent uncontrolled arrivals.
    - Establish a stable shooting platform before any exposure around cover.
- **Exits**:
    - Conduct scans and evaluations before movement; relocate deliberately to superior positions.
    - In dynamic contexts, integrate "fighting off the X" via suppressive fire or bounding overwatch.
    - Incorporate shooting on the move during exits where feasible.
- **Use of Terrain and Obstacles**: Instruct on "slicing the pie" for gradual sector clearance upon exit.
- **Teaching Tip**: Introduce timed drills with simulated threats to bridge theory and application, reinforcing decision-making under moderate pressure.

Advanced Level: Tactical and Strategic Application

- **Key Objective**: Hone entries and exits for optimal advantage under duress, encompassing engagement timing, threat response, and deceptive tactics.
- **Entries**:
    - Balance speed and stealth: Employ explosive bounds under fire or methodical advances for surprise.
    - Prep the trigger pre-engagement if contact looms.
    - Leverage footwork for minimal exposure, protruding only essential elements (e.g., one eye and muzzle).
    - Merge entries with brief-exposure firing (peek, engage, retract).
- **Exits**:
    - Facilitate contact breaks with angular maneuvers, suppression, or obscurants like smoke.
    - Pre-map exit routes to evade entrapment.
    - Handle reloads and malfunctions within cover prior to departure.
    - Train lateral shifts and fallback cover options.
- **Tactical Deception**: Deploy feints, such as simulated movements or auditory diversions, to mislead adversaries.
- **Teaching Tip**: Simulate high-stress scenarios with force-on-force elements, analyzing post-drill debriefs to refine instinctive responses.

III. Movement Techniques: Key Principles for All Levels

Adhere to these universal principles to ensure safe, effective maneuvers regardless of proficiency.

Principle	Application
Maintain Weapon Readiness	Orient the muzzle toward threat sectors; index the trigger finger until ready to fire.
Avoid Crowding Cover	Position at arm's length to facilitate mobility and versatile angles.
Minimize Exposure	Expose only necessities via angular positioning—typically one eye and muzzle.
Slice the Pie	Clear sectors incrementally around edges to control visibility and risk.
Balance Speed and Control	Prioritize rapid transit to cover without compromising weapon stability or awareness.

Definitions and Contrasts

Entering Cover

Entering cover constitutes the tactical transition from an exposed state to a protected one capable of withstanding or deflecting threats like projectiles or fragments. This maneuver aims to:

- Curtail personal vulnerability.
- Secure a vantage for observation, engagement, or resupply.
- Attain positional superiority.

Refined Instructor-Level Definition: Entering cover is the intentional relocation to a ballistic protective site, performed with restraint to uphold awareness, readiness, and advantage.

Key Elements:

1. **Purposeful Movement**: Guided by threats, terrain, and objectives—not haphazard.
2. **Angular Approaches**: Mitigate exposure en route.
3. **Weapon Orientation**: Sustain muzzle alignment with threats.
4. **Distance Control**: Offset from cover for maneuverability.
5. **Engagement Preparedness**: Ready to fire during transit or upon arrival.

Distinctions: Unlike concealment (visual hiding sans protection) or mere occupation (static presence), entry focuses on the transitional phase.

Exiting Cover

Exiting cover involves the purposeful departure from protection to an exposed or repositioned state, often to:

- Secure superior sightlines.
- Adjust proximity to threats.
- Relocate to enhanced cover.
- Sustain or terminate engagement.

Refined Instructor-Level Definition: Exiting cover is the calculated abandonment of ballistic shelter for repositioning, engagement, or withdrawal, preserving awareness, readiness, and exposure management.

Key Elements:

1. **Decision-Making**: Necessity-driven, not impulsive.
2. **Threat Assessment**: Precede with scans for current and potential hazards.

3. **Controlled Movement**: Calibrate pace—deliberate or explosive—while stabilizing the weapon.
4. **Muzzle Management**: Direct toward threats throughout.
5. **Angular Discipline**: Employ oblique paths to diminish predictability.
6. **Preparation**: Address weapon status or communications beforehand.

Distinctions: Avoid conflating with blind breaks (reckless) or panicked retreats (unplanned); tactical exits are premeditated.

Instructional Contrast: Quick Summary Table

Aspect	Entering Cover	Exiting Cover
Definition	Transition into ballistic protection	Departure from ballistic protection
Purpose	Gain safety and advantage	Reposition, engage, or disengage
Movement Style	Cautious, angle-conscious	Explosive or deliberate, threat-based
Weapon Readiness	High—poised for entry engagement	High—muzzle forward post-movement
Common Error	Crowding or over-commitment	Unassessed or unplanned departure

Detailed Expansion: Moving Into Entry Position, Posting Up, and Posting Off

I. Moving Into an Entry Position Behind Cover

Definition: Approaching and assuming a preparatory stance adjacent to cover for subsequent actions like engagement or surveillance.

Pre-Entry Considerations:

1. **Threat Awareness**: Index muzzle deeply for known threats; proceed cautiously for unknowns.
2. **Cover Assessment**: Gauge type (hard/soft), dimensions, and orientation.
3. **Approach Route**: Select paths minimizing exposure via angular or offset trajectories.

Technique:

- **Weapon Ready**: Two-handed grip, muzzle aligned with eye-line toward threats.
- **Eyes Lead**: Visual precedence guides muzzle tracking.
- **Angular Entry**: Oblique paths preserve orientation and profile reduction.
- **Speed Modulation**: Slow near cover to avoid overruns.
- **Offset Maintenance**: Arm's-length spacing for flexibility.

II. Posting Up On Cover

Definition: Adopting a static, engagement-ready posture in direct proximity to cover.

When Applicable: Mid-to-long-range threats, maximal concealment needs, or constrained movement.

Technique:

- Body Alignment: Proximity without restriction; enable pie-slicing via shifts.
- Weapon Extension: Minimal protrusion beyond edges.

- Footwork: Forward foot toward threats, rear for stability.
- Mindset: Vigilant scanning with readiness for transitions.

Risks: Tunnel vision, immobility, unintended exposures.

III. Posting Off Cover

Definition: Utilizing cover from a standoff (1–3 feet), enhancing maneuverability at partial protection cost.

When Applicable: Broad-sector engagements, dynamic needs, or low-cover scenarios.

Technique:

- **Separation**: 1–3 feet for agility.
- **Stance**: Athletic, bent knees for readiness.
- **Indexing**: Muzzle to threats; off-line exposure for unpredictability.

Advantages: Superior angles, disengagement ease, reduced static risks.
Tradeoffs: Diminished protection, heightened awareness demands.

Comparison Table: Posting On vs. Off Cover

Factor	Posting On Cover	Posting Off Cover
Protection	Maximal ballistic	Moderate to low
Mobility	Restricted	Enhanced
Exposure Management	Anchored minimization	Deliberate lean control
Tactical Use Case	Static/suppressive	Dynamic/scanning
Situational Risks	Stagnation, flanking	Angle vulnerabilities

Exiting from Posted Positions

I. Definition: Exiting a Position Behind Cover

The calculated departure from protection to reposition, engage, or withdraw, prioritizing initiative recovery.

II. Exiting from On Cover

Context: Close-contact posture with high protection but limited options.

Rationale: Threat evolution, cover compromise, or sector shifts.

Technique:

1. **Preparation**: Scan, resolve weapon issues, map paths.
2. **Break**: Leg-driven, smooth disengagement.
3. **Muzzle**: Threat-oriented; suppress if needed.
4. **Angles**: Diagonal exits for profile reduction.

Errors: Crowding-induced delays, blind steps, muzzle lag, hesitation.

III. Exiting from Off Cover

Context: Offset posture for mobility.

Rationale: Flanking, advancement, or evasion.

Technique:

1. **Setup**: Reconfirm threats; load rear foot.
2. **Movement**: Context-matched pace; engage en route if trained.
3. **Angles**: 45° or lateral for visibility and evasion.
4. **Re-engagement**: Planned destinations; avoid open halts.

Errors: Excessive exposure, muzzle neglect, mental delays, fixation.

Comparison Table: Exiting On vs. Off Cover

Criteria	Exiting On Cover	Exiting Off Cover
Starting Distance	Close contact	Offset (1–3 feet)
Initial Movement	Compressed shift	Preloaded acceleration
Mobility Potential	Limited	High
Typical Purpose	Contact break, angle shift	Flank, aggressive reposition
Risk Factors	Slow disengagement	Overexposure, mismanagement

V. Drill Integration: Instructor Progressions

Beginner: Dry-fire walk-backs; verbal-cued scans and exits.
Intermediate: Timed live-fire posts, shoots, and relocations.
Advanced: Cue-driven moving threats; multi-cover bounding with decisions.

VI. Instructor Tips

- Emphasize cognitive aspects: "Why" alongside "how."
- Use cues like "Threat left!" to condition responses.
- Assess exposure and muzzle in evaluations.

Cover Versus Concealment: A Tactical Imperative

In the realm of tactical training and self-defense, distinguishing between cover and concealment is not merely academic—it is a matter of survival. This chapter delivers a professional dissection of these concepts, tailored for instructors, law enforcement professionals, military personnel, and advanced civilian shooters. Drawing on established ballistic principles and empirical data focused on common pistol calibers (such as 9mm Luger, .40 S&W, and .45 ACP), we explore definitions, contrasts, real-world applications, and instructional strategies. The analysis underscores the critical need for terrain awareness, informed by rigorous testing from sources like the National Institute of Justice (NIJ), FBI Ballistic Research Facility, and independent evaluations.

I. Definitions

Cover

Cover refers to any physical barrier or environmental feature capable of halting or substantially mitigating the penetration of projectiles, thereby affording genuine ballistic protection to the individual utilizing it. This protection is contingent upon the barrier's material composition, thickness, and the specific threat level posed by incoming fire.

- **Key Characteristic**: Inherent ballistic resistance, calibrated to withstand anticipated threats, such as handgun rounds or, in more robust cases, rifle projectiles.
- **Function**: It safeguards life by physically intercepting, deflecting, or absorbing bullets, minimizing the risk of injury and enabling sustained defensive or offensive actions.

Concealment

Concealment encompasses any object, terrain element, or environmental condition that impedes visual detection of a shooter's position without providing substantive ballistic defense against projectiles. It serves as a temporary veil rather than a shield.

- **Key Characteristic**: Solely visual obfuscation, lacking the structural integrity to resist penetration.
- **Function**: It hinders an adversary's ability to locate, track, or accurately engage a target, facilitating maneuvers, repositioning, or the initiation of countermeasures.

II. Professional Comparative Analysis

To facilitate instructional clarity, the following table delineates the core distinctions between cover and concealment, emphasizing their tactical implications for pistol-centric engagements.

Aspect	Cover	Concealment
Primary Function	Ballistic protection against projectiles	Visual obstruction to evade observation
Ballistic Protection	Affirmative—arrests or decelerates rounds based on material properties	None—offers no resistance to penetration
Tactical Use	Defensive positioning, sheltering during exchanges, or firing from relative safety	Evasive maneuvering, ambush setup, or undetected repositioning
Examples (Pistol Threat)	Engine blocks, reinforced concrete walls (8 inches or thicker), steel I-beams, substantial tree trunks (12 inches or more in diameter)	Bushes, interior drywall, curtains, smoke, furniture, or shadows
Movement Consideration	Often immobile or restrictive, necessitating deliberate navigation	Enhances mobility through lightweight or transient barriers
Effect on Opponent	Impedes effective targeting and lethality	Prolongs target acquisition time but does not neutralize threats

This framework highlights that while both elements contribute to survivability, cover provides a tangible edge in direct confrontations, whereas concealment excels in asymmetric or fluid scenarios.

III. Empirical Data: Ballistic Performance Against Pistol Rounds

Ballistic evaluations, grounded in standards from the NIJ (e.g., Standard-0101.06 and updates through 2025) and FBI protocols, assess material efficacy against common pistol ammunition. Tests typically involve:

- **9mm Luger**: 124-grain full metal jacket (FMJ) or jacketed hollow point (JHP) at velocities of approximately 1,150–1,200 feet per second (fps).
- **.40 S&W**: 180-grain FMJ or JHP at around 950 fps.
- **.45 ACP**: 230-grain FMJ at roughly 850 fps.

These calibers exhibit comparable penetration in soft barriers due to similar kinetic energies (typically 300–400 foot-pounds), though 9mm often demonstrates slightly deeper penetration in gel or thin materials owing to higher velocity

Independent tests, such as those from The Box O' Truth and Pew Pew Tactical, simulate household and urban environments, revealing that most pistol rounds penetrate multiple layers of concealment but are halted by dense cover

.The table below synthesizes performance data from these sources, categorizing materials as cover or concealment for pistol threats.

Material	Ballistic Performance Against Pistol Calibers	Cover Status
Drywall (1–2 layers, ½–⅝ inch)	Easily penetrated; 9mm, .40, and .45 traverse 10–12 inches or more (equivalent to 5–6 interior walls)	Concealment
Interior Wood Doors (hollow-core)	Readily penetrated with minimal deflection; all calibers pass through multiple doors	Concealment
Office Desks or Furniture (wood/particleboard)	Penetrated; offers slight deflection but no reliable stop	Concealment
Concrete (8-inch block or wall)	Effectively stops all tested pistol rounds; may produce spall or fragments but prevents through-penetration	Cover
Engine Block (automotive)	Superior resistance; halts 9mm, .40, and .45; may partially deflect rifle rounds	Cover
Vehicle Doors (standard steel)	Frequently penetrated, though angle and layering may cause deflection or fragmentation (penetration depths 0.5–5.5 inches post-impact)	Partial Cover
Steel Plate (⅜-inch mild steel)	Stops pistol rounds at typical engagement distances; ineffective against rifles close-range	Cover (Pistol)

Cinder Block Wall	Generally arrests pistol projectiles; potential for fragmentation or ricochet
Cover (Partial)	
Large Trees (12-inch+ trunk)	Effective against pistol calibers; wood density absorbs energy (e.g., 9mm penetrates ~8–10 inches of pine, .45 ~7 inches)
Cover	
Refrigerators or Appliances	Unreliable; may slow velocity via internal components but rarely stops bullets outright
Limited Cover	

These findings, corroborated through 2025 by ongoing NIJ and FBI validations, emphasize that everyday urban or residential elements often default to concealment, necessitating rapid transitions to verified cover

IV. Instructor-Level Considerations

For educators in tactical firearms training, imparting the nuances of cover and concealment demands experiential learning to bridge theory and application.

Teaching Tips

- Incorporate live-fire barricade exercises to vividly illustrate material limitations, such as drywall's ineffectiveness against 9mm penetration

- Stress adaptive decision-making: In scenarios where only concealment is accessible, leverage it for evasion or repositioning.
- Advocate integration: Train students to exploit concealment en route to cover, fostering layered defensive strategies.

Contextual Applications

- **Law Enforcement/Close-Quarters Battle (CQB)**: Residential structures predominantly offer concealment; prioritize speed, aggression, and dynamic entry to exploit this disparity.
- **Concealed Carry/Self-Defense**: Identify household cover (e.g., engine blocks in garages) and use concealment to disengage or flank threats.
- **Military/Tactical Units**: Conduct pre-operational terrain mapping to delineate cover-concealment zones, accounting for exposure angles and structural vulnerabilities.

V. Summary: Professional Takeaways

The essence of cover and concealment distills to these foundational principles, guiding tactical proficiency:

Principle	Cover	Concealment
Can Save Your Life	Yes	No
Useful Tactically	Yes	Yes
Stops Bullets	Yes	No
Buys Time and Space	Yes	Yes
Requires Terrain Awareness	Yes	Yes

Mastery of these distinctions empowers shooters to navigate threats with precision, transforming environmental awareness into a decisive advantage. Instructors should reinforce that while concealment provides opportunity, only true cover delivers protection— a lesson validated time and again in ballistic research and real-world engagements.

Shooting On Cover vs. Off Cover

A Professional Comparative Analysis with Teaching Context

I. Definitions and Tactical Intent

Shooting *On* Cover

The act of engaging threats from a position where the shooter remains in **direct physical contact or proximity to cover**, using it as both **ballistic protection and a support element**.

- Common in defensive hold, barricade engagements, and static fighting positions.
- Emphasizes **maximizing protection while minimizing exposure**.
- Cover is part of the firing position: vertical walls, doorways, vehicles, barriers.

Shooting *Off* Cover

The act of **deliberately moving away from hard cover** to engage a threat from an **offset, open, or flanking position**, often to gain a better angle, improve field of fire, or maintain mobility.

- Common in aggressive maneuvering, bounding, team movement, or when cover is not available at the point of decision.
- Emphasizes **mobility, initiative, and tactical problem-solving**.
- Involves *temporary exposure* for tactical advantage.

II. Comparison: On Cover vs. Off Cover

Factor	Shooting On Cover	Shooting Off Cover
Primary Purpose	Maximize ballistic protection	Gain angle, mobility, or dominate a threat area
Protection Level	High (if used correctly)	Low to none
Exposure Management	Minimal exposure, slice the pie, tight presentation	Greater exposure; relies on speed, aggression
Shooting Position	Anchored, controlled, stable	Dynamic, may require alternate or compromised stance
Tempo and Initiative	Reactive or defensive	Proactive or offensive
Use Case	Holding, defending, or stalling	Advancing, flanking, bounding, or clearing

III. Common Shooter Errors and Instructor Notes

Shooting On Cover – Common Errors

Error	Description	Corrective Strategy
"Crowding" Cover	Shooter is too close to cover, limiting visibility, mobility, and increasing risk of deflection	Teach the **"one arm's length rule"** or **elbow space buffer** to maintain maneuverability

Error	Description	Corrective Strategy
Improper Exposure	Exposing unnecessary body parts—shoulders, elbows, head	Reinforce **slicing the pie** and using offset angles
Muzzle/weapon flash on cover	Muzzle or optic telegraphs position by protruding past cover	Use barricade drills to develop spatial awareness of weapon position
Leaning instead of shifting	Over-leaning causes instability and fatigue	Instruct to shift hips and knees, not just lean from the waist
Predictable patterning	Repeated exposure from same point increases risk	Train alternating firing positions and movement around cover
Failure to move laterally	Shooter stays locked behind one piece of cover	Teach micro-movement: **"cover to cover" transitions**

Shooting Off Cover – Common Errors

Error	Description	Corrective Strategy
Overexposure	Poor use of terrain; body fully exposed with no protection	Teach use of angles, fleeting exposure, and **bounding techniques**
Lack of commitment to movement	Shooter hesitates mid-transition, stopping in a poor spot	Reinforce the principle: **"Move with purpose or stay behind cover."**

Error	Description	Corrective Strategy
Failure to scan or identify	Shooter moves off cover without a plan or without identifying threats	Emphasize **"move with eyes first"** and incorporate cognitive drills
Shooting while moving without control	Rounds miss or go wild due to poor movement fundamentals	Use step-and-shoot drills, **"shoot, then move"** tactics to develop control
No plan to return to cover	Engages from open terrain with no path back to protection	Teach **"off cover, onto cover"** movement patterns (use of bounding landmarks)
Misuse of concealment as cover	Taking a flanking shot from concealment assuming safety	Clarify distinction in all drills between **ballistic vs. visual protection**

IV. Teaching Context and Progression

Beginner Level:

- Teach **cover as protection**; reinforce understanding of what is and is not cover.
- Static cover shooting from upright, kneeling, and braced positions.
- Introduce visual angles: slice the pie, angle of exposure, muzzle discipline.

Intermediate Level:

- Add **movement to and from cover**.
- Off cover shooting introduced in structured drills with timing and spacing.

- Decision-making: when to stay on cover vs. break contact and maneuver.

Advanced Level:

- Introduce **mixed terrain drills**: shoot from on-cover, off-cover, while bounding.
- Add **stress inoculation**: time pressure, low-light, non-standard positions.
- Scenarios where **shooters must decide dynamically** between staying or moving off cover.

Instructor Guidance:

- Emphasize **principles before techniques**: cover is not a static object; it's a tactical decision point.

- Use force-on-force to drive home the **lethality of improper use of cover**.
- Integrate **After Action Reviews (AARs)** to assess exposure, muzzle discipline, and tactical effectiveness.

V. Final Professional Takeaways

"Cover is not safety unless you understand how to use it. And mobility is not freedom unless you have a reason to move."

- **On-Cover** favors survivability and control. Use when defending or holding.
- **Off-Cover** favors initiative and tempo. Use when maneuvering or breaking the engagement rhythm.

True tactical proficiency lies in knowing when to use each.

Target Transitions

Target transitions are the deliberate and controlled movement of the shooter's attention, vision, and firearm from one threat or target area to another. This skill is essential in dynamic engagements that demand speed, efficiency, and precision when addressing multiple threats or aiming at different anatomical zones on the same target.

A common example is the **Mozambique Drill** fire two rounds to the thoracic cavity followed by one to the cranial vault. This classic drill not only tests marksmanship but also reinforces the need to transition accurately and decisively between high-value zones on a single target.

A more advanced application of this principle is the **Crisscross Drill**, which layers movement, precision, and complexity:

- Begin with three targets spaced laterally.
- Fire two rounds to the body of Target 1.
- Transition and fire one round to the head of Target 2.
- Transition again and fire two rounds to the body of Target 3.

For those seeking a greater challenge, incorporate an **emergency reload** after completing this sequence, and reverse the drill:

- After the reload, fire **one round to the head of Target 3**,
- Then **two rounds to the body of Target 2**,
- Finish with **one round to the head of Target 1**.

This drill challenges the shooter to manage complex motor tasks under time and cognitive pressure while maintaining visual and trigger discipline.

Mechanics of Target Transitions

Efficient transitions require a seamless integration of **vision, firearm manipulation**, and **trigger control**. While multiple techniques exist, their application is largely dictated by the shooter's skill level, situational awareness, and tempo of engagement. Below are three progressive methods of transitioning between targets:

1. Vision-Led Transitions (Fundamental Level)

At the foundational level, the shooter fires the designated rounds on Target 1, then shifts visual focus to Target 2. The pistol is then indexed onto the new target, aligning the sight package to the new line of sight.

Key Points:

- Move the eyes—not the head.
- The firearm follows the eyes.
- Begin prepping the trigger during movement to reduce split times.

This method emphasizes safety and control. It is the most widely taught and understood approach, suitable for both beginners and intermediates seeking repeatable, accountable performance.

2. Recoil-Riding Transitions (Intermediate Level)

As the shooter gains confidence and control over recoil, transitions can begin **as the sight package lifts** from Target 1. Rather than allowing the pistol to return to the original point of aim, the shooter "rides" the recoil and directs the firearm toward Target 2.

Advantages:

- Saves time by eliminating return-to-zero.
- Maintains efficiency without sacrificing accuracy.

This method relies on predictable recoil behavior and requires the shooter to have a well-established grip, posture, and visual tracking ability.

3. Trigger-Break Transitions (Advanced Level)

The most efficient—and advanced—method involves initiating the transition **at the precise moment the trigger breaks**, just before the sight package lifts. In this technique, the shooter is already shifting visual focus and beginning physical movement as the round is being discharged.

Performance Requirements:

- High-level kinesthetic awareness ("feel").
- Extreme familiarity with recoil timing and sight lift.
- Trust in predictive shooting and subconscious gun handling.

This level of transition allows minimal time between shots and is ideal for shooters operating at a subconscious competence level. However, it demands exceptional discipline in **eye-first transitions**—the eyes must always lead the gun to the next target.

Vision is the Driver

Regardless of the technique employed, **vision must be the primary driver of target transitions**. The eyes must always move before the gun. The more precisely and rapidly the pistol can follow the visual cue, the more efficient the transition becomes.

In a defensive or tactical context, poor visual control during transitions can lead to excessive time on target, delayed threat engagement, or unintended rounds on non-threats. Efficient transitions, therefore, are not only about speed—but also about visual accountability, precision, and disciplined gun handling.

Low Light Fundamentals for Everyday Carry (EDC)

Why Low Light Skills Matter

Most violent encounters happen in reduced or limited light—after sunset, indoors, in parking garages, or in other shadowed environments. In these conditions, you cannot engage a threat you cannot clearly identify. Shooting at shadows, silhouettes, or sudden flashes of light is both unsafe and legally indefensible. In a real defensive encounter, the combination of time pressure, adrenaline, and the instinct to survive can lead to tragic mistakes if you misidentify a person.

Why Carry a Light

A quality flashlight is as important to the prepared civilian as a quality handgun.
You carry light for four main reasons:

1. **Navigation** – In the dark, your first priority is moving without tripping, stumbling, or running into obstacles. This keeps you upright, balanced, and in control.
2. **Identification** – You must confirm exactly *what* and *who* you are seeing before you even think about touching the trigger. A good light allows you to detect and recognize potential threats while keeping them from pinpointing your position.
3. **Control and Influence** – The concentrated beam ("hot spot") of a flashlight can disrupt an aggressor's vision, slow their approach, or direct their movement.
4. **Communication** – In some situations, a flashlight beam can be used to signal or indicate direction to others without speaking. However, misuse or overuse can reveal your position.

Search and Scan Techniques

If you believe there's a potential threat but don't know exactly where it is, avoid moving with the light in a fixed position.

- Change the beam's angle often—up, down, side to side—to make it harder for someone to locate you.
- Use walls, floors, and ceilings to bounce light indirectly into an area, revealing details without exposing your exact location.
- Be aware of **backlighting**—light sources behind you that can silhouette your body and make you an easy target. This could come from open doors, streetlights, headlights, or even another flashlight.

Avoid **self-blinding** by controlling beam direction near reflective surfaces like mirrors or light-colored walls.

- **Suggested output**: 60–225 lumens for indoor use; 225–500 lumens for outdoor or open-area work.

Backlighting Awareness

One of the most common—and dangerous—mistakes in low light is accidentally standing where a light source behind you makes you clearly visible. Criminals don't need to see much to aim at you or close distance quickly. Always consider what's behind you and reposition when necessary.

Principles of Low Light Use for Civilians

1. Read the Light: Before acting, take a moment to understand the lighting environment. Note shadows, reflections, light sources, and dark corners. Being aware of these factors gives you an immediate tactical advantage.

One Light is No Light!
Run a weapons Light
But always
have a
Handheld
backup light
Be Prepared

2. Stay in the Shadows

Operate from the lowest possible level of light while still being able to see and move safely. Force potential threats to leave their concealment rather than stepping into it yourself.

3. Think Like the Threat

Ask yourself: “If I were the bad guy, could I see me right now?” This perspective helps you decide when to move, when to stay still, and where to position yourself for safety.

4. Light and Move

Use short bursts of light to scan an area, then turn it off before moving to a new position. This makes it harder for anyone to track you while still allowing you to gather visual information.

5. Power with Light

- **Hot Spot Disruption** – Aim the brightest part of the beam into a potential aggressor's eyes to momentarily disrupt their vision. This can create a window to move, communicate, or disengage.
- **Confined Space Awareness** – In close quarters, combine *Power with Light* and *Light and Move* to prevent overexposing your location.

6. Disorientation

Using rapid side-to-side movement or a strobe function can interfere with an attacker's depth perception and coordination. This is most effective if you're also changing your position.

7. Alignment

Whenever possible, keep your eyes, light, and firearm aimed in the same direction. In many situations, a handheld light will be your primary tool until you have a confirmed threat in sight.

8. Redundancy

Carry more than one light. Your primary flashlight could fail, be dropped, or be out of reach when you need it most. A smaller backup light ensures you're never left in the dark.

Handheld Flashlight One-Handed Pistol Shooting Techniques

Low-light encounters present unique challenges for armed citizens, especially those who carry concealed. Criminal activity often thrives under the cover of darkness, where reduced visibility hinders threat recognition and target discrimination. A concealed carrier who cannot positively identify a target risks tragic mistakes and legal consequences. Handheld flashlight techniques empower individuals to locate, assess, and, if necessary, engage threats while preserving mobility and situational awareness. For instructors, mastery of these methods is not optional—it is essential. Teaching proper light discipline, grip adaptations, and one-handed shooting skills ensures students can defend themselves with precision and confidence, even when the environment works against them.

Purpose

In low-light or no-light conditions, handheld flashlight techniques allow a shooter to:

- Positively identify threats before engaging (avoiding catastrophic mistakes)
- Control where light is directed independently from muzzle orientation
- Maintain flexibility in confined spaces or around cover
  while weapon-mounted lights (WMLs) are faster to deploy, handheld techniques remain essential for those without WMLs or when using light in non-gun contexts where pointing a gun is unsafe.

Foundational Concepts

Before selecting a specific method:

1. **Light Discipline** – Use intermittent bursts (light on → identify → light off → move) to avoid becoming a fixed target.

2. **Grip Priority** – Accept that light control compromises ideal two-handed grip. Train for one-handed recoil management.
3. **Muzzle–Light Separation** – Keep light beam and muzzle aligned only when engaging, otherwise maintain offset to avoid unintentional muzzle coverage.

Primary Techniques

1. FBI Technique

- **Method:** Flashlight held high and away from body, arm extended slightly to the side.
- **Body Mechanics:** Pistol arm fully extended in shooting stance; flashlight arm bent at ~100–120°, angled away from head.
- **Advantages:**
    - Moves light source off shooter's body line, making it harder for adversary to aim at you.
    - Effective for scanning without muzzling unknowns.
- **Disadvantages:**
    - Less stability for aiming.
    - Fatiguing over time.
- **Best Use:** Searching and identification before engagement; open areas.

2. Harries Technique

- **Method:** Flashlight in support hand, back of hand pressed against back of shooting hand wrist or forearm; wrists locked to form an isometric tension.
- **Body Mechanics:** Strong hand grips pistol; support hand rotated palm-up holding flashlight; back of hands pressed together.
- **Advantages:**
    - Creates a semi-two-handed platform with more recoil control.
    - Works well in confined spaces.
- **Disadvantages:**
    - Muzzles anything you illuminate—requires strict threat identification discipline.

- **Best Use:** Static engagements, when you need maximum control.

3. Neck Index

- **Method:** Flashlight held near jawline or under chin, indexed to neck/cheek.
- **Body Mechanics:** Strong hand extended with pistol; support hand flashlight pressed lightly against jawline with light projecting forward.
- **Advantages:**
  - Excellent for navigating tight spaces and using cover.
  - Quick to transition between scanning and shooting.
- **Disadvantages:**
  - Light very close to head—adversary can target your position.
- **Best Use:** Indoor clearing, tight hallways.

4. Rogers/SureFire Technique

- **Method:** Uses a flashlight with a tail-cap switch, held between index and middle fingers of support hand; allows partial two-handed grip.
- **Body Mechanics:** Support hand fingers wrap around flashlight and also contact pistol grip; light activated by squeezing fingers.
- **Advantages:**
  - Most stable shooting platform for handheld light.
  - Quick on/off with natural hand squeeze.
- **Disadvantages:**
  - Requires specific flashlight design.
  - Fine motor skills can degrade under stress.
- **Best Use:** When equipment is matched to the shooter's skill level.

5. Chapman Technique

- **Method:** Similar to a two-handed grip; flashlight held like a syringe grip between index and middle fingers with thumb on switch.
- **Body Mechanics:** Support hand partially wraps pistol grip with flashlight in between.
- **Advantages:**
    - Provides strong two-handed control.
- **Disadvantages:**
    - Works best with longer flashlights and specific switch placement.
- **Best Use:** Outdoor engagements, prolonged low-light patrol.

6. Ayoob Technique

- **Method:** Named after Massad Ayoob. The flashlight is held in an icepick grip (lens projecting down), support hand backs against shooting hand knuckles, forming a modified Harries without full wrist lock.
- **Advantages:**
    - Works with small flashlights.
    - Easier to transition between light and empty-hand control.
- **Disadvantages:**
    - Less stable than Harries.
    - Reduced reach for light beam.
- **Best Use:** Close quarters, when frequent hand transitions are needed.

7. Syringe Grip

- **Method:** Similar to Rogers/SureFire, but flashlight body is held like a syringe, with thumb or finger operating a tail-cap or pressure switch.

- **Advantages:**
    - Allows partial two-handed grip.
    - Works with certain flashlight designs that have ring or groove for grip.
- **Disadvantages:**
    - Requires flashlight with proper diameter.
- **Best Use:** Mixed environment—searching, then rapid engagement.

8. FBI Modified / Temple Index Light

- **Method:** Variation of the FBI technique—light held close to the side of the head, pointed forward, mimicking a "temple index."
- **Advantages:**
    - Keeps light aligned with head movement.
    - Fast transition from search to shoot.
- **Disadvantages:**
    - Clearly marks shooter's head location.
- **Best Use:** Tactical building searches with frequent head movement.

9. Underhand / Mag-Lite Technique

- **Method:** Flashlight (often long-bodied like a Mag-Lite) held under the pistol hand, supporting the pistol from below.
- **Advantages:**
    - Can use flashlight as a striking tool in close quarters.
    - Very stable with heavy lights.
- **Disadvantages:**
    - Outdated for small modern tactical lights.
    - Adds bulk and slows transitions.
- **Best Use:** Security work, law enforcement with baton-style lights.

10. FBI Arc Sweep

- **Method:** FBI-style light position, but the support hand sweeps the beam in a wide arc to disorient adversaries or search multiple areas quickly.
- **Advantages:**
  - Excellent for disorientation and wide-area searching.
- **Disadvantages:**
  - Burns battery quickly.
  - Risk of giving away position repeatedly.
- **Best Use:** Outdoor area searches, tracking suspects.

11. Reverse Harries

- **Method:** Flashlight held palm-down in support hand, crossing under the pistol arm instead of behind it.
- **Advantages:**
  - May be more comfortable for shooters with limited wrist flexibility.
  - Similar recoil control to Harries.
- **Disadvantages:**
  - Can block some muzzle clearance.
- **Best Use:** Adaptation for injury or limited wrist range.

12. Modified Neck Index (Jaw Index)

- **Method:** Flashlight indexed against jawline rather than under chin—creates a consistent point of aim with less neck exposure.
- **Advantages:**
  - Slightly safer than full neck index in terms of target aiming at light.
  - Retains rapid deployment.

- **Disadvantages:**
    - Still close to head; can become a bullet magnet.
- **Best Use:** Hallways, doorways, short movements between cover.

13. FBI Off-Set Hip

- **Method:** Flashlight held low and off to the side at hip level, angled upward.
- **Advantages:**
    - Less visible from a distance.
    - Light splash can still illuminate threats without revealing exact position.
- **Disadvantages:**
    - Limited beam reach.
- **Best Use:** Stealth movement in low light.

Handheld Flashlight One-Handed Pistol Techniques – Strengths & Weaknesses

Technique	Stability for Shooting	Light Control / Search Ability	Muzzle–Light Separation	Speed to Engage	Strengths	Weaknesses
FBI	Low	High	Excellent	Moderate	Keeps light off body line; great for searching without muzzling	Fatiguing; less recoil control
Harries	High	Moderate	Poor	Fast	Semi-two-handed stability; works in confined spaces	Light always on muzzle line; slower to move between targets

Technique	Stability for Shooting	Light Control / Search Ability	Muzzle–Light Separation	Speed to Engage	Strengths	Weaknesses
Neck Index	Medium	High	Poor	Very Fast	Fast transitions; consistent beam alignment	Light close to head makes shooter easy to target
Rogers/SureFire	High	High	Moderate	Very Fast	Strong control; quick light activation with grip	Requires specific flashlight; grip-sensitive
Chapman	High	High	Moderate	Fast	Two-handed control; comfortable for prolonged use	Works best with certain flashlight lengths
Ayoob	Medium	Moderate	Moderate	Fast	Works with small flashlights; quick to transition to empty-hand	Less stability than Harries; shorter beam reach
Syringe Grip	High	High	Moderate	Fast	Allows partial two-hand grip; intuitive for some	Needs proper flashlight shape; can be awkward with gloves
Temple Index	Medium	High	Poor	Very Fast	Follows natural head movement; quick from search to shoot	Clearly reveals head location

Technique	Stability for Shooting	Light Control / Search Ability	Muzzle–Light Separation	Speed to Engage	Strengths	Weaknesses
Underhand/Mag-Lite	High	Low	Poor	Slow	Very stable with long, heavy lights; can double as impact tool	Bulky; outdated for small modern lights
FBI Arc Sweep	Low	Very High	Excellent	Moderate	Sweeps large area; can disorient threats	Burns battery; reveals position repeatedly
Reverse Harries	Medium	Moderate	Poor	Moderate	Good for limited wrist mobility; similar control to Harries	Can interfere with muzzle clearance
Modified Neck Index	Medium	High	Poor	Very Fast	Slightly less exposure than full Neck Index	Still close to head; moderate stability only
FBI Off-Set Hip	Low	Moderate	Excellent	Slow	Keeps light low; can illuminate indirectly for stealth	Limited beam reach; poor recoil control

Handheld Flashlight One-Handed Pistol Techniques – Quick Reference

Technique	Grip Type	Stability	Primary Tactical Purpose
FBI	Standard pistol + flashlight held high/away	Low	Search and identify without muzzling unknowns; reduce risk of being targeted
Harries	Wrist-to-wrist lock	High	Stable shooting in confined spaces; quick engagement
Neck Index	Flashlight indexed to jaw/neck	Medium	Fast ID-to-shoot indoors; tight hallways
Rogers/SureFire	Syringe grip with pressure switch	High	Maximum control with rapid light activation for trained users
Chapman	Modified two-hand with flashlight in support hand	High	Prolonged low-light patrol or engagements
Ayoob	Icepick grip, back of hands together	Medium	Works with small lights; flexible for hand-to-hand transition
Syringe Grip	Syringe grip (thumb/finger activation)	High	Search and engagement with partial two-hand control
Temple Index	Flashlight aligned at temple/head	Medium	Quick ID indoors, natural with head movement
Underhand/Mag-Lite	Support hand under pistol, baton-style	High	Heavy flashlight stability; close-quarters striking option
FBI Arc Sweep	Standard pistol + high arc light sweep	Low	Wide-area searching and threat disorientation
Reverse Harries	Palm-down cross-under	Medium	Adapted Harries for injury/limited mobility
Modified Neck Index	Flashlight indexed to jawline	Medium	Slightly less exposure than full neck index; fast indoors
FBI Off-Set Hip	Low, off-hip hold	Low	Stealth movement with indirect illumination

Training Considerations

- **Dry Fire:** Practice drawing pistol and activating flashlight separately, then together.
- **Live Fire:** Alternate strong-hand only shooting with each light technique under time pressure.
- **Movement Drills:** Practice "light on → ID → move → engage" to prevent light-tracking by adversary.
- **Cover Integration:** Use cover edges to shield light until ready to expose and engage.
- **Low-Light Decision-Making:** Train scenarios where light is used but no shots are fired, reinforces threat identification discipline.

Mastering handheld flashlight techniques transforms low-light shooting from a liability into a tactical advantage. The concealed carrier gains the ability to identify threats, control visual dominance, and maintain readiness without compromising safety. Instructors who fully understand these methods can bridge the gap between daylight proficiency and real-world defensive capability, giving their students skills that extend far beyond the range. This subject demands deliberate practice, informed instruction, and disciplined application because in the darkness, the one who controls the light controls the fight.

Use of a Weapon-Mounted Pistol Light for Everyday Carry (EDC)

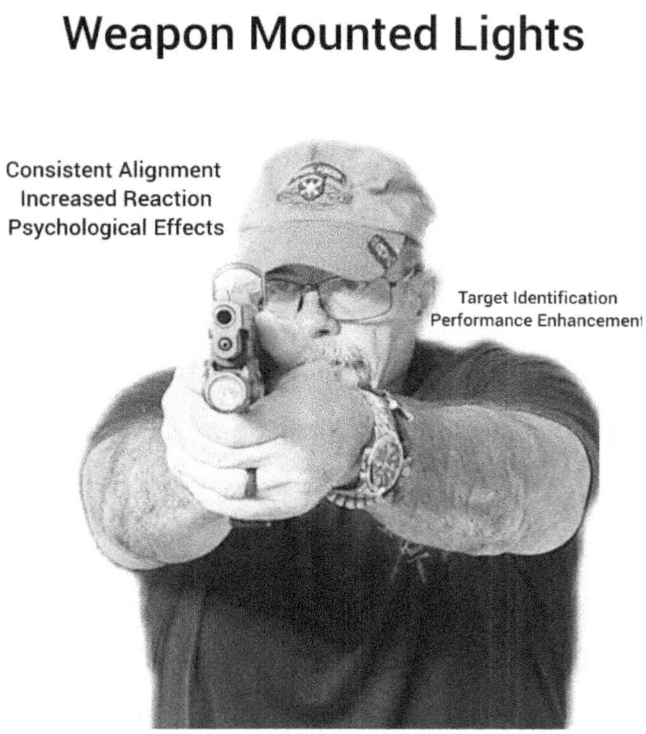

Purpose and Justification

A weapon-mounted pistol light (WML) is a force-multiplying accessory that serves two primary functions for the armed citizen:

1. **Target Identification** – You cannot lawfully engage what you cannot clearly identify. In a defensive shooting, proper illumination allows the carrier to distinguish between a legitimate threat and a non-threat in low light.
2. **Low-Light Performance Enhancement** – A WML increases the shooter's ability to apply accurate fire in reduced visibility conditions by enabling clear sight alignment, sight picture, and positive target acquisition.

Statistics and field data indicate that the majority of violent criminal assaults occur in diminished light—either at night, indoors, or in transitional spaces. This makes illumination capability not optional, but a core element of a comprehensive EDC setup.

Advantages

- **Hands-Free Target Illumination** – A WML frees the support hand for tasks such as opening doors, using a phone, manipulating a child or dependent, or stabilizing oneself.

- **Consistent Alignment** – The light beam is automatically aligned with the muzzle, ensuring that if the target is illuminated, it is also in the gun's potential line of fire.
- **Increased Reaction Speed** – Immediate access to light without the need to deploy and orient a separate flashlight can reduce the time between recognition and response.
- **Better Weapon Retention** – Two-handed grip is maintained, reducing the risk of disarmament compared to some handheld flashlight shooting techniques.
- **Psychological Effect on Threats** – High-lumen light can temporarily overwhelm an aggressor's night-adapted vision, creating a brief tactical advantage.

Limitations and Considerations

- **Muzzle Discipline Risk** – A WML illuminates only where the muzzle is pointed. This can create serious legal and safety issues if the user violates Rule 2 ("Never point the muzzle at anything you are not willing to destroy") when searching or clearing.
- **Holster Requirements** – Carrying a pistol with a WML requires a purpose-built holster with proper retention and clearance. This can limit holster availability and concealment options.
- **Weight and Balance Changes** – Adding a light changes the pistol's balance and may affect recoil characteristics. While often beneficial for recoil control, it can alter draw stroke feel and sight tracking.
- **Light Discipline** – Overuse of light can reveal your position or give the threat time to react. Training must emphasize intermittent, controlled use rather than continuous beam projection.

- **Battery Dependence** – WMLs are only effective if properly maintained with charged batteries. A failure to inspect and replace power sources can render them useless when needed most.

Best Practices for Civilian EDC

1. **Combine WML with a Handheld Light** – A WML is a supplement, not a replacement. A handheld flashlight allows for low-profile searching and navigation without pointing a firearm at unknowns.
2. **Train for Multiple Activation Methods** – Learn to activate the WML with both the support-hand thumb and index finger, and to manipulate it under stress while maintaining a combat grip.
3. **Scenario-Based Training** – Practice home-defense and public-space scenarios that require positive target identification, engagement, and decision-making under varying lighting conditions.
4. **Understand Legal Implications** – Illumination and aiming at an individual in public can be interpreted as a use of force. Know your jurisdiction's laws regarding brandishing, threat display, and the use of deadly force.
5. **Integrate into the Draw Stroke** – Incorporate WML activation into your draw practice so that the light is employed instinctively when appropriate, without disrupting sight alignment.

Conclusion

For the responsibly armed citizen, a weapon-mounted pistol light offers significant advantages in threat identification, accuracy, and control during low-light encounters. When paired with proper training, a WML enhances both safety and effectiveness in defensive situations. However, it demands disciplined handling, consistent practice, and a clear understanding of its limitations. The armed professional and the everyday carrier alike should view the WML as a tool that extends capability—not as a substitute for sound tactics, judgment, or firearm fundamentals.

Instructor Foreword: The Importance of Dry Fire

I am a proponent of dry firing and have been since the beginning of my shooting journey. My introduction came through the US Army Special Forces Special Operations and Techniques (SOT) and the Advanced Reconnaissance, Target Analysis, and Exploitation Techniques Course (SFARTAETC). In both programs, dry fire was not optional. After 10-hour live fire days, we were still required to conduct **two hours of dry fire each night** before pistols could be turned in to the arms room.

This repetition forged consistency, discipline, and most importantly—**confidence**. These are not just military skills; they are foundational skills that apply to **every armed citizen and student**, regardless of background.

Safety Note: In dry fire, the way you handle your pistol with no ammunition is the exact way you will handle it with live ammunition. **Do not compromise safety protocols**.

Core Dry Fire Principles to Instill in New Shooters

1. **Dry Fire Builds Everything but Recoil Management** Dry fire develops **grip**, **trigger control**, **presentation**, **sight alignment**, **transitions**, **draw strokes**, and **reloads**. The only element it cannot replicate fully is **recoil management**.
2. **Dead Trigger Use for Grip Evaluation** A properly executed dead trigger rep allows instructors to assess **how the pistol behaves under pressure**. If the shooter's grip is weak or unbalanced, the sight package will move. If it's correct, it won't. This creates a perfect diagnostic environment.

3. **Consistency, Predictability, Repeatability (CPR)** Every movement should become:
   - **Consistent**: Same input each time
   - **Predictable**: Same result each time
   - **Repeatable**: Sustainable under time, fatigue, or stress
4. **Time + Dedication = Proficiency** Repetition drives mastery. Studies show it takes roughly **10,000 reps** to create deep neurological imprinting that transitions a task from conscious to subconscious execution. Dry fire is where these reps happen affordably and safely.

Teaching Dry Fire to Beginning Shooters

- **Start Simple**: Introduce dry fire only after clear explanation of **gun safety**, **muzzle awareness**, and **range commands**.
- **Introduce Realism Gradually**: Many new shooters struggle when transitioning from dry to live fire. They've trained without recoil, flash, or noise. Counter this by explaining upfront: *"Dry fire builds mechanics. Live fire builds reaction and recoil control."
- **Build Initial Confidence**: Start with exercises like wall drills or trigger press reps on large, close targets.
- **Language Matters**: Use plain, precise terms like "press" instead of "pull," and "target-focused" or "sight-focused" when introducing visual alignment.
- **Grip Pathway Evaluation**: Teach students to ensure their **grip is identical each time**. Instruct them to slow down and feel the buildup of grip pressure before drawing.

Teaching Dry Fire to Intermediate Shooters

- **Layer in Complexity**: Introduce tasks such as concealed carry draw, reloads, and transitions.
- **Introduce Pressure**: Add time standards, decision drills, and stress inoculation (e.g., verbal cues or distraction noise).
- **Refine Mechanics**: Use video feedback or mirrors to ensure movement paths are clean, pistol presentation is on the eye-target line, and sight packages are acquired cleanly.
- **Dead Trigger Diagnostic Drills**: This is where intermediate shooters should be introduced to aggressive, violent trigger inputs using a dead trigger. This highlights flaws in grip integrity, hand placement, and sympathetic pressure.

Practical Dry Fire Examples (All Levels)

1. **Draw to Sight Picture Drill**
    - Build consistent draw path.
    - Sight package must land on the intended spot without floating or diving.
2. **Dead Trigger Grip Check Drill**
    - Use a dead trigger and press violently. Instructors watch for sight disruption. If the dot moves, grip is flawed.
3. **Transition Drill**
    - Drive pistol between two targets while keeping the sight package level. Do not replicate recoil.
4. **Reload Reps**
    - Repeated mag changes with eyes on target. Ensure consistent mag index and insertion.

5. **Structure and Movement Rehearsals**
    - "Dirt dive" a stage, a room clearing, or movement sequence. Dry fire the transitions, posture changes, and movement efficiency.

How to Set Up for Dead Trigger Press by Pistol Type

- **Double Action Pistols**:
    - Press through the DA trigger. After hammer fall, keep pressing without resetting.
- **Single Action Pistols**:
    - After first press, do not reset the trigger. Conduct subsequent reps on the dead trigger.
- **Striker-Fired Pistols**:
    - Disable the reset by placing a rubber band or index card in the breech with slide slightly out of battery.

Instructor Tip: Instruct students to **press with intensity**—the harder they press, the more likely they are to reveal subtle grip deficiencies.

Final Word to Instructors

Dry fire is not a substitute for live fire—it is the **foundation** for it. An instructor must:

- Explain clearly what dry fire does and does not do.
- Build dry fire into every level of instruction.
- Diagnose grip, trigger control, and presentation issues more efficiently than on the range.

Reinforce this principle:

"Dry fire is where we program. Live fire is where we test."

When a student is able to execute dry fire reps that are clean, consistent, and critique-resistant, they are ready to bring that skill into the real world—with live fire confidence, control, and composure.

Here's a **detailed comparison** of **Live Trigger Dry Fire**, **Dead Trigger Dry Fire**, and **Ball and Dummy Fire**, including definitions, purposes, differences, and use cases.

1. Live Trigger Dry Fire

Definition

Dry fire where the shooter **presses the trigger until the striker or hammer releases**—just like during a real shot. The trigger is "live," meaning it has resistance and breaks.

Common in striker-fired and hammer-fired firearms. The slide must typically be cycled between reps to reset the trigger.

Purpose

- Train **trigger press mechanics**
- Identify and correct **anticipation, flinch, or heeling**
- Reinforce sight alignment/stability through the **trigger break**
- Build neuromuscular memory for **smooth, controlled press**

Feedback Mechanism

- Sights or red dot movement at the break show error

- Can be enhanced with dry fire lasers or dot tracking

2. Dead Trigger Dry Fire

Definition

Dry fire where the trigger is already spent and **does not break** (no striker fall). This occurs after the gun has been dry-fired once, and the trigger hasn't been reset.

In a striker-fired pistol, after the first trigger press, the trigger becomes "dead" unless you rack the slide. In DA/SA guns, you may get DA trigger pull. For striker guns, it's just slack or resistance with no break.

Purpose

- Practice **mechanics that don't require a trigger break**
- Build consistency in:
  - Draw stroke
  - Grip presentation
  - Reloads
  - Target transitions
  - Recoil follow-through

Feedback Mechanism

- Observes **visual consistency and hand movement**, but not trigger control
- Enables **high-volume reps without slide reset**

3. Ball and Dummy Fire (Live Fire or Simulated)

Definition

A mix of **live rounds and inert dummy rounds** in the magazine (or dry fire reps with expected vs unexpected outcomes). The goal is to expose **anticipation or flinch** under conditions of uncertainty.

In live fire: When the dummy comes up, the shooter presses the trigger and the gun doesn't fire—revealing any pre-ignition movement.

In dry fire: Can be simulated with coach-led "click/bang" calls, or unpredictable dead trigger reps.

Purpose

- Diagnose and correct **flinch or recoil anticipation**
- Build **mental discipline** under stress
- Reinforce **trigger consistency regardless of outcome**

Feedback Mechanism

- If shooter dips, flinches, blinks, or jerks the trigger when the gun doesn't fire, it becomes **instantly visible**

COMPARISON CHART

Feature	Live Trigger Dry Fire	Dead Trigger Dry Fire	Ball & Dummy Fire
Trigger Status	Functional (breaks)	Non-functional (no break)	Mixed (some break, some don't)
Slide Reset Required	Yes (striker-fired guns)	No	No (dry fire) / Yes (live fire)
Primary Focus	Trigger control, sight stability	Mechanics, grip, transitions	Anticipation, mental discipline
Best For	Precision dry fire drills	Volume reps, reloads, transitions	Diagnosing flinch in live/dry fire
Feedback Type	Visual on sights/dot at break	Visual/motion (not trigger)	Shooter reaction to unexpected result
Risk of Poor Habit	Low if done slowly and correctly	Medium if repeated with poor form	High if flinch is not corrected immediately
Need for Live Ammo?	No	No	Yes (traditional) / No (simulated variant)

I. INSTRUCTOR-LEVEL UNDERSTANDING OF DRY FIRE

What Is Dry Fire?

Dry fire is the **intentional practice of firearms manipulation and marksmanship fundamentals without live ammunition**. It is **neuromuscular, cognitive, and**

procedural programming—where skill is built **without recoil**, which allows for **deep isolation of errors**.

Purpose at the Instructor Level:

- Create **flawless, automatic repetitions** of fundamental shooting behaviors
- Remove distractions like recoil, sound, and range pressure to **diagnose micro-errors**
- Train sight picture, trigger control, grip, draw, reloads, and transitions at **perfect tempo**
- Condition **emergency, movement, and concealment skills** safely and efficiently
- Build **decision-making under pressure** via dry "decision drills" or mental reps

Dry fire is where you program the gunfighter's blueprint—live fire is where you test it.

II. WHAT INSTRUCTORS SHOULD BE LOOKING FOR

During student dry fire, look for:

1. Trigger Press Mechanics

- **Straight to the rear** with no lateral movement
- Finger **placement** appropriate for the gun (not too deep or shallow)
- Watch for **"prepping" and staging** on compressed positions

2. Sight Stability at Break

- Dots/sights should **not jump** or shift as the trigger breaks
- Red dot should remain **centered in the window** through press and follow-through

3. Grip Integrity

- Isometric tension between hands
- No **collapse or compensation** as trigger is pressed
- High tang grip remains in position—**no walking down** the backstrap

4. Visual Discipline

- Shooters should be **target-focused or dot-focused** based on the task
- No **glancing at the gun**, especially during reloads or draws
- Look for **target focus override**—are they lifting their head before pressing?

5. Efficient Mechanics

- Draw stroke: Is it **repeatable, close to the body, aggressive, and straight-lined**?
- Reloads: Is the **mag index consistent**, or are they slapping or fishing?
- Transitions: Are they **snapping or dragging the muzzle**?

6. Mental Engagement

- Are they just "going through the motions," or actively **processing and visualizing**?
- Is **internal dialogue** working for or against them?

III. HOW TO TEACH DRY FIRE TO A NEW SHOOTER

Start with this explanation:

"Dry fire is how we make shooting second nature—without the pressure, cost, or noise of live ammo. This is where you get perfect. Every rep builds a habit your body will follow under stress."

Then simplify the idea with **three core principles**:

1. Work Fundamentals Without Interference

"You don't have recoil or blast to distract you. So we're looking for total control—your grip, sights, and trigger must move as one. If you can't do it here, you won't do it at speed with live fire."

Key tip for new shooter:
"Watch your front sight (or red dot). If it moves when you press the trigger, that's your body anticipating. Your job is to press smoothly and keep that sight still."

2. You're Programming Muscle Memory

"Think of dry fire like writing code. What you repeat is what you'll do under stress. So every rep needs to be perfect—speed comes later. Quality builds speed."

Key tip for new shooter:
"We're not rushing. We're engraving perfect reps. You'll be amazed how fast your body adapts when every rep is clean."

3. Use Realistic, Repetitive Scenarios

"You'll work your draw, reloads, malfunction drills, and transitions in the exact order they happen in a fight. You're not pretending—you're preparing."

Key tip for new shooter:
"This is a dress rehearsal. Every time you draw, you should imagine you're responding to a real threat."

COMMON STUDENT MISTAKES TO CORRECT:

Error	What It Looks Like	Correction Strategy
Rushing reps	Choppy draw, poor grip	"Slow is smooth. Get it perfect first."
Glancing at gun	Visual confirmation of slide or magwell	"Trust your index. Focus on the threat."
Slapping trigger	Dot/sight movement on break	"Press to the wall. Control the press."
Overgripping	Shaky sights, tension	"Firm grip, relaxed arms. Don't choke the gun."

Dead Trigger Dry Fire offers a highly valuable opportunity to evaluate and refine a shooter's **grip structure**, because it allows for **repetitive practice** without interruption, and isolates **grip performance under mechanical stress** without recoil or reset distraction.

BENEFITS OF DEAD TRIGGER DRY FIRE FOR GRIP EVALUATION

1. High-Volume Repetition without Slide Reset

- With striker-fired pistols, traditional dry fire requires racking the slide between each live trigger press.
- Dead trigger dry fire allows for **multiple reps without interruption**, which means you can **observe how the grip holds up over time** (e.g., during sustained fire simulation).

Benefit: You're evaluating not just the initial grip, but its **durability across reps**—whether it collapses, loosens, or fatigues.

2. No Trigger Movement = Pure Grip Observation

- Since the trigger doesn't break, the shooter is not anticipating or flinching. Their grip isn't compensating for a "shot."
- This lets the instructor focus solely on:
  - **Grip pressure balance (support vs firing hand)**
  - **Thumb placement and tension**
  - **Heel gap or voids**
  - **"Walk down" of the backstrap over time**

Benefit: You get a clean visual of grip behavior **without the confounding variable of trigger press errors**.

3. Supports Dynamic Grip Evaluation During Movement or Transitions

- Dead trigger dry fire is ideal for **draw drills**, **target transitions**, or **reloads,** where the trigger isn't critical but grip retention is.
- You can monitor whether the shooter:
  - Maintains **grip consistency** through movement
  - Has to **rebuild the grip unnecessarily** between actions
  - Grips harder with one hand to overcompensate for the trigger not breaking

Benefit: You can test **functional integrity**—does the grip hold under stress without the artificial breaks of slide reset?

4. Red Dot Tracking for Grip Diagnosis

- In a red dot-equipped pistol, you can have the shooter simulate recoil tracking (dead trigger dry fire allows rapid consecutive presses without racking).
- Watch how the **dot returns to center** or drifts—this reveals:
  - Grip imbalance
  - Finger isolation errors
  - Torque from one hand

Benefit: Evaluate how well the **grip manages recoil return**—even without real recoil.

5. Isolates and Diagnoses Grip-Related Inconsistencies

Because the only variable being moved is the shooter's **hand and gun**, not internal mechanical movement, you can isolate:

Observation	Possible Grip Issue
Muzzle drifts left/right between reps	Uneven support hand tension
Dot disappears or floats	Poor grip pressure or finger curl
Gun walks low in the hand	Weak backstrap contact / recoil shelf breakdown
Recoil management inconsistent	Lack of grip compression and muscular indexing

A **highly effective training ratio** for most defensive pistol shooters, especially those focused on **skill-building**, is:

Dry Fire to Live Fire Ratio: 5:1 to 10:1

This means for **every 1 round fired live**, you should complete **5 to 10 dry fire reps**.

WHY THIS RATIO WORKS

1. Dry Fire Builds Skill, Live Fire Confirms It

- Dry fire isolates fundamentals (grip, draw, sight picture, trigger press) **without recoil interference**.
- Live fire adds stress, recoil, noise, and pressure—**not the best time to learn** a skill, but the perfect time to validate it.

Dry fire is where you fix problems. Live fire is where you expose them.

2. Dry Fire Allows Massive Repetition Without Cost or Fatigue

- You can do 100+ reps in a dry fire session without ammo or fatigue.
- Live fire (especially with recoil) limits reps due to cost, fatigue, and environmental constraints.

3. Neurological and Motor Learning Requires Repetition

- Building **neuromuscular pathways** for complex movements (draw, reload, transition) requires **hundreds or thousands of correct reps**.
- Dry fire is the only practical way to achieve that volume consistently.

SAMPLE DRY FIRE TO LIVE FIRE RATIO BREAKDOWNS

Shooter Type	Dry:Live Fire Ratio	Example
Civilian CCW / Self-defense	7:1 to 10:1	700 dry reps per 100 live rounds
Competitive shooter	5:1 to 7:1	500 dry reps per 100 live rounds
Law enforcement (qual focus)	4:1 to 6:1	400 dry reps per 100 live rounds

Shooter Type	Dry:Live Fire Ratio	Example
New shooter (early learning)	10:1+	Heavy dry fire emphasis early on

Yes—**beyond the standard "stand and press the trigger" dry fire**, there are several **lesser-known but highly effective dry fire methods** that can enhance real-world performance, especially for concealed carriers, instructors, and high-performance shooters.

These approaches often blend **visual processing**, **problem-solving**, **cognitive stress**, and **environmental realism**.

LESSER-KNOWN TYPES & METHODS OF DRY FIRE TRAINING

1. Cognitive or Processing-Based Dry Fire

Add a **mental decision-making task** before or during the draw/engagement.

Examples:

- Use colored targets—**draw and engage red only if green is present**
- Use numbered or lettered targets—**draw and engage based on a verbal or visual prompt**
- Integrate a **deck of cards**, **dice**, or an **app** that changes the task mid-rep

Purpose: Builds OODA Loop speed, decision-making under time, and target discrimination—**not just motor memory**.

2. Visual Acuity & Perception Dry Fire

Uses dry fire to train **sight clarity, focus transitions**, and **dot acquisition speed**

Examples:

- Use **tiny visual targets (1/4" dots or pencil dots)** at eye level to work high-precision reps
- Rapid focus change drills: alternate between two target distances or sizes
- Use red dot occlusion (with tape or film) to train **target-focused shooting**

Purpose: Improves **dot acquisition**, **confirmation levels**, and **sight-picture processing**—especially under visual noise.

3. Compressed-Time or Micro-Drill Dry Fire

Focus on **only one specific movement**, repeated at high rep counts

Examples:

- **Hand-only mag reloads** from belt to magwell without pistol (mag index training)
- **Draw stroke reps** from concealment to presentation—no trigger press
- **Trigger prep drills** from compressed ready, working the wall only

Purpose: Builds **perfect micro-movements** that are too fast to isolate in live fire.

4. Startle-Flinch Override Dry Fire

Teaches how to recover from a **startle response or flinch** using dry rep scenarios

Examples:

- Start from a **"startle stance"**: hands away, posture off-balance
- Train draw and fire after a **verbal "GO!"** cue or timer with unpredictable delays
- Add pushback, sudden motion, or a bump from a coach just before the rep

Purpose: Conditions the shooter to **override SNS response** and re-engage task focus after disruption.

5. Low Light or No Light Dry Fire

Trains visual and physical handling in light-restricted conditions

Examples:

- Use flashlight techniques (Harries, neck index, or WML) in dry runs
- Perform reps in dim or red-light rooms with target silhouettes
- Practice drawing and engaging using **ambient audio cues only**

Purpose: Builds **low-light orientation**, flashlight handling, and **search/fire transitions**—crucial for home defense training.

6. Dynamic Positional Dry Fire

Simulate movement-based or real-world positions not typically used on a square range

Examples:

- Practice dry fire from **seated, kneeling, prone, or supine** positions
- Draw and engage while **stepping offline, sidestepping, or pivoting**
- Practice from **inside vehicles, doorways, or confined spaces**

Purpose: Conditions **non-static shooting mechanics**—what you'll likely use in real life.

7. Unstable Platform Dry Fire

Builds grip consistency and visual alignment under instability

Examples:

- Stand on a **balance board or foam pad** while performing draw and dry press
- Engage from a **moving or swaying position** (e.g., inside a vehicle or on a platform)
- Shoot one-handed while holding an object in the support hand

Purpose: Trains **control under imbalance**, simulating stress and imperfect conditions.

8. Timer-Based Micro-Goal Dry Fire

Puts specific time-pressure on isolated actions

Examples:

- "Draw to first shot in under 1.50 seconds" (using shot timer dry fire mode)
- "Reload to dry press in under 2.0 seconds"
- "Dot acquisition and press from compressed ready in 0.80 seconds"

Purpose: Develops **explosive speed + discipline**, making dry fire goal-driven.

Bonus: Combine These into Dry Fire Blocks

Use a layered approach:

1. **Technical block** (e.g., draw, reload, press)

2. **Cognitive block** (target ID, decision)
3. **Disruption block** (startle, movement, light)

This creates a **complete performance prep system**, far beyond basic dry fire.

Dry fire training empowers concealed carriers to master essential skills through relentless, ammunition-free repetitions, forging automatic responses that prove vital in life-threatening encounters. Practitioners actively cultivate precise grips, seamless draws, and unflinching trigger presses, while integrating cognitive challenges to accelerate decision-making and adaptability. This disciplined regimen, rooted in neurological imprinting via thousands of targeted iterations, elevates performance far beyond live fire's limitations, minimizing errors amid chaos. Instructors, equipped with exhaustive knowledge of dry fire methodologies—from dead trigger diagnostics to dynamic positional drills—champion this foundation, guiding students toward subconscious excellence and unyielding composure. Ultimately, dry fire's paramount significance lies in its capacity to program survival instincts, ensuring concealed carriers and their mentors alike wield the tools for decisive, responsible action.

Instructor Knowledge: Current Methodologies and Terminologies in Pistol Shooting

As a shooting instructor, maintaining proficiency in contemporary methodologies and terminologies is essential. In the realm of competitive and tactical pistol shooting, certain concepts and naming conventions are attributed to influential figures such as JJ Racaza and Ben Stoeger. While the origins of these ideas may spark debate—much like the attribution of various shooting drills—their precise provenance is secondary to their practical utility. What matters most is a thorough understanding of the terms, conventions, and underlying principles, enabling instructors to effectively convey them to students.

I have tried to provide a structured breakdown and comparison of key visual processing and decision-making models: JJ Racaza's "Attack vs. Control," Ben Stoeger's "Predictive vs. Reactive" shooting, his Visual Confirmation Levels (1–3), and the generalized 5 Levels of Focus. These frameworks are particularly relevant to transitions, visual processing, and performance under speed and pressure in pistol shooting.

1. JJ Racaza's Attack vs. Control

JJ Racaza's model articulates the dynamic balance between velocity and precision in high-stakes shooting scenarios.

- **Attack Mode**
  - Characterized by aggressive, rapid movements.
  - Employed for low-difficulty targets, such as those at close range or with open presentations.
  - Requires minimal visual confirmation.
  - Emphasizes speed at the expense of meticulous precision.
- **Control Mode**
  - Focuses on deliberate, precision-driven actions.
  - Applied to challenging shots, including distant targets, partials, or those adjacent to no-shoots.
  - Demands heightened visual confirmation before and during the shot.
  - Prioritizes accuracy over rapidity.

Purpose: This dichotomy equips shooters to discern when to accelerate aggressively ("attack") and when to moderate pace ("control"), thereby minimizing avoidable errors or excessive verification.

2. Ben Stoeger's Predictive vs. Reactive Shooting

Ben Stoeger's approach delineates visual and temporal strategies contingent on target characteristics and shooter assurance.

- **Predictive Shooting**
  - Involves discharging the firearm in anticipation of an adequate sight picture.
  - Suitable for straightforward targets or scenarios where confidence in sight alignment is high.
  - Commonly utilized during transitions or while in motion.
- **Reactive Shooting**
  - Entails withholding the shot until the sight picture is visually verified.
  - More methodical and slower; reserved for demanding shots.
  - Relies on explicit visual cues to affirm alignment prior to firing.

Purpose: The framework differentiates shots amenable to intuitive rhythm and proprioception (predictive) from those necessitating explicit validation (reactive).

3. Ben Stoeger's Visual Confirmation Levels (1–3)

This tiered system quantifies the extent of visual input required prior to trigger break, calibrating effort to target demands.

- **VC 1 (Minimal Confirmation)**
    - Involves scant or absent clear sight picture.
    - Aligns with predictive shooting.
    - Ideal for expansive targets at proximity.
    - Sufficient peripheral awareness permits confident firing without intensive aiming.
- **VC 2 (Moderate Confirmation)**
    - Features distinct visibility and alignment of the front sight or dot, though briefly.
    - Appropriate for intermediate distances, partials, or moderate-risk engagements.
    - Alignment is verified, but the shot is executed promptly thereafter.
- **VC 3 (Extensive Confirmation)**
    - Demands a sustained, deliberate sight picture.
    - Essential for extended ranges, hard cover, or stringent no-shoots.
    - Necessitates reactive shooting protocols.

Purpose: It enables shooters to modulate visual rigor according to target complexity, avoiding both under- and over-verification.

4. The 5 Levels of Focus (Attributed to Steve Anderson; Generalized Framework)

This progressive model elucidates stages of visual engagement and cognitive integration in shooting.

- **Level 1: No Focus**
  - Absence of directed attention; minimal awareness.
  - Results in frequent misses without comprehension of causation.
- **Level 2: Target Focus**
  - Attention confined to the target, yielding broad but superficial detail.
  - Prevalent among novices or under duress.
- **Level 3: Sight Awareness**
  - Sights enter the field of view but lack fixation.
  - Common in developing shooters.
- **Level 4: Front Sight Focus**
  - Precise alignment is observed, fostering reliable accuracy.
  - Enables consistent shot calling; correlates with VC 2 and VC 3.
- **Level 5: Visual Patience/Mastery**
  - Comprehensive perception encompasses target, sights, motion, and transitions.
  - Facilitates real-time adaptations.
  - Exemplifies elite proficiency, blending reactive and predictive elements as warranted.

Purpose: The levels cultivate heightened awareness and command over visual focus, progressing from rudimentary to sophisticated application.

Comparison Matrix

The following table synthesizes these concepts, highlighting emphases on speed, accuracy, target dependency, visual processing, and typical applications.

Concept	**Speed-First**	**Accuracy-First**	**Based on Target Difficulty**	**Visual Processing Emphasis**	**When Used**
JJ Attack	Yes	No	Yes	Moderate	Close/fast targets
JJ Control	No	Yes	Yes	High	Hard/technical shots
Predictive	Yes	No	Yes	Moderate	Close/familiar targets
Reactive	No	Yes	Yes	High	Long/tight targets
VC 1	Yes	No	Yes	Low	Hoser stages
VC 2	Balanced	Balanced	Yes	Moderate	Most targets
VC 3	No	Yes	Yes	High	Far/partial targets
Focus Levels 1–2	No	No	No	Poor	Novice/poor performance
Focus Level 3	Balanced	Balanced	Inconsistent	Moderate	Mid-level
Focus Levels 4–5	No	Yes	Yes	Excellent	Expert shooters

Nuanced Breakdown for Instructors and Advanced Shooters

Beyond foundational comprehension, instructors must delve into the subtleties of these methodologies. This deeper analysis illuminates the rationale, timing, and integration of each, fostering adaptive instruction for advanced practitioners.

JJ Racaza's Attack vs. Control

- **Attack Mode**
  - **Mindset**: Emphasize aggressive pacing, propelling the firearm through sequences with elevated confidence and low error tolerance.
  - **Applications**: Proximity engagements (<7 yards), rapid steel arrays (3–5 yards), or ambulatory shooting where exactitude is subordinate.
  - **Visual Behavior**: Prioritize target fixation over sight-centric detail; rely on kinesthetic indexing from extensive repetition.
  - **Risks**: Outpacing visual acuity or premature trigger breaks sans stabilization.
  - **Prerequisites**: Robust indexing and autonomic firearm handling; hallmark of elite performers.
- **Control Mode**
  - **Mindset**: Adopt a respectful, measured approach to ensure sight dominance.
  - **Applications**: Constricted partials, extended distances (15–25+ yards), or unstable postures (e.g., barricades or kneeling).
  - **Visual Behavior**: Constrict focus to the dot or front sight, incorporating intentional pauses for validation.
  - **Risks**: Excessive scrutiny leading to hesitation or anxiety-induced disruption.

Integration: Proficiency emerges from fluid alternation, even mid-array—escalating to attack when viable, reverting to control as exigencies demand.

Ben Stoeger's Predictive vs. Reactive Shooting

- **Predictive Shooting**
  - **Definition**: Trigger activation synchronized with anticipated alignment, bypassing exhaustive confirmation.
  - **Traits**: Optimal for oscillating targets, close doubles, or sequential arrays; involves preemptive grip and trigger preparation.
  - **Visual Element**: Awareness of projected sight trajectory via biomechanics.
  - **Success Indicators**: Tight groupings and efficient splits absent pursuit.
  - **Pitfalls**: Erroneous assumptions yielding misses or recoil-induced flinching if fundamentals falter.
- **Reactive Shooting**
  - **Definition**: Deferral of the shot pending visual affirmation of alignment.
  - **Necessity**: Precision demands like distant headshots, obscured dots, or single-shot evaluations.
  - **Timing**: Perceived as slower yet efficient by averting corrections.
  - **Risks**: Prolonged fixation or immobilization under competitive strain.

Pro Tip: Hybridize by prepping predictively during transitions while reserving reactive confirmation for the shot itself.

Ben Stoeger's Visual Confirmation Levels (1–3)

The table below details visual cues, contexts, and exemplary drills for each level.

VC Level	What You See	Used When	Example Drill
VC 1	Fleeting glimpse of dot/sight in vicinity	Expansive targets at close range	3-yard Bill Drill
VC 2	Distinct entry of front sight/dot into target center	10–15 yards with adjacent no-shoots	15-yard Accelerator Drill
VC 3	Sustained, intentional sight picture	20–30 yards on diminutive steel or tight partials	25-yard Head Box (Static)

The 5 Levels of Focus: Detailed Framework

This model transcends mere observation, probing the depth of visual assimilation and its influence on decision-making. It empowers instructors to pinpoint deficiencies, customize interventions, and guide evolution from deliberate to instinctive execution.

Overview Table:

Level	Focus Description	Shooter Behavior
Level 1	No visual focus	Looking without perceiving
Level 2	Target-focused only	Disregarding sights
Level 3	Sights enter awareness	Inconsistent sight utilization
Level 4	Conscious sight alignment	Initiation of accurate shot calling
Level 5	Visual control mastery	Intuitive, responsive management

- **Level 1: No Visual Focus**
    - **Description**: Indiscriminate gaze or erratic scanning; prevalent in novices or amid overload.
    - **Mental State**: Overwhelmed reactivity sans planning or anchors.
    - **Visual Behavior**: Open eyes yield no actionable data; possible recoil-induced blinking.
    - **Instructor Notes**: Incapacity for shot calling; tied to inexperience, poor preparation, or exhaustion.
    - **Remediation**: Employ dry-fire with focal points; query post-shot observations to instill engagement.
- **Level 2: Target Focus Only**
    - **Description**: Exclusive target fixation, evoking instinctive point shooting.
    - **Mental State**: Prioritizing haste over precision, often stress-induced.
    - **Visual Behavior**: Alignment overlooked; reliance on indexing or urgency.
    - **Instructor Notes**: Viable at ultra-close ranges (3–5 yards) but deficient beyond.
    - **Remediation**: Introduce dot drills or graduated-distance controlled pairs with mandatory calling.
- **Level 3: Sights Enter Awareness**
    - **Description**: Emerging sight recognition without full exploitation; a pivotal intermediate stage.
    - **Mental State**: Dividing attention, with resultant indecision on shot timing.
    - **Visual Behavior**: Transient sight appearances, susceptible to overrides or blinks.
    - **Instructor Notes**: Prone to excessive validation; hesitation risks.
    - **Remediation**: Incorporate VC 2 exercises (7–15 yards on partials); advocate firing upon acceptable sights.
-

- **Level 4: Conscious Sight Alignment and Shot Calling**
  - **Description**: Intentional sight prioritization, leveraging visuals for informed actions.
  - **Mental State**: Directed focus yields a feedback cycle.
  - **Visual Behavior**: Tracks dot elevation and recovery; sustains on complexities.
  - **Instructor Notes**: Enables modality blending (predictive/reactive); handles diverse arrays.
  - **Remediation**: Accelerate under duress via Accelerator Drills, Dot Torture, or El Presidente variants.
- **Level 5: Visual Mastery (Focus on Demand)**
  - **Description**: Adaptive focus allocation across multiple elements in real time.
  - **Mental State**: Subconscious mechanics liberate consciousness for strategy.
  - **Visual Behavior**: Multifaceted perception (e.g., dot path, recoil, target contours).
  - **Instructor Notes**: Attained by few; vital for pinnacle performance and adaptability.
  - **Remediation**: Reinforce with advanced regimens like 3-2-1 Drills, partial transitions, or reactive scenarios.

Principles Over Techniques

Instructional Philosophy: Principles Over Techniques

Professional Definition and Rationale

As a firearms instructor, your primary objective extends beyond teaching students to execute specific tasks; it is to arm them with the foundational "why"—the guiding principles that underpin all effective actions under duress. Techniques represent mere applications of these principles, tailored to particular scenarios, body types, mission requirements, or environmental factors.

Why Principles Matter More Than Techniques

- Techniques are situational; principles are universal.
- Techniques falter when contexts shift; principles adapt seamlessly.
- Principles cultivate problem-solvers; techniques breed rote performers.
- Principles endure under stress; isolated techniques erode.

By emphasizing principles, instructors empower students to critically assess their actions, improvise in fluid situations, and transcend inflexible methodologies.

Core Firearms Principles (with Examples of Supporting Techniques)

Principle	Description	Techniques That Support It
Efficient Movement	Movement should minimize exposure while maximizing survivability.	- Slicing the pie - Lateral movement off the X - Bounding overwatch
Consistent Sight Alignment and Visual Control	The ability to align sights or dot predictably with the eyes, irrespective of position or pace.	- High-ready presentation - Compressed ready - Temple index for movement
Trigger Control Relative to Visual Confirmation	Precision in trigger manipulation must align with visual input and target size/distance.	- "Confirmation 1–2–3" model - Prep and press vs. fast slap reset shooting

Principle	Description	Techniques That Support It
Situational Awareness and Cognitive Processing	Shooters must detect threats, process data, and decide in real time.	- OODA loop-based drills - Reactive steel drills - Shoot/no-shoot scenario-based training
Balance of Speed and Precision	The shooter must discern when to accelerate or decelerate, harmonizing accuracy with exigency.	- Failure-to-stop drills - Bill drill vs. Dot Torture - Speed reload vs. retention reload decision-making

Example for Instructional Use: Drawing the Firearm Technique-Oriented Approach (Limiting)

"You must always draw from the 3 o'clock outside-the-waistband (OWB) holster using this exact step-by-step sequence: 1. Clear cover garment, 2. Establish master grip, 3. Lift and rotate, 4. Join hands, 5. Extend to target."

Principle-Oriented Approach (Flexible)

"The governing principle is an efficient, consistent draw that orients the muzzle toward the target and aligns the sights as swiftly as the situation demands. Techniques—whether from OWB, appendix inside-the-waistband (AIWB), or concealment—must accommodate your attire, holster configuration, and threat distance. While steps may vary subtly, the principle endures: clear, grip, draw, orient, engage."

Guidelines for Instructors

1. **Always Explain the Why Behind the How**
   Link every technique to its principle. For instance: "Why index this way? To maintain control and minimize profile."
2. **Present Multiple Valid Techniques When Possible**
   Provide options suited to diverse physiques, gear, or expertise levels. This enables students to tailor their approach while remaining anchored in principles.
3. **Use Failure Points to Reinforce Principles**
   When a technique falters, redirect to the principle. Example: "Your reload stalled due to lost visual control of the magwell—let's revisit the principle of visual indexing."
4. **Evaluate Progress by Principle Application, Not Mere Drill Performance**
   Probe: "Can they articulate why they selected this method?" or "Can they adapt amid evolving conditions?"

Summary Statement for Instructor Use

"Techniques are tools in the toolbox, but principles form the blueprint. My role isn't to stock your toolbox solely with my tools—it's to furnish the blueprint, enabling you to select the optimal tool for the moment."

A Deeper Dive into the Principles of Combat and Their Influence on Pistol Shooting

Combat—whether in military operations, law enforcement encounters, or personal defense—adheres to timeless principles that shape the deployment of tactics, techniques, and tools such as the pistol. Fundamentally, these principles revolve around securing and sustaining superiority in volatile, high-risk settings. This exploration is structured to facilitate instructor-level discourse, bridging conceptual divides for civilian and professional shooters alike.

I. Core Combat Principles (Strategic and Tactical)

1. **Violence of Action**
   - **Definition**: Swift, overpowering force to stun, disrupt, and overpower the adversary.
   - **Influence on Pistol Shooting**:
     - Rapid, resolute engagements.
     - Aggressive target transitions.
     - Unwavering commitment to each shot.
2. **Speed**
   - **Definition**: Achieving tempo superiority; outpacing the opponent's response.
   - **Influence on Pistol Shooting**:
     - Prioritizes draw velocity, target acquisition, and firing rhythm.
     - Stresses streamlined manipulations: reloads, clearances, and movement.
     - Aligns with visual Confirmation Level 1 (high-speed shooting).
3. **Surprise**
   - **Definition**: Attacking in unanticipated ways to generate exploitable edges.
   - **Influence on Pistol Shooting**:
     - Exploitation of angles, motion, and timing.
     - Concealed carry strategies: masked draw strokes, misleading stances.
     - Firing from atypical positions or while in transit.

4. **Security / Force Protection**
    - **Definition**: Safeguarding one's operational capacity during engagement.
    - **Influence on Pistol Shooting**:
        - Utilization of cover and concealment.
        - Post-engagement assessments and vigilance.
        - One-handed techniques for injury or constrained scenarios.
5. **Offensive Action (Initiative)**
    - **Definition**: Proactively imposing one's intent to control engagement dynamics.
    - **Influence on Pistol Shooting**:
        - Preemptive preparedness (OODA cycle leverage).
        - Instant counteroffensive exercises.
        - Psychological ascendancy via posture and pace.
6. **Adaptability (Flexibility)**
    - **Definition**: Rapid recalibration to evolving battle elements—terrain, foe strategies, equipment issues.
    - **Influence on Pistol Shooting**:
        - Seamless malfunction resolutions.
        - Effortless shifts between dominant and support-hand firing.
        - Agile cognitive handling amid duress (decision-making under fire).
7. **Economy of Force**
    - **Definition**: Deploying minimal essential power at pivotal junctures.
    - **Influence on Pistol Shooting**:
        - Ammunition conservation.
        - Prioritizing precision over barrage.
        - Measured application of burst fire or suppressive volleys.

II. Translating Combat Principles into Pistol Shooting Fundamentals

These combat tenets morph into the bedrock principles of proficient pistol handling. Instructors must convey that pistol shooting transcends mechanical proficiency—it embodies combat conduct, steeped in these immutable truths.

III. Pistol Shooting Principles Shaped by Combat Realities

Combat Principle	Pistol Shooting Translation	Instructional Focus
Violence of Action	Commit unequivocally to the shot. Eliminate hesitation. Bridge the mental divide.	Foster assurance via force-on-force simulations.
Speed	Attain swift sight pictures and controlled triggers.	Instruct on confirmation tiers and shot responsibility.
Surprise	Employ concealment, misdirection, and novel draw paths.	Highlight mindset and tactical positioning.
Security	Maintain unwavering weapon command. Avoid outpacing your sights.	Incorporate compressed ready positions, retention firing, and single-hand proficiency.
Initiative	Position yourself as the aggressor, not merely the reactor.	Promote anticipatory choices and immersive scenarios.
Adaptability	Navigate, fire, and resolve issues with fluidity.	Prioritize kinetic range work and mental stress exercises.

Combat Principle	Pistol Shooting Translation	Instructional Focus
Economy	Fire only as necessary. Ensure hits with every round.	Bolster accuracy, discipline, and resource stewardship.

IV. Layered Teaching Framework

Beginner Level

- Frame pistol mechanics as self-preservation tools.
- Concentrate on controlled fundamentals: stance, grip, sight alignment, trigger control.
- Introduce basic combat contexts (e.g., pressured draws from concealment).

Intermediate Level

- Integrate judgment calls and timed exercises.
- Advance to mobility, multi-target engagements, and malfunction handling.
- **Accentuate principles such as speed, initiative, and economy of force.**

Advanced Level

- Incorporate role-based simulations (force-on-force, shoot/no-shoot).
- Demand combat ethos amid exhaustion.
- Challenge against intricate principles like adaptability and surprise.

Instructor Level

- Train practitioners to reason in principles, eschewing rote techniques.
- Elucidate the stress-resilience of each principle.

- Tailor exercises to isolate targeted combat tenets.

V. Example Drill: Principle Integration

Drill Name: Combat Triad Engagement

- **Setup**: Three laterally spaced targets.
- **Purpose**: Fuse Violence of Action, Speed, and Economy of Force.
- **Sequence**:
    1. Draw and deliver two rounds to Target 1 (combat-effective accuracy).
    2. Swiftly shift to Target 2 with one precise round (economy emphasis).
    3. Relocate offline to cover while addressing Target 3 (adaptability and security).
- **Debrief**: Evaluate decisiveness, purposeful movement, and shot accountability.

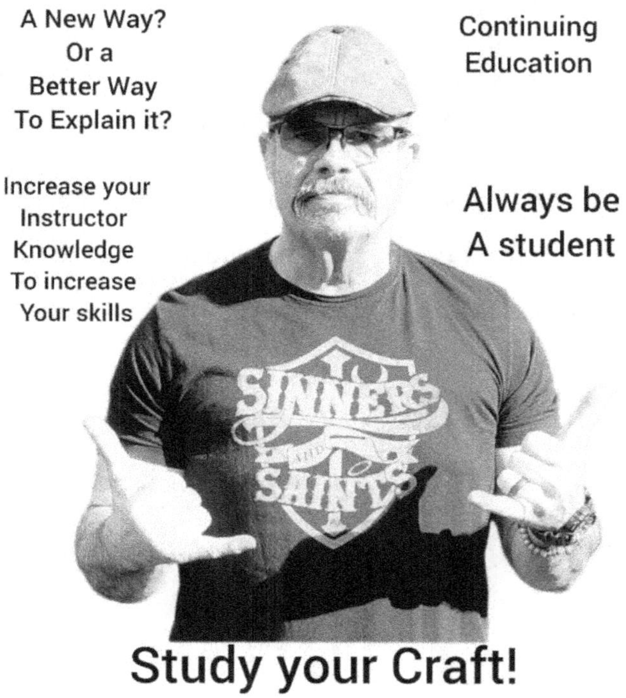

VI. Final Thoughts

Divorcing pistol instruction from combat principles is akin to teaching swimming in arid conditions. Every discharge, maneuver, and choice in pistol employment must stem from a combat-honed perspective. The ultimate aim transcends marksmanship excellence—it is triumph in adversity.

Finished for Now

As a firearms instructor, I am satisfied with the information contained within this book. I know that I have missed something, but I did have to make certain assumptions. The reader and user of this book now has access to a great deal of information, just not everything that I wanted to include.

This book was written for the Every Day Carry individual and the Instructors that teach this subject matter, so I attempted to stay in that lane. I know I veered off the path and included some information that will apply to multiple shooting disciplines.

For Drills and Courses of fire please check out my second book: ***A Green Beret's Guide to Enhanced Pistol Shooting Skills*** **(ISBN: 9798218640354)**

As an author, I learn something new on every outing. This will help me with my next book which I have started to work on so that I can add more depth to many of the subjects that have been presented in this book.

Finished for Now!

Kyle "Panda"Barrington

Instructor Glossary

A

- **Accuracy:** Precision of shot placement on the intended point of aim.
- **Action:** Mechanism that loads, fires, and ejects cartridges.
- **Aiming:** Directing sights toward a target.
- **Aftermarket:** Non-OEM parts added to modify or upgrade performance.
- **Appendix Carry (AIWB):** Carrying a concealed pistol at the front of the waistband.
- **Armor-Piercing:** Ammunition designed to penetrate armor or ballistic shields.
- **Auto-Indexing:** Feature in some pistols that rotates a magazine or cylinder automatically.
- **Automatic Fire:** Continuous fire with one trigger press (rare in pistols, often confused with semi-auto).
- **Axis Shift:** Change in bore axis height affecting recoil control.

B

- **Backstrap:** Rear portion of the grip.
- **Ball Ammunition:** Standard full-metal-jacket training ammo.
- **Ballistics:** Study of projectiles in motion.
- **Barrel:** Tube through which the bullet travels when fired.
- **Battery (In Battery):** Condition where the slide is fully forward and the pistol is ready to fire.
- **Beavertail:** Flared rear section of the frame to prevent slide bite.
- **Bite (Slide Bite):** Injury caused by slide contact with shooter's hand.
- **Blowback:** Simple action design where slide is forced rearward by recoil alone.
- **Bore Axis:** The vertical distance between the bore and the shooter's grip.
- **Break (Trigger Break):** Moment the trigger releases the sear and fires the shot.

C

- **Caliber:** Diameter of the bullet or bore, typically in inches or millimeters.
- **Carry Optic:** Red dot optic designed for concealed carry pistols.
- **Centerfire:** Ammo with a centrally located primer.
- **Clear (the weapon):** Ensuring the firearm is unloaded and safe.
- **Compensator:** Device to redirect gas and reduce muzzle rise.
- **Concealed Carry:** Carrying a hidden firearm on the body.
- **Controlled Pair:** Two deliberate shots with sight picture confirmation in between.

- **Co-Witness:** When iron sights are visible through an optic.
- **Creep:** Unwanted movement in the trigger before the break.
- **Crown:** Muzzle end of the barrel; crucial to bullet stability.

D

- **DAO (Double Action Only):** Each trigger pull both cocks and releases the firing mechanism.
- **Decocker:** Mechanism to safely lower the hammer.
- **Defensive Shooting:** Firearms use for self-protection.
- **Disconnector:** Mechanism that prevents out-of-battery firing.
- **Double Action (DA):** Trigger press both cocks and releases the hammer.
- **Double Feed:** Two rounds attempting to enter the chamber.
- **Double Tap (Hammer Pair):** Two rapid shots, one sight picture.
- **Drop Safety:** Safety that prevents discharge when the pistol is dropped.
- **Drift (Sight Drift):** Adjusting sights laterally for windage.

E

- **Ejection Port:** Opening on the slide where spent cases are expelled.
- **Ejector:** Fixed or spring-loaded part that throws spent casings clear.
- **Elevator Drill:** Exercise that builds target acquisition from various elevations.
- **Extractor:** Mechanical claw that pulls the spent casing from the chamber.
- **Eye Dominance:** The dominant eye used for aiming.
- **Eye Relief:** Distance from optic to eye while maintaining full field of view.

F

- **Failure to Eject (Stovepipe):** Casing remains in ejection port.
- **Failure to Feed:** Next round doesn't enter the chamber.
- **Failure to Fire:** Trigger pull does not result in a shot.
- **Firearm:** A portable gun, in this case, a pistol.
- **Flash Sight Picture:** A fast, rough sight alignment used at close range.
- **Flinch:** Anticipatory reaction that disrupts accuracy.
- **Follow-Through:** Maintaining technique after the shot breaks.
- **Front Sight Focus:** Visual concentration on the front sight.
- **Front Strap:** Forward section of the grip frame.
- **Funnel Magwell:** Flared magwell to speed reloads.

G

- **Gas-Operated:** Pistol action powered by combustion gas pressure.
- **Grip:** Hand interface with the pistol, essential for recoil management.
- **Grip Angle:** The angle between the barrel and the grip frame.
- **Grip Panel:** Side section of the grip, often removable.
- **Grip Safety:** Safety disengaged only when proper grip is applied.
- **Group Size:** Measurement of the spread between multiple hits on target.
- **Guide Rod:** Component that guides recoil spring motion.

H

- **Hair Trigger:** Very light trigger pull weight.
- **Half-Cock:** Hammer partially cocked for added safety or reduced trigger pull.
- **Hammer:** Part that strikes firing pin or primer in hammer-fired guns.
- **Headspace:** Distance between the breech face and chamber shoulder.
- **Hot Range:** Training environment where firearms are loaded.
- **Hydrostatic Shock:** Tissue damage from high-velocity bullets.

I

- **Immediate Action:** Quick malfunction-clearing technique (Tap-Rack-Bang).
- **Indexing:** Consistent hand placement or sight alignment.
- **Inside the Waistband (IWB):** Holster position carried inside the pants.
- **Iron Sights:** Traditional front and rear aiming system made of metal.
- **ISPC/IDPA:** Sport shooting disciplines focused on defensive pistol skills.

J

- **Jam:** Informal term for a malfunction.
- **Jerking the Trigger:** Abrupt movement of the trigger, disturbing aim.

K

- **Keyhole:** An oblong hole on target indicating unstable bullet flight.

L

- **Lanyard Loop:** Attachment point for a retention lanyard.
- **Laser Sight:** Projects a visible laser dot on the target.
- **Lead (the target):** Aiming ahead of a moving target.

- **Lead Exposure:** Health risk from shooting indoor ranges without ventilation.
- **Live Fire:** Practice with real ammunition.
- **Locking Block:** Component that locks barrel and slide together during firing.
- **Low Ready:** Muzzle-down ready position just below line of sight.

M

- **Magazine:** Ammunition-feeding device inserted into the pistol.
- **Magazine Catch/Release:** Mechanism to remove the magazine.
- **Magwell:** Magazine well or opening for insertion.
- **Malfunction:** Any failure of the pistol to fire or operate correctly.
- **Match Grade:** Components manufactured to precise tolerances.
- **Minute of Angle (MOA):** Unit used to measure shot group dispersion.
- **Muzzle:** The front end of the barrel where bullets exit.
- **Muzzle Device:** Accessories like brakes, compensators, or suppressors.
- **Muzzle Flip/Rise:** Upward motion of the barrel under recoil.
- **Muzzle Discipline:** Always keeping the muzzle pointed in a safe direction.

N

- **Natural Point of Aim (NPOA):** The position your body naturally aligns with the sights.
- **Negligent Discharge (ND):** Unintentional firing due to user error.
- **Night Sights:** Sights equipped with tritium or photoluminescent inserts.

O

- **Offset:** Vertical distance between bore and optic.
- **Open Carry:** Carrying a firearm visibly on the body.
- **Optic:** An aiming device, typically a red dot or holographic sight.
- **Overtravel:** Trigger movement after the sear releases the hammer.
- **Overpressure (Ammo):** Higher-pressure ammunition exceeding standard specs.

P

- **Parallax:** Optical distortion in optics that can affect aim.
- **Pistol:** A semi-automatic or single-shot handgun.
- **Pistol Brace:** Stabilizing device attached to the rear of some pistols.
- **Plinking:** Informal recreational shooting.
- **Point Shooting:** Firing without sight alignment, relying on natural aim.
- **Porting:** Barrel modification to reduce recoil.

- **Press Check:** Partially racking the slide to verify chambered round.
- **Primer:** The ignition component at the base of a cartridge.
- **Puncture Cavity:** The wound track left by a bullet.

Q

- **Quick Draw:** Rapid presentation of the pistol from the holster.
- **Qual (Qualification):** Test or standard for shooting proficiency.

R

- **Rack the Slide:** Operating the slide to chamber a round or clear a malfunction.
- **Recoil:** Backward force from a fired round.
- **Recoil Management:** Techniques to reduce the effects of recoil.
- **Recoil Spring:** Absorbs and returns energy in recoil cycling.
- **Red Dot Sight (RDS):** A non-magnified optic projecting a red aiming point.
- **Reset (Trigger):** Point at which the trigger re-engages the sear after firing.
- **Retention:** Ability of the holster to hold the pistol securely.
- **Riding the Reset:** Deliberately releasing trigger only to the reset point.

S

- **Safety:** Mechanical feature preventing unintentional firing.
- **Sear:** Component that holds the hammer or striker in place.
- **Semi-Automatic:** Fires one round per trigger pull and automatically reloads.
- **Sight Alignment:** Front and rear sights aligned correctly.
- **Sight Picture:** Sights aligned on the target.
- **Slide:** Upper part of the pistol that reciprocates during fire.
- **Slide Lock:** Lever or button that holds the slide open.
- **Snap Cap:** Inert cartridge used for dry fire practice.
- **Stance:** Shooter's posture and body positioning.
- **Striker-Fired:** System using a spring-loaded firing pin instead of a hammer.

T

- **Take-Up:** Initial slack in the trigger before resistance.
- **Tap-Rack-Bang:** Immediate action drill to clear malfunctions.

- **Three-Dot Sight System:** Common iron sight configuration.
- **Thumb Safety:** Safety mechanism operated by the thumb.
- **Timer (Shot Timer):** Training tool that records draw and shot times.
- **Trigger Control:** Smooth, consistent manipulation of the trigger.
- **Trigger Guard:** Frame surrounding and protecting the trigger.
- **Trigger Pull Weight:** Force required to activate the trigger.
- **Trigger Shoe:** Aftermarket trigger face enhancement.

U

- **Unload and Show Clear:** Safety procedure to prove firearm is unloaded.
- **Undertravel:** Incomplete trigger movement that fails to fire the gun.
- **Undercut Trigger Guard:** Relief cut beneath trigger guard to aid grip.

V

- **Vertical Stringing:** Grouping of shots in a vertical line, often due to recoil issues.
- **Vision (in shooting):** Using sight focus and target acquisition effectively.
- **Visual Indexing:** Aligning the gun visually to the target without sights.

W

- **Wall (Trigger Wall):** Point in the trigger pull where resistance increases before the break.
- **Weaver Stance:** Staggered shooting stance with bent elbows.
- **Windage:** Horizontal sight adjustment to compensate for shot drift.
- **Witness Marks:** Factory or custom alignment indicators.
- **Weak Side:** Non-dominant side of the body for shooting or carrying.

X

- **X-Ring:** Center scoring zone on a target.

Y

- **Yield Point:** Structural limit in parts under stress (rarely referenced).

Z

- **Zero:** Calibrating sights or optics for point-of-impact alignment.

www.ingramcontent.com/pod-product-compliance
Lightning Source LLC
Chambersburg PA
CBHW080632230426
43663CB00016B/2843
9798218785864